e-commerce: law, business and tax planning

Julian JB Hickey
Barrister
with contributions by
Robin Mathew QC
and
Christopher Rose

JORDANS
2000

Published by
Jordan Publishing Limited
21 St Thomas Street
Bristol BS1 6JS

Important Notice
The information given and the views expressed herein are for further consideration only and should not be acted upon without independent consideration and professional advice. Neither the publishers nor any person involved in the editing or authorship of this publication can accept any responsibility for any loss occasioned to any person no matter however caused or arising as a result of or in consequence of action taken or refrained from in reliance on the contents hereof.

British Library Cataloguing-in-Publication Data
A catalogue record for this book is available from the British Library.

ISBN 0 85308 562 5

Typeset by Mendip Communications Ltd, Frome, Somerset
Printed by MPG Books Ltd, Bodmin, Cornwall

Preface

The purpose of this book is to provide a guide from a UK perspective on the business and tax law framework which applies to information technology and e-commerce. This book is the product of a variety of articles and conferences in which I have been involved. It is intended to be of use to both the domestic and international multi-disciplinary practitioner, and for this reason a number of general areas are included.

The book is not intended to be a tax planning manual. Instead, it is designed to ease the non e-commerce specialist into the framework of business and tax law which will apply to their chosen method of e-commerce business. Inevitably, it is impossible to give definitive guidance on an area which is being developed in a piecemeal and somewhat unsatisfactory way. However, it is possible to deal with the basic framework which will apply to e-commerce.

As a starting point for dealing with clients' problems the book is as succinct and as user-friendly as possible. It is hoped that both multi-disciplinary and specialist practitioners will find it of interest in guiding them into this interesting new world.

I would like to thank several people for their assistance and comments in the writing of this book. Foremost, I am grateful to Stephen Honey of Jordan Publishing Ltd for his commitment to publication of this work. My thanks go to Dr David Southern (University of London) for providing useful suggestions, and also for the assistance provided by Gary Mills and Gareth Green (Ernst & Young) who commented on the transfer pricing chapter. I am also indebted to Robin Mathew QC and Dr Christopher Rose for agreeing to contribute their respective chapters.

No doubt, despite the considerable endeavours which have been made in ensuring accuracy, some errors will remain. Any suggestions for improvement in the material are welcomed, and should be addressed care of my publishers.

Finally, a special thank you to my mother for her support and encouragement during the writing of this book.

Julian JB Hickey, Barrister
The Intellectual Property Institute
London
November 1999

Contents

Table of Cases

References are to paragraph numbers. References to a Table are followed by the page number where the Table is set out, for example Table 13 at p 104.

Table of Statutes

References are to paragraph numbers. References to a Table are followed by the page number where the Table is set out, for example Table 13 at p 104.

Table of Statutory Instruments

References are to paragraph numbers. References to a Table are followed by the page number where the Table is set out, for example Table 13 at p 104. See also Appendix 2.

Table of Foreign Statutes

References are to paragraph numbers.

Table of EC Legislation

References are to paragraph numbers. References to a Table are followed by the page number where the Table is set out, for example Table 13 at p 104.

Table of Other Material

References are to paragraph numbers. References to a Table are followed by the page number where the Table is set out, for example Table 13 at p 104.

Table of Abbreviations

Full title	*Abbreviation used in this book*
advance pricing agreement	APA
Alternative Investment Market	AIM
American Standard Code for Information Interchange	ASCII
BInery digiT	BIT
Binding Tariff Information	BTI
Capital Allowances Act 1990	CAA 1990
combined nomenclature	CN
Common Agricultural Policy	CAP
Committee of Fiscal Affairs (OECD)	CFA
Companies Act 1985	CA 1985
comparable uncontrolled price	CUP
Customs and Excise Management Act 1979	CEMA 1979
double taxation agreement	DTA
electronic commerce	e-commerce
electronic data interchange	EDI
electronic mail	e-mail
enterprise investment scheme	EIS
European Court of Justice	ECJ
European Economic Interest Grouping	EEIG
European Union	EU
Finance Act 1994	FA 1994
Finance Act 1995	FA 1995
Finance Act 1996	FA 1996
Finance Act 1997	FA 1997
Finance Act 1998	FA 1998
Finance Act 1999	FA 1999
first year allowance	FYA
General Agreement on Tariffs and Trade	GATT
Group of 7 leading industrial nations	G7
generally accepted accounting principles	GAAP
Harmonised System	HS
Hypertext markup language	HTML
Income and Corporation Taxes Act 1988	ICTA 1988
Insolvency Act 1986	IA 1986
integrated services digital network	ISDN
International Mobile Satellite Organisation	Inmarsat
International Monetary Fund	IMF

International Telecommunications Satellite Organisation	Intelsat
Internet Explorer	IE
Internet service provider	ISP
joint academic network	JANET
Limited Partnership Act 1907	LPA 1907
local area network	LAN
low direct tax jurisdiction	LDTJ
Model Tax Convention on Income and Capital	Model Convention
mutual agreement procedure	MAP
operating system	OS
Organisation for Economic Co-operation and Development	OECD
Partnership Act 1890	PA 1890
random access memory	RAM
research and development	R&D
software development subsidiary	SDS
Taxation of Chargeable Gains Act 1992	TCGA 1992
Trade Marks Act 1994	TMA 1994
treaty jurisdiction company	TJC
Uniform Resource Locator	URL
value added tax	VAT
Value Added Tax Act 1994	VATA 1994
venture capital trusts	VCT
wide area network	WAN
World Trade Organisation	WTO

Part I

INTRODUCTION

Chapter 1

INFORMATION TECHNOLOGY AND E-COMMERCE

1.1 INFORMATION TECHNOLOGY

1.1.1 Introduction

The interaction of tax with information technology ('IT'), especially Internet transactions, has sparked considerable commercial, academic and professional interest.[1] This is not surprising given that the sums involved in this area of commerce offer significant rewards both for entrepreneurs and tax authorities throughout the world. It is estimated that the market for information and communication technologies is £48 billion per year.[2] It has also been predicted that, within five years, electronic commerce ('e-commerce') will top US$800 billion.[3] At this point in time, no specific scheme of taxation exists in respect of IT and Internet commerce. As a result, transactions must be slotted into the general framework of tax law.[4] The purpose of this chapter is to explain the nature and basic terminology of the IT and Internet world.

1.1.2 Towards a definition of IT

IT has not at the time of publication been considered judicially within the courts of the UK. However, the term has received statutory recognition in two Acts of Parliament. The most recent interpretation is provided by the Carriage of Goods By Sea Act 1992. This provides in s 5 that:

> '"information technology" includes any computer or other technology by means of which information or other matter may be recorded or communicated without being reduced to documentary form.'

---

1 Intertax has devoted a specific issue dealing with 'International Tax Issues in Cyberspace' (vol 25, April 1997) with contributions from the UK, Japan, USA, Canada, Germany and France. Also see *The Bulletin for International Fiscal Documentation* (November 11/12, vol 50, 1996) which contains articles in respect of tax and the Internet. See Frances M. Horner and Jeffrey Owens, 'Tax and the Web: New Technology, Old Problems' (1996) *The Bulletin for International Fiscal Documentation* p 516 and David R. Tillinghast, 'The Impact of the Internet on the Taxation of International Transactions' (1996) *The Bulletin for International Fiscal Documentation* p 524. Another article on the Internet is to be found M. Loten 'Doing Business on the Internet' (Issue No 361/June 1996).

2 See *Internet Business* (April 1997) Issue 3, p 26.

3 Prediction by Killen & Associates. See *Internet Business* (June 1997), Issue 5, p 43.

4 In October 1998 the Inland Revenue and HM Customs and Excise issued a policy statement on UK tax policy regarding e-commerce. See Appendix 1.

For the purposes of Sch 1, para 14 to the Local Government Act 1988, the term has the following meaning:

> '"information technology" means any computer, telecommunications or other technology the principal use of which is the recording, processing and communication of information by electronic means.'

IT is the bedrock of the Internet. IT enables information of varying types, such as sound, voices and raw data to be passed over long distances in the twinkling of an eye. There can be no doubt that IT has revolutionised the work place. The rapid evolution of SOHO[1] as a result of the development of mobile computing has transformed the way people work.

1.1.3 Components of IT

IT is the technology we use to manipulate information. It is not the information itself.

This technology comprises hardware, which is the physical boxes, wires, keyboards and screens with which we are familiar. Everything we see when a computer is turned off is hardware. When the computer is turned on, like many other pieces of equipment, it follows a series of instructions. These instructions are called programs which enable the computer to perform a wide variety of tasks. Usually, programs (a collection of programs, working together to perform a common task like stock control or word-processing is called software) are not created by the individual user of the computer, but either come already installed with the computer, or are purchased separately and installed (copied) onto the computer at a later date. Software can be bought on the high street, by mail order and, increasingly, by 'downloading' (copying) from the Internet. Computer programs can contain thousands, sometimes millions, of separate instructions.

When a programmer writes a line of a program, it will look something like:

if item:stocklevel < 100, then reorder(item)

It may not make easy reading, but, to us, it does have recognisable words and, sometimes, an understandable sequence of logic. A computer, however, cannot understand instructions in this form. The instruction has first to be converted (using a special piece of software called a compiler or interpreter) into a form that the computer can process. This form is binary notation and it is used for storing computer programs and data.

Binary notation uses only two digits: 0 and 1, compared to the ten digits in decimal notation. However, these two digits can be combined to form infinite variations of numbers, or codes, which are used to convey messages to the computer.

Computers are powered by electro-magnetism. Regardless of the voltage, an electrical current within the computer, or a section of computer disk or CD-ROM, is either ON or OFF, or magnetised or not magnetised, or up or down, etc. Because of this two-state principle of electro-magnetism, computers can 'read' the on/off messages of binary codes.

---

1 Small Office Home Office.

In decimal notation, we recognise the value of the number 215, almost without thinking. The last digit, 5, denotes the number of single units, the middle digit, 1, the number of tens and the first digit, 2, the number of hundreds. More digits to the left indicate ten times the value of the digit to the right: thousands, tens of thousands, etc.

In binary notation, the far right digit, as with decimals, denotes the number of single units. The next digit from the right denotes the number of twos, the next the number of fours, eights, sixteens, thirty-twos, sixty-fours, one-hundred-and-twenty-eights, and so on. So, the decimal number 215 would be expressed, in binary notation, as:

1 1 0 1 0 1 1 1

Reading from the left, there is one 128, one 64, no 32, one 16, no 8, one 4, one 2 and one 1.

128 + 64 + 16 + 4 + 2 + 1 = 215.

A computer needs many programs to function. When it is switched on an operating system ('OS') is initiated. This takes care of the nuts and bolts of the computer: how to respond to key presses, mouse clicks, how to read the magnetic media such as disks and tape drives, whether a CD-ROM[1] drive is present, how to allocate document and data files to disk space, and so on. Popular operating systems are MS-DOS,[2] the all-conquering MS-Windows in its various versions (3.1, '95, '98 and 2000), OS/2 and Unix.

When the OS has done its initial start up work, the computer user can select, from an on-screen menu, or by clicking an icon, an application system to run 'on top' of the OS. This could be an accounts system, word-processing, stock control, or any of thousands of other off-the-shelf systems.

As information is entered into a computer, a combination of the application system which is currently being used, and the OS, will convert the key-presses into binary code and allocate resources for the data to be processed (in 'RAM' (Random Access Memory)) then permanently stored, if necessary, on disk, either inside the computer or somewhere else via a network connection.

The software will have been programmed to recognise what type of data is being input, and to what real-world entity it relates. A stock-control system, for example, will store the number of an item in stock, number on order, delivery times, etc as purely numeric binary values. A stock item description is stored as a series of binary codes representing letters and other characters. There are various universal coding systems for this, the most well-known being ASCII (the American Standard Code for Information Interchange) in which capital A is represented by 65, B by 66, etc. There are other codes for lower-case letters and characters such as punctuation. In a word-processing system, almost all input will be stored this way. Other types of data are programmed to hold dates (usually as an internal numeric value which is then interpreted and displayed as a date), logical values (simply Yes or No which can be represented by one BInary digiT, or 'BIT'), even pictures and sound. Each of these separate pieces of data is stored in a 'field'.

1 Compact Disc Read-Only Memory.
2 MicroSoft Disk Operating System.

A collection of fields, holding information about, say, one stock item, is called a 'record'; many records holding information about all stock items are held in a file.

People familiar with spreadsheets tend to view records as 'rows' and fields as 'columns'. Often, several files storing related data, are called a 'relational database'. This would include files for stock movements, suppliers, orders placed, usage, sales, etc, which are linked together to enable the user to view information from various viewpoints.

Software is written by developers, who may be individuals or huge organsiations such as Microsoft, and is distributed via floppy disks, CD-ROMs or the Internet. Floppy disks and CD-ROMs are inserted into a computer, which then copies and installs the program onto the internal storage of the computer, or network of connected computers. These physical information carriers raise specific tax issues.[1]

The sale of a CD-ROM or floppy disk does not represent a sale of the software on it. This is protected by a range of intellectual property rights, such as copyright or a patent. Thus, inherent in the transaction is the distinction between the sale of the physical carrier, such as the CD-ROM, a coated piece of plastic, and the software, the use of which is licensed.

The following is a typical licensing clause which accompanies the physical carrier:

> 'Ownership of Software: As licensee, you own the media upon which the software is fixed, but [the owner] retains title and ownership of the software recorded on the original media and all subsequent copies of the Software regardless of the form or media in which or on which the original and other copies may exist. This licence is not a sale of the Software or any copy.'

The drafting of such a clause is important because many tax jurisdictions make a distinction between a licence for intellectual property rights, such as copyright, and a sale or lease of physical property. In some situations, the person paying for the use of a licence, ie the licensee, must deduct tax at source for the use of the right. In some cases, the hardware, such as a replacement micro-processor (the central processing unit of a computer) is sold outright, whilst the software permanently encoded on it will be licensed.[2] In this situation, it is arguable that 'withholding tax' should not be applied in respect of the payment, which can be attributed to the right to use the software which forms part of the physical micro-processor. However, in recent years, tax authorities have shown a keen interest in deconstructing 'package prices'. A package price is an inclusive price for the use of the physical goods and the intangible property such as a licence to use computer software. Tax administrations which disaggregate package prices are usually those which impose withholding taxes on payments for the use of intangible property.

Example 1

X Ltd sells 10,000 hardware components to an associated company trading in a country in Asia. The hardware components contain a software element which is the

---

1 For example, the value of software encoded on physical carriers is excluded for the purposes of customs duties provided the value of the software is declared separately from the physical carrier and any accompanying documentation, and packaging.

2 See C. Reed *Computer Law* (Blackstone Press, 3rd edn, 1996).

subject of intellectual property. The price of £100,000 for the hardware components is a package price which includes an amount for a licence to use the software element. The tax authority of the Asian country disaggregates the package price and requires the purchaser to apply withholding tax to the amount attributable to the software licence.

1.1.4 Interaction of hardware and software

It is important to remember that the software stored on a CD-ROM, floppy disk or the 'hard' disk within the computer, is nothing more than binary codes which are read into the computer's micro-processor from where instructions are distributed to the computer's components so that they may perform the tasks required to accomplish the purposes of the specific program.

1.1.5 Analog and digital

Writing is, in many languages, analogous to the sound of the words when spoken. The spoken word itself is analogous to the thing or concept that it represents. Pictures are analogous to the scenes they portray. These things have no meaning to the computer, however sophisticated the software. Many of the peripherals, therefore, of a computer are concerned with converting data or instructions held digitally (using binary-based codes, as described) into a simulation of analogous information, with which the human brain is more immediately familiar, such as text on the computer screen or printer, or sound from a speaker.

Some early computers used variable media (either mechanical or by varying electrical frequency or voltage) to effect the actual internal calculations and to represent values analogously. Although requiring less processing power, these did not offer the same flexibility and potential for programming as binary-based digital coding and are largely a thing of the past. Over the last decade or so, other, previously analog[1], technologies, such as music reproduction, telephones and radio and television, have moved to digital-based technologies, largely due to the phenomenal increase in processor power and dramatically falling prices.

1.1.6 Computer networks

A network of computers is two or more computers connected in some way, usually by simple wiring or fibre-optic cable. Each computer attached to a network contains the necessary connection circuitry and software. Often the computers are connected to a central store called a 'server' which serves the computers in the network with available software and data. This allows each computer to have access to the same software and to the same data as necessary. In addition, the network allows communication between individual computers within the business organisation via e-mail (electronic mail). In a computer network, most processing is carried out locally (on the individual computers) and the results of the processing is returned to the server for storage. Larger mini or mainframe computers carry out all their processing centrally, and communicate with users via 'dumb' terminals. If any computer attached to a network fails, the network normally continues to function, and, as most data and

1 The American spelling of analog, is, like program, usually used in the context of IT.

programs are 'backed up'[1] automatically on the server, the failed computer can be replaced quite easily.

A Local Area Network ('LAN') normally covers a single site within a business. A Wide Area Network ('WAN') covers several disparate sites, but usually with dedicated cable connections, often using existing telephone lines. A LAN, or WAN, is an effective and efficient method of updating and sharing information between individuals for business purposes. The cost of installing a LAN network can often qualify for tax relief as an expense of carrying on a trade.[2]

1.1.7 Fixed networks

The network through which information passes may be fixed in the sense that there are permanent links between the computers, such as in the case of a LAN, or where a mixture of internal 'hard-wired' and external connections are used, such as a WAN. In the past, networks had to use common operating systems and normally be able to access information stored in a way specific to their type of computer and the software co-ordinating their network. With the advent of the Internet (see below), however, it was realised that Internet technology, which is able to share information between a wide diversity of hardware and software technologies, could be used on a local fixed basis, at a fraction of the cost of alternatives, and the concept of the 'Intranet'[3] was born.

1.1.8 Flexible networks

In a flexible network, the passage of information from source to recipient will not always follow the same route. Each message and request for access to particular information carries an address, or locator. The routers built into a flexible network will find a route for the message or request, in theory the fastest, to its destination.

1.2 THE INTERNET

1.2.1 Introduction

An examination of the history of the Internet is beyond the scope of this book. Many valuable works exist that explore its evolution. One particular work worthy of mention is *The Internet Book.*[4] Chapters 7 and 8 explore the early years of Internet development. Another useful introduction is a book by Davey Winder *All you need to know about the Internet.*[5]

---

1 Back up – copy of software and data which can be re-loaded in the event of a technology failure.
2 See Chapter 5.
3 See *Internet Business* (April 1997) Issue 3, p 29 which describes the intranet developed for BP to share oil well engineering and drilling information with other businesses within the BP network of companies.
4 Douglas E. Comer (Prentice Hall International, 1995).
5 (Future Publishing Ltd, 1996).

1.2.2 Internet structure

There is no statutory definition of the Internet, and no specific legislation governing its operation within the UK. *The Road Ahead* describes the Internet and its historical background in the following terms:

> 'The Internet is a loose collection of interconnecting commercial and non-commercial computer networks. The constituent networks are tied by telecommunications lines and by their shared reliance on standard communication protocols (rules). This decentralised structure makes sense when you consider the origin of the Internet.
>
> The Internet is an outgrowth of a government network called the ARPANET, which was created in 1969 by the Defense Department so that defense contractors and researchers could continue to communicate even after a nuclear attack. Rather than try to harden the network against nuclear weapons, ARPANET's designers decided to make it resilient by distributing its recourses in a completely decentralized way – so that destruction of any part of the network, of even of most of it, wouldn't stop the overall flow of information. The network quickly found favour among computer scientists and engineers in industry and universities, and it became a vital communication link among far-flung collaborators.'[1]

The US has however defined the Internet for the purposes of the Internet Tax Freedom Act.[2] Under s 155(6) the Act defines the term 'Internet' as meaning:

> '. . . the combination of computer facilities and electromagnetic transmission media, and related equipment and software comprising the interconnected worldwide network of computer networks that employ the Transmission Control Protocol/Internet Protocol, or any predecessor or successor protocol, to transmit information.'

The Internet is, in simple terms, a vast flexible network of networks. This is possible because of the development of software which is not 'platform-dependent', in other words, computers of differing architectures and operating systems are able to communicate and understand each other. A basic illustration of the Internet is shown in Diagram 1 below.

1.2.3 Telecommunication infrastructure

The Internet is dependent upon a vast telecommunication infrastructure incorporating copper cables, fibre-optic cables, radio, and satellite communication. The first transatlantic cable was laid between Scotland and Newfoundland in 1956. Many more cables have since been laid across the North Atlantic and Pacific Oceans and digital technology has enabled far more separate 'messages' to be conveyed over one cable. For example, the submarine cable known as TAT-9 has a capacity of up to 15,000 voice circuits.[3] It seems likely, though, that the future of a worldwide communication lies with geostationary satellite communication, which requires no physical transmission medium over most of its course.

Telecommunication suppliers make their profits by offering their network as a conduit for the transfer of data, or for carrying voice signals or images. Money is made from

---

1 (Penguin, 1996) pp 110 and 111.

2 HR 4105. See US Code, Title 4, Chapter 6 – Moratorium on certain taxes, ss 151–155.

3 For an extensive list of submarine cables see G. Langley and J. P. Ronayne *Telecommunication Primer* (Pitman Publishing, 4th edn, 1993).

Diagram 1: Basic structure of the Internet

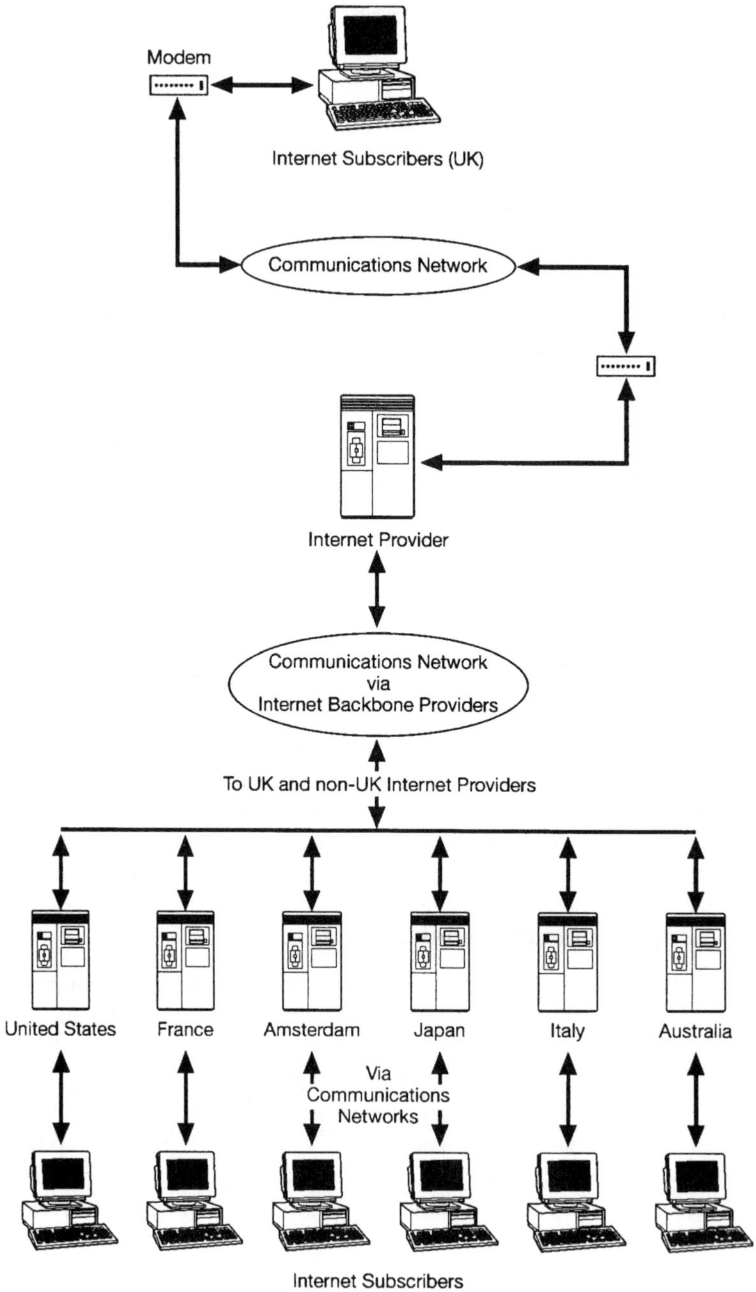

rental income paid by individuals for use of the telecommunication network, and from leasing permanent lines with the capacity to carry large data traffic to Internet service providers[1] ('ISPs').

In a domestic context agreements will exist between telecommunication providers, such as Mercury and British Telecom for the reciprocal use of parts of each other's network. Leasing agreements will also exist with business entities, such as ISPs, for the permanent use of specific lines on the network. Telecommunication providers will also provide special number services to business entities. One example of this is the '0800' prefix, which indicates that a freephone service is offered. A person who dials this number is not charged. Instead the call is charged to the recipient organisation.

Some phone numbers designated by a telecom provider represent a premium rate service. These are indicated typically by a '0839', '0660', '0881' or a '0336' prefix in the UK. Calls made to these numbers are at premium rate to cover the costs of the company providing the service. This is typically access to a live conversation forum, to financial information or to computer support services. The call charge is at a high rate to cover the costs of providing the service, and the costs of the telecom provider in ensuring that the facilities to run these special services are in place. Agreements exist between the telecom provider and the service company. These agreements will have their own tax implications.

1.2.4 Internet backbone structures

In order to achieve fast, efficient and stable connectivity within Europe for the purposes of transferring information various telecommunication backbones were formed. One such backbone is operated by a company known as Ebone Inc, which operates a network linking specific parts of Europe together, coupled with permanent access to various countries outside Europe.[2] Each customer of Ebone Inc pays a fee which is used to maintain the network, pay for staff, and pay lease payments for telecommunication lines. The Ebone Inc network is used by commercial ISPs as their entry to the worldwide Internet. The costs of subscribing to such a network can be relieved for tax purposes as an expense in carrying on a trade.

The Ebone Inc network is one of many 'open' networks, which means that information can be exchanged with other networks within Europe and throughout the world.

For example, when a UK individual sends electronic mail to a friend in Paris, the message is first transmitted to his ISP, then to a network such as that operated by Ebone Inc in the UK where it is passed to a connection in Paris. The data is then passed to the ISP in Paris, and thence to the individual recipient's computer.

---

1 Individuals and all but the largest companies do not maintain their own Internet network. Instead they use an ISP which allows an individual computer to become, usually via a telephone line, connected to a large network. ISPs include CompuServe, AOL, Demon, FreeServe.

2 Further information on Ebone Inc can be obtained from the company's web site, which is at: http://www.ebone.net.

1.2.5 Routers

Networks such as that operated by Ebone Inc interconnect with other networks throughout Europe and the world. In this way, information can be transferred around the world. The points of connection between the networks are linked by what are known as 'routers'. A router is simply a computer with a single purpose: to seek out the fastest route by which to send information. Often this information is broken down into small 'packets' which may themselves be sent via different routes, re-assembling themselves into a coherent whole at the recipient's end.

1.2.6 Satellite network

Increasingly, satellites are used to transmit information using radio and microwaves. Radio and microwaves can usually only travel in straight lines, so a geo-stationary satellite is used, which can 'see' over the horizon, to receive messages and instantly re-transmit them to another part of the Earth. The satellite is controlled and maintained in a constant position above the Earth by a control centre. The satellite and its control centre tend to be owned by international organisations, such as Intelsat (International Telecommunications Satellite Organisation) and Inmarsat (International Mobile Satellite Organisation) or government bodies, whereas the sending and receiving stations are typically owned by telecommunication companies within each country.

Intelsat is an organisation of 135 national members which operates on the basis of a 'not for profit co-operative'.[1] Each nation contributes an amount of capital, which corresponds to the amount of use of the Intelsat system, who then receive a return on their investment. According to the Intelsat web site 'INTELSAT operates as a wholesaler, providing services to end-users through the INTELSAT member in each country'.[2] The Intelsat system is a provider of a wide spectrum of services to all types of business throughout the world. To place in perspective the type of traffic carried by satellite providers, the following passage is reproduced from the Intelsat web[3] site, headed 'Who uses the INTELSAT system':

> 'INTELSAT serves a growing number of customers around the globe. These customers are the major telecommunications operators throughout the world. They include providers of basic long distance telephone services like BT, Cable and Wireless, France Telecom and Deutsche Telekom. They include the world's major broadcasters such as CBS, BBC, CNN, the European Broadcasting Union, and the Asian Broadcasting Union, who depend on INTELSAT to transmit news, sports and entertainment programmes.
>
> Airlines for transcontinental booking arrangements, international banks for credit verification and authorization. Multinational manufacturers, petroleum companies, news

---

1 See Intelsat's web site at http://www.intelsat.com.

2 Ibid.

3 A web site forms part of the World Wide Web (www). Web sites, or pages, along with e-mail, are the reason for the popularity of the Internet. Usually they consist of information created by companies, organisations and individuals which can be accessed by web 'surfers'. The word 'web' is used because pages have 'hyperlinks' to other, related, documents, which could be on other sites in other parts of the world. A company in London could have a site with a link to an associated company in New York. The New York company may have a link to the New York Tourist Information site. This site may include a link to, for example, a Monet exhibition at the Metropolitan Museum, with a link to, say, the Louvre, in Paris, and so on.

> and financial information services like Reuters (UK), Agence France Presse (France), and ITAR Tass (Russia) to faciliate their global operations.
>
> International newspaper distributors like International Herald Tribune, the Financial Times, the Wall Street Journal, for simultaneous remote printing of daily editions on several continents.'[1]

In addition to these organisations, some satellites are operated by private entities. One example of this is the PanAmSat Corporation based in the USA. The satellite system is a distribution centre for information. The operators make their profits by permitting others to use the system as a conduit for the transfer of information. The Internet site of the PanAmSat Corporation illustrates the type of use to which a satellite can be put for business purposes.[2] The web site describes the following uses.

(1) Broadcasters, both US and foreign based, use the system for the distribution of their television programmes to cable systems and home-viewers.
(2) Corporations. Satellites are used for private business communication networks.
(3) Telecommunication service providers. A satellite is used as a conduit for communications traffic originating from national telecom suppliers.
(4) News organisations use the satellite for the purposes of distributing information worldwide.
(5) Internet service providers use it to enable their customers to gain access to Internet sites in other countries.

Satellite system operators gain revenue from a number of sources. Agreements exist between national telecom providers and the satellite system operators, and businesses, which use the satellite system directly for the purposes of, for example, data sharing within a closed private network within a corporate structure. Agreements of this type with satellite system providers will have tax implications. As described above, some countries and entities within those countries have invested in internationally-operated satellite systems such as Intelsat. Intelsat members contribute capital sums, and receive capital repayments and compensation for the use of capital in proportion to their investment share.[3] The investing entities which contribute to the Intelsat system under the umbrella of UK membership include British Telecommunications plc and Cable & Wireless plc.[4]

1.2.7 Dial-up access

Internet service providers such as AOL, CompuServe and many others use permanent networks. Revenue is made by permitting others to use these networks. Individuals and companies are able to access the Internet by subscription to the services of an ISP. This link is achieved using either a modem (which converts digital codes into telephone-compatible impulses) and an ordinary telephone line or the newer, faster, ISDN lines (integrated services digital network) which can transmit data digitally over their entire length. When connected, the individual's computer becomes, in

1 See Intelsat's web site at http://www.intelsat.com/(1998).
2 See the PanAmSat Internet site at: http://www.panamsat.com/(1998).
3 See Intelsat's 1995 Annual Report at http://www.intelsat.com (1998).
4 For a complete list of UK investing entities, and those who invest under the umbrella of other national memberships see the Intelsat web site at http://www.intelsat.com.

effect, a part of the ISP's network, and has access to its various services, including the ability to connect with other ISPs via organisations such as Ebone Inc. In this way, individuals and businesses can communicate with other people for the purposes of sharing information and selling products.

1.2.8 Internet search engines

As the Internet grows, so do the problems of locating relevant information. Where finding a book among a random selection on a single bookshelf is easy, but locating one in a library, with no indexes or references could take weeks, 'Search engines'[1] on the Internet provide an index of subjects available. All web pages have a description embedded into them of the general nature of the page and certain key words. A bed manufacturer in Lincoln would probably include the words, *bed, bedding, furniture, furnishing, bedroom, bedrooms, lincoln, lincs lincolnshire, england, uk, manufacture, company, distributor* in their web page. These words are registered with the search engine provider and anyone searching for BEDROOM FURNITURE in LINCOLN would be presented with this site. A search for, simply, BEDROOM FURNITURE or for UK COMPANY, however, would still find the site, but would almost certainly find several hundreds, or thousands, of others, too.

The main revenue of these operators, which will be subject to direct taxation such as corporation tax, is at the moment derived from banner advertisement of web sites operated by businesses.[2] The second main source of revenue is the licensing of mirror sites. In other words, someone else acquires the right to use the search engine database and acts as the host in another country. The advantage of this is that the search engine site is local to a particular country offering quicker performance times. The advertisement banners will also reflect the market of that country. The licensing of the search engine site will involve tax related issues in respect of intellectual property. Copyright may exist in a database and it is possible that any payment made for the use of a search engine by a licensed party could represent payment of a royalty on which a withholding tax may be applied. In addition to payments for copyright, the licence agreement will involve issues relating to trade mark use, and goodwill. The terms of the licence payment may either be based on a royalty or lump sum.

An additional source of income to Internet search engine providers are through 'value added links'. This is where a search engine provider pays for every link made by it to another Internet provider's site. For example, Yahoo is Alta Vista's biggest customer in this respect.[3] Payments such as these will have both domestic and international tax implications.

1.2.9 Browsers

'Browser technology' is the basis of the recent success of the Internet, and, more recently, of Intranets. A browser is the software which an individual uses to access information held on the Internet. The most widely used are Netscape's Navigator and

---

1 Examples of these searchable databases are 'Altavista' at www.altavista.com and 'Yahoo' at www.yahoo.com.

2 See *Internet Business* (April 1997) Issue 3, p 82.

3 Ibid.

Communicator and Microsoft's Internet Explorer ('IE'). These similar-looking programs enable the user to type in a web page address (or Uniform Resource Locator, URL) such as www.bbc.co.uk which is then located and displayed on screen. Web pages are written using HTML[1] which encrypts the document with information about how it should be displayed, and with information about links to other pages elsewhere on the Internet. One problem with HTML is that different browsers display pages slightly differently. Add to this the fact that computer screens themselves vary considerably in their size, quality and user settings, and it is often very difficult for designers of web pages to be certain of exactly how their work will appear to every potential user.

1.3 INTERNET PARTICIPANTS

1.3.1 Introduction

The following paragraphs highlight some of the central players within the world of the 'global information superhighway'. Interesting tax issues arise in the context of their particular activities. For example, what are the circumstanes in which an offshore trader can be taxed? Could an Internet service provider, or the operator of an electronic shopping mall be held accountable as agents for the profits generated by businesses using their services? Where software is given away without charge what are the tax consequences of such activities?

1.3.2 Internet service providers ('ISPs')

The gateway to the Internet for most individuals and for many companies is via one of a range of ISPs. Examples of commercial providers are CompuServe, Demon Internet, Microsoft, Pipex and AOL. Non-commercial entities such as universities or charities may also provide access to the Internet. The UK university joint academic network ('JANET') existed long before the word 'Internet' was in everyday use. ISPs provide access to a network which is linked to outside networks owned by other ISPs, usually via network backbones such as those operated by Ebone Inc.

In exchange for the facility offered by ISPs, subscribers pay a monthly fee of typically £5 to £15. There is also a new wave of companies providing free access, paid for by advertising revenue, such as FreeServe. The Internet access provider comes in many forms. Some simply provide access to the Internet. Others, such as CompuServe and AOL have a range of facilities and information accessible only by their subscribers. Some represent a joint venture company between two domestic Internet providers who are developing an international Internet service and others may simply be a single business established for providing access to a particular market. These smaller operators will normally lease line capacity from other larger Internet access providers. The costs incurred in establishing an Internet access business are usually deductible for tax purposes. The area of Internet business is still in the early stages of growth. No doubt in time there will be mergers, acquisitions and amalgamations of these businesses. Such activities attract tax charges and reliefs.

---

1 Hypertext markup language.

1.3.3 e-commerce

The basic mechanics of how IT is used to transfer instructions for the production of specific types of output, such as text, sound and images has been touched upon in the early parts of this chapter. E-commerce represents the application of this technology for the purposes of carrying on a trade within a country and between continents. E-commerce takes many different forms, some of which are identified in the list below.[1] Also contained in this list is an illustration of the businesses which make e-commerce possible.

Categories of e-commerce

(1) Advertising (estimated market of US$1 billion by the year 2000).
(2) Auctions (for example, sale of second hand and surplus PC products).
(3) Electronic mailing lists (employment agency services).
(4) Subscriptions (for example, in the USA the *Wall Street Journal* operates a subscription service on the Internet).
(5) Commissions (for example, a web site which provides links to another web site operator receives from the latter a commission for each person who uses the link and subscribes to the service offered by that web site operator).
(6) Demographic analysis (for example, game sites on the web collect data from players who complete on screen questionnaires. The data is then sold to game companies etc).
(7) Tendering.
(8) Shopping sites.

Internet application software businesses

(9) Web browsers and associated software.
(10) Secure payment systems.
(11) Video-conferencing systems.

Computer and associated suppliers

(12) Computer and associated hardware component manufacturers.
(13) Software developers and manufacturers.

Telecommunication suppliers

(14) Telecommunication manufacturers.

Network operators

(15) Internet access providers, such as AOL and Ebone Inc.
(16) Telecommunication suppliers.

---

1 See an article written by J. Nugent 'Models Wanted' in *Internet Business* (June 1997) Issue 5, p 42.

The US has defined the term 'electronic commerce' for the purposes of the Internet Tax Freedom Act.[1] Under s 155(4), the Act defines the term 'electronic commerce' as meaning:

> 'any transaction conducted over the Internet or through Internet access, comprising the sale, lease, licence, offer, or delivery of property, goods, services, or information, whether or not for consideration, and includes the provision of Internet access.'[2]

1.3.4 Fiscal issues

The fiscal consequences of the Internet is a complex area. From the outset a distinction must be made between:

(1) the persons who develop, manufacture and operate IT; and
(2) the application of IT for the purposes of carrying on e-commerce with individuals and businesses.

The tax rules which apply in respect of (1) will be those which are common to any type of business activity. For example, the circumstances in which a company will be taxed by a jurisdiction, the extent to which relief is given for expenditure on technology used in a business, the amalgamation of businesses are all issues that arise on a day-to-day basis within the tax system.

The tax issues which arise in respect of (2), in other words, from the application of IT (such as e-commerce) is an area which represents difficulties far removed from day-to-day tax issues. Issues of particular difficulty include the circumstances in which a tax authority can tax offshore e-commerce, and the circumstances in which value added tax ('VAT') applies to Internet transactions. When can profits derived from a satellite unit be taxed, if at all? When can an Internet access provider be charged to tax in the name of an offshore trader?

---

1 HR 4105.
2 Internet Tax Freedom Act, s 155(4).

Part II

BUSINESS VEHICLES AND INTERNET ACTIVITY

Chapter 2

BUSINESS VEHICLES

2.1 INTRODUCTION

The available range of vehicles for carrying on activities in respect of IT and Internet trade are summarised in Table 1. As the Table illustrates, the range of business entities is both wide and diverse. A privately financed economic activity can be carried on in the UK via the medium of either a company, partnership, or European Economic Interest Grouping ('EEIG').

A foreign business might consider establishing a branch within the UK, ie physical offices. The decision of whether to use a business vehicle within a trading jurisdiction must now be balanced against the benefits offered by e-commerce. The growth in IT means that it may be necessary only for certain types of business to establish a physical location in the country where profits are to be remitted and nowhere else.

The purpose of this chapter is to:

(1) summarise the range of available business vehicles for carrying on IT and e-commerce related business; and
(2) provide a summary of the tax consequences which arise from those choices.

The UK tax legislation offers, in limited circumstances, the opportunity to encourage external investment by individuals in some business entities. These are referred to later in the chapter.

Table 1: Summary of UK business vehicles

Vehicle	*Formation*	*Nature of economic activity*	*Type(s) of business vehicle available*	*Members' liability*	*Owner of business property*	*Type of members' interest*
Registered company	Under the Companies Act 1985, as amended	Any form of economic activity	PUBLIC Public company (limited by shares) CA 1985, s 1(3) Share capital must not be less than £50K (CA 1985, s 118) Must be more than 2 members PRIVATE Private company. No minimum share capital. May be only 1 member: the Companies (Single Member Private Limited Companies) Regulations 1992, SI 1992/1699	PUBLIC Limited by shares PRIVATE Limited with share capital or by guarantee or unlimited Unlimited companies can be registered with or without the capital divided into shares	Company and not the members: *Macaura v Northern Assurance Co Ltd* [1925] AC 619 Company possesses single legal personality *Salomon v Salomon and Co Ltd* [1897] AC 22	A company may divide its capital into different classifications The share capital may reflect the following classes: 1. Ordinary shares: provide the right to a dividend and capital 2. Preference shares: provide a right to a dividend and/or the capital in priority to holders of other share classes
Branch (permanent establishment) of a non-resident corporation	A fixed place of business through which the business of an enterprise is wholly or partly carried on: Art 5 of OECD Model Tax Convention	Any form of economic activity	No legal personality. The permanent establishment is purely a physical base through which the economic activity is carried on by an enterprise of another State	Depends upon law of foreign State	Company by which the permanent establishment is created	Depends upon law of foreign State

Vehicle	Formation	Nature of economic activity	Type(s) of business vehicle available	Members' liability	Owner of business property	Type of members' interest
General partnership Persons who carry on a business in common with a view of profit PA 1890, s 1	Two or more persons (artificial or natural) Regulated by the PA 1890	Any form of economic activity	Group partnership (partnership between partnerships: each one linked by a partnership deed to the 'head' office) Two types of agreement: head partnership and branch partnership Sub-partnership (a partnership where one of the partners agrees to divide his share of the main partnership profits and losses with other persons) An illustration of how partnerships have been used in transactions is provided by *Ensign Tankers (Leasing) Ltd v Stokes* [1992] STC 226	All partners are jointly and severally liable for all debts and obligations incurred by the firm while the partner is a member, PA 1890, s 9 A company may be a partner	Property held and applied by the partners for the purposes of the partnership, PA 1890, s 20 Property must be applied in accordance with the partnership agreement, PA 1890, s 20 Partnership does not have SLP but each partner does	According to percentage of interest in partnership profits as provided in the partnership agreement. In the absence of an express or implied agreement there are special rules, PA 1890, s 24. A partner has a beneficial interest in the property of the partnership. There is no interest capable of assignment. *Hadlee v Commissioner of Inland Revenue* [1993] STC 294 PC
Limited partnership 'Silent partner'	Two or more persons (artificial or natural) One of the persons must be a general partner (who is liable for all the debts and obligations of the firm), LPA 1907, s 4(2) One of the persons must be a limited partner. This person contributes money or property, valued at a stated amount, LPA 1907, s 4(2)	Any form of economic activity	Partnership Act 1890 Limited Partnerships Act 1907 Group partnership (partnership between partnerships: each one linked by a partnership deed to the 'head office') Two types of agreement: head partnership and branch partnership Sub-partnership (a partnership where one of the partners agrees to divide his share of the main partnership profits and losses with other persons) An illustration of how limited partnerships have been used in transactions is provided by *Reed (Inspector of Taxes) v Young* [1986] STC 226, HL	Restricted to extent of capital contribution, LPA 1907, s 4(2) A company may be a limited partner, LPA 1907, s 4(4)	As for partnerships generally Partnership does not have SLP but each partner does A partner has a beneficial interest in the property of the partnership. There is no interest capable of assignment. *Hadlee v Commissioner of Inland Revenue* [1993] STC 294, PC	According to percentage of interest in partnership profits, PA 1890, s 24 A limited partner cannot take part in the management of the partnership business Neither does the limited partner have power to bind the firm A partner who participates in the management of the firm will become liable for all debts and obligations of the firm incurred while it takes part in the management, LPA 1907, s 6(1)

Vehicle	***Formation***	***Nature of economic activity***	***Type(s) of business vehicle available***	***Members' liability***	***Owner of business property***	***Type of members' interest***
European Economic Interest Grouping (Neither a partnership nor a company) Formed on the basis of a contract. Art 1 Council Regulation (EEC) 2137/85	Created under the 1985 EC Regulation European Interest Grouping Regulations 1989, SI 1989/638 Formed by at least two persons who carry on economic activities in different states The persons may either be natural or artificial. Art 4 Council Regulation (EEC) 2137/85	Any form of economic activity Designed to facilitate cooperation across frontiers Preamble to Council Regulation (EEC) 2137/85 It is not designed to make profits for itself. Art 3(1) Council Regulation (EEC) 2137/85	An EEIG has legal personality if registered in a Member State. It is therefore capable of holding IP reg 3 EEIGR 1989 An EEIG must not carry on any activity outside the economic activities of its members. The activity must not be more than ancillary to those activities. Art 3(1) Council Regulation (EEC) 2137/85 The use of 'limited', 'unlimited' or 'public limited company' by an EEIG is prohibited, reg 10 EEIGR 1989 An EEIG is prohibited from exercising management functions over its members' activities, or holding shares in them, or be a member of another EEIG. Art 3(2)(a), (b) Council Regulation (EEC) 2137/85	Members have unlimited joint and several liability for the EEIG's debts and liabilities. Art 24 Council Regulation (EEC) 2137/85 This is however subject to their own limited liability	EEIG	Profits arising from activities paid to members in accordance with the contract of formation. Art 21(1) of Council Regulation (EEC) 2137/85

2.2 COMPANY INCORPORATION

A company is for all purposes a person. The law has created a legal fiction. A company can enter into contracts, borrow money, rent buildings and carry on a trade in e-commerce. A company can buy another company. A company can lose money just like an individual and go bankrupt. Capital, ie finance is contributed to the company by persons in exchange for shares which makes them members of the company. Each shareholding carries various rights such as the right to appoint the management of the company. The advantages of creating and using a company for the purposes of carrying on a business in respect of IT or e-commerce are examined later in this chapter. First let us consider the nature of a company within the UK.

A company can be formed by registration in accordance with the Companies Act 1985 ('CA 1985'). This statutory regime applies to England, Wales and Scotland, although the Companies Acts apply with some modifications in Scotland.

Forming a company brings with it a number of obligations. A company is required to produce annual accounts, and the directors are required to produce a report each year.[1] Each year the directors of a company are required to send to the Registrar of Companies a copy of the company accounts, directors' report and an auditors' report.[2] Companies can be acquired 'off-the-shelf' from formation agents. The method by which a company must be administered is governed by the constitution which comprises the memorandum and articles of association.

2.3 PUBLIC AND PRIVATE COMPANIES

CA 1985 distinguishes between a public and private company. A company is a public company if it is stated to be such in the memorandum of association.[3] A company, which is not a public company, is deemed to be a private company. The name of any public company ends with the words 'public limited company' or the abbreviation 'plc'. One advantage of using a public company for an e-commerce or IT business is that it is the first step necessary to obtain a listing on the UK Stock Exchange.

It is also possible to form a private company. The name of any private company must end with the words 'limited' or the abbreviation 'Ltd'.[4] One of the advantages of using a private company is that there are no minimum share capital requirements, and the conditions for the allotment and payment for share capital are less strict. Private companies are usually incorporated first to carry on a business. When the resources of the members are insufficient to meet the capital requirements of the business venture, the private company is then typically converted into a public company. In this way, capital can then be raised from the public.

---

1 CA 1985, ss 226 and 234.
2 Ibid, s 242.
3 Ibid, s 1.
4 Ibid, ss 25 and 27.

Example 2

A Ltd is formed by three individuals who each contribute £50,000 to the finances of the company. Each hold an equal number of shares in the company in proportion to their capital contributions. After two years of successful trading the management decide that it is time to expand the business by raising finance from the general public. This objective is to be achieved by converting the private company into a public company and seeking a listing on the UK Stock Exchange.

2.4 MANAGEMENT

The management of a company is governed by two documents known as the memorandum of association and articles of association. These documents contain the rules of how the company is to be managed. CA 1985 provides model articles of association, which are to be used in default of other articles being registered by the company, or insofar as not excluded.[1] Once registered, they are binding upon the company and its members.[2] The articles usually provide for a number of things, for example, how meetings are to be called, how the management are to be appointed, and transferability of shares.

2.5 CORPORATE PERSONALITY AND MEMBERSHIP LIABILITY FOR CORPORATE OBLIGATIONS

A company has single legal personality distinct from its members.[3] In other words, a company can enter into contracts, for example, for the hire of plant or machinery, or for the lease of telecommunication lines to permanent Internet backbone networks. The effect of this is that the obligations of the company are limited to the company and not directly extended to the members. The concept of single legal personality is pierced 'where special circumstances exist indicating that the company is a mere façade concealing the true facts'.[4] This usually happens where a company is used for the purposes of carrying on fraudulent activity. Otherwise the assets, debts and obligations are those of the company and not the members. Creditors do not generally have a claim against the assets of a company's members.

Example 3

A Ltd enter into contracts with consumers in the UK and abroad via the Internet for the sale of goods. The company receives payment for £20,000 worth of goods. However, as a result of trading difficulties the company passes into insolvency owing £50,000 to its trade suppliers. In this scenario the individual consumers will generally only have a claim against the company for the undelivered goods, as will the trade creditors.

---

1 CA 1985, s 8, SI 1985/805 and the Companies (Tables A to F) Regulations 1985, SI 1985/805, Table A.

2 CA 1985, s 14.

3 *Salomon v Salomon & Co* [1897] AC 22.

4 *Woolfson v Strathclyde Regional Council* (1978) SLT 159 at 161, per Lord Keith.

The liability of a company's members is determined by reference to the nature of their shareholding. Shares are issued by a company in exchange for finance. Shares in companies usually carry limited liability so that the members are liable only for the amount (if any) unpaid on the shares.[1] The concept of limited liability may only be of notional value where the business is small and has borrowed to finance its operations. In these circumstances, it is common for the bank to obtain personal guarantees from the directors and/or shareholders in respect of the finance granted to the company. The members would then be liable in their capacity as guarantors.

2.6 SHAREHOLDER RIGHTS

The rights that attach to shares vary. A company is usually permitted to create different classes of shares carrying various rights or restrictions under its articles of association.[2] For example, a company may issue preference shares that give the holder a right to a dividend or capital in priority to holders of ordinary shares in the company. Shares are personal property of the member.[3] As such, shares can be transferred by sale, or under a will. Shares normally carry the right to vote at shareholders' meetings for the purposes of appointing directors, sanctioning pay policy and any alteration to the company's share capital. A share normally carries the right to a proportion of the proceeds of the company when it is wound up.

2.7 MINIMUM SHARE CAPITAL REQUIREMENTS AND RAISING CORPORATE EQUITY FINANCE

A registered public company must meet minimum share capital requirements, otherwise it will not be granted a trading certificate. The authorised minimum capital is currently £50,000 (1999).[4] The capital of a public company can be raised from public or private sources. Capital can be raised from the public through the issue of shares in one of two ways. The available options are by admission to the Official List of the London Stock Exchange, or by admission to the Alternative Investment Market ('AIM').

2.8 TRANSFERABILITY OF COMPANY SHARES

Shares in a company are transferable.[5] A company can refuse to register a transfer only insofar as is allowed under its constitution (ie so far as permitted by the articles of association). For example, under the model articles provided for by CA 1985, Table A, reg 24, a transfer may be refused where shares are only partly paid up and the directors do not approve of the person to whom the transfer is made.

---

1 Insolvency Act 1986, s 74(2)(d).
2 See the Companies (Tables A to F) Regulations 1985, SI 1985/805, Table A, reg 2.
3 CA 1985, s 182.
4 Ibid, s 118.
5 Ibid, s 182.

A public company cannot impose restrictions on fully paid-up shares if it wishes to have its shares quoted on the Stock Exchange. It is not uncommon to find restrictions in the articles of a private company that enable the directors to refuse a registration in their absolute discretion or upon specified grounds. Shares in a company can be held by any person irrespective of nationality. Partnerships may hold shares in the name of the firm.

2.9 REGISTER OF MEMBERS

Every company is required to maintain a register of its members.[1] The particulars to be registered by the company include: name and address of members; date of registration and cessation of membership; and the number of shares held. Failure to comply with these requirements exposes the company to a fine.[2] The register must be kept at its registered office.[3] All members of a company are entitled to inspect the register free of charge. CA 1985 does not recognise the existence of bearer shares in respect of a company.

2.10 SHAREHOLDER CONTROL

UK law permits shareholders to enter into agreements between themselves, which, for example, determine how voting rights will be exercised by them in a general meeting. Shareholders may contract with each other to exercise their votes to prevent alteration of their company's share capital.[4] Alternatively, the shareholders' agreement could relate to how they are to vote on specific management issues.

2.11 FORMATION REQUIREMENTS FOR A PUBLIC COMPANY

A public company must be formed by two persons subscribing their names to a memorandum of association.[5] CA 1985 does not impose conditions on the type of person who can form a company. Thus, a natural or legal person, UK national or foreign national can form a UK registered company. After formation, a public company must continue to have at least two members because otherwise after six months of one-person membership that person is liable for the debts of the company.[6] Upon registration of the company's memorandum, the registrar issues certificates to the effect that the company is incorporated, that it is a limited liability company and a public company.

1 CA 1985, s 352.
2 Ibid.
3 Ibid, s 353.
4 *Russell v Northern Bank Development Corporation* [1992] 3 All ER 294.
5 CA 1985, s 1.
6 Ibid, s 24.

A public company cannot commence to trade or exercise any borrowing powers unless the registrar has issued a trading certificate.[1] Such a certificate is issued only where the registrar is satisfied that the nominal value of the company's share capital is at least equal to the authorised minimum (at the time of publication this is £50,000). CA 1985 only requires that at least one-quarter of the nominal value of the share capital be paid up plus any premium.[2] A public company with a share capital of £50,000 may therefore only require £12,500 to be paid up by its members, leaving £37,500 of share capital to be called up. By contrast, a private company can commence business upon its incorporation.

The memorandum must state the name of the company sought to be registered, the location of the company and its objects.[3] Since a public company may only be a company limited by shares, it must state that the liability of its members is limited. In respect of the share capital, it is also necessary to state the amount of the share capital and its division. A company is required to have a nominal share capital. Additionally, each subscriber must take at least one share, and the total number of shares taken by the subscribers must be reflected in the memorandum against their names.[4] Where a company states that its object is to carry on business as a general commercial company, CA 1985 provides that:[5]

- the object of the company is to carry on any trade or business; and
- it has the power to do anything for the purposes of carrying on that business.

The articles of association of a company govern the relationship between the company, directors and members. Model articles, known as 'Table A' are deemed to be a company's articles insofar as other articles are not registered, or insofar as they do not modify or exclude Table A.[6] The model articles are contained in the Companies (Tables A to F) Regulations 1985.[7] Table A includes articles dealing with the issue of share capital, share certificates, transfer of shares, the procedure for general meetings, the voting rights of members, and the appointment and powers of directors etc.

2.12 FISCAL INCENTIVES

The UK provides a range of fiscal incentives to attract investment directly into the shares of companies. The incentives are achieved through schemes such as the enterprise investment scheme ('EIS') and venture capital trusts ('VCT').

---

1 CA 1985, s 117.
2 Ibid, s 101.
3 Ibid, s 2.
4 Ibid.
5 Ibid, s 3A.
6 Ibid, s 8.
7 SI 1985/805, as amended by SI 1985/1052.

2.13 ENTERPRISE INVESTMENT SCHEME COMPANY

Incentives for persons to invest in an IT or Internet business can be achieved through the use of an enterprise investment scheme company. The EIS scheme can also be used for the purposes of financing research and development activities related to IT and Internet business. The advantage of organising a business programme through an EIS company is that it offers a fiscal reward to those who invest in it.[1] The relief is in the form of a set-off against income tax liability of the subscriber calculated by reference to the value of shares subscribed for in an EIS.[2] The minimum subscription in any year is £500. The maximum subscription is up to £150,000.[3] The relief is the amount which corresponds to the lower rate of taxation[4] on the amount subscribed for in the company.[5]

Example 4

A person subscribes for shares worth £40,000 in an EIS company which specialises in IT. The individual is entitled to income tax relief of £8,000.[6]

The relief operates to reduce tax liability on total income for the year in which the shares are subscribed.[7] In certain circumstances, part of the subscription can be carried back to a preceding year.[8] The relief is available to a person whether or not resident in the UK. No claim for relief against income tax is allowed unless the company has carried on the trade or a research and development activity for a period of at least four months.[9] Neither is relief available unless the shares were subscribed and issued for bona fide commercial purposes, and not as part of an arrangement the main purpose of which is tax avoidance.[10] On disposal of the shares, no capital gains tax liability arises if the shares are held for the relevant period.[11] Where a chargeable gain does arise in respect of EIS shares, it is possible to defer the tax liability by reinvestment.[12]

---

1 The provisions governing an enterprise investment scheme company are contained in Part VII, Ch III of the Income and Corporation Taxes Act 1988 and Part IV of the Taxation of Chargeable Gains Act 1992. See generally *Simon's Direct Tax Service* (Butterworths, loose-leaf, 1997) Part E3.1, and Update Commentary at U1.8008. See the Inland Revenue guidance manual *Inspector's Manual* 6925, and CA 5002 (published by Butterworths).

2 Income and Corporation Taxes Act 1988 ('ICTA 1988'), s 289A.

3 ICTA 1988, s 290.

4 The lower rate is currently 20 per cent and will remain so until at least the financial year 1997–98.

5 ICTA 1988, s 289A(2).

6 Ie 20 per cent (lower rate of income tax) of £40,000.

7 ICTA 1988, s 289A(2). See generally s 289A(5).

8 Ibid, s 289A(3), (4). The provision allows on a claim made by an individual for part of the subscription to be attributed to the preceding year in which it is incurred. Carry-back is available for up to half of any share issue, and in respect of no more than a subscribed value of £25,000.

9 Ibid, s 289A(6),(7).

10 Ibid, s 289(6).

11 Taxation of Chargeable Gains Act 1992 ('TCGA 1992'), s 150A. The relevant period is five years from the issue of the shares. (See s 312(1A)(a) of ICTA 1988.)

12 TCGA 1992, s 150C and Sch 5B.

To qualify for income and capital gains tax relief a person must invest in a qualifying EIS company.[1] It is therefore necessary for those seeking to use this incentive to ensure that the company is a qualifying company carrying on a qualifying trade[2] as required under ICTA 1988. A company can qualify under the EIS umbrella even though it is not resident in the UK.[3]

A qualifying trade is one which does not consist of, inter alia, the following activities, or if they do so, the activity must not represent a substantial part of the trade:[4]

- dealing in land, commodities, futures, shares, securities or other financial instruments;
- dealing in goods otherwise than in the course of an ordinary trade of wholesale or retail distribution;
- banking, insurance, money-lending, debt-factoring, hire-purchase financing or other financial activities;
- oil extraction industries;
- leasing, receiving royalties or licence fees;
- providing legal or accountancy services;
- providing services or facilities for any trade carried on by another person which consist to a substantial extent of activities described above.

There are many more conditions which must be satisfied to qualify as an EIS. See generally Part VII, Chapter III of ICTA 1988.

2.14 PARTNERSHIP

Another vehicle by which a business in IT or e-commerce may be carried on is through the use of a partnership. This is essentially a mechanism by which two or more persons carry on business together. As Table 1 shows that a partnership can take different forms. The UK recognises two types of partnership: these are a general and a limited partnership. The former is regulated by statute under the Partnership Act 1890 ('PA 1890'), and the latter by the Limited Partnership Act 1907 ('LPA 1907'). The statutory provisions are not a complete codification of the law relating to partnerships.

A partnership is a legal relationship between two or more persons. A partnership does not possess legal personality separate from its members like a company. Generally, the rights and obligations referred to under PA 1890 are capable of alteration with the consent of the partners (whether express or inferred from a course of dealing).[5] In this

---

1 ICTA 1988, s 289.

2 The Inland Revenue provide guidance on this matter in *Revenue Interpretation*, RI 120 (August 1995). A company carrying on a trade which is engaged in research and development will not be prevented from qualifying as an EIS company where the trade consists to a substantial extent of receiving royalties or licence fees, and those receipts are derived from the research and development which the company has carried out (ICTA 1988, s 297(5)). Special rules govern film production and royalty receipts (see s 297(4)).

3 ICTA 1988, s 293(1) (qualifying companies).

4 Ibid, s 297(2).

5 PA 1890, s 19.

context, PA 1890 is like a voluntary code, whereas the provisions of CA 1985 are generally mandatory.

2.15 GENERAL AND LIMITED PARTNERS

The legislation draws a distinction between a general and a limited partner. If a general partnership exists, each person who is a partner is liable jointly and severally for the acts of the other partners. A person who chooses the status of a limited partner is only liable for partnership debts and obligations to the extent of the capital contribution. A limited partner will lose this protection where it participates in the management of the partnership. There is no prohibition on the type of person who can be a partner. For example, a partnership can exist between an individual and a company, or possibly a resident and non-resident corporation.[1] All partners are agents for one another. The liability of partners is therefore potentially unlimited. By contrast, the liability of members of a company is limited to the extent of their shareholding. The debts and obligations incurred by the company are solely those of the company. LPA 1907 offers a degree of limited liability for partners. Unless indicated otherwise, the provisions of PA 1890 also regulate limited partnerships.[2]

Example 5

A Ltd is in partnership with Roy who is a limited partner. A Ltd is the general partner. Roy contributed capital of £40,000 to the partnership, and does not participate in the operation of the partnership business. Debts of £80,000 are incurred. Because Roy is a limited partner his liability for the partnership debts cannot exceed his contribution of £40,000.

Further protection against exposure to debts and obligations resulting from membership of a partnership can be obtained by incorporating a company to fulfil the role of a partner. The persons who are members of a partnership are collectively referred to as a 'firm'.

2.16 PARTNERSHIP PROPERTY

Property acquired for the purposes of the partnership business is deemed to be partnership property. As such, it must be applied by the partners for the purposes of the partnership and in accordance with the partnership agreement.[3] A partnership can hold shares in a company in the name of the firm. A partner may assign his share in the partnership by sale, mortgage or redeemable charge.[4] A limited partner may also assign his share in the partnership.[5]

---

1 ICTA 1988, ss 114 and 115(4).
2 LPA 1907, s 7.
3 PA 1890, s 20.
4 Ibid, s 31.
5 LPA 1907, s 6.

2.17 PARTNERSHIP FORMATION

Under PA 1890, a partnership exists where:

(1) two or more persons, for example, individuals or companies irrespective of nationality, or country of incorporation;
(2) carry on a business;
(3) in common; and
(4) with a view of profit.[1]

A partnership is usually formed under a contract, known as a partnership agreement. It is also possible for a partnership to be created informally from a course of dealings.[2] PA 1890 specifies a number of circumstances that are relevant in ascertaining whether or not a partnership is in existence.[3] These include the following:

(1) co-ownership of property does not in itself create a partnership;
(2) sharing of gross returns between persons does not in itself create a partnership;
(3) a share in the profits of a business is prima facie evidence of a partnership;
(4) a contract which provides for the remuneration of an employee linked to a share of the profits of the business does not in itself make the employee a partner in the business;
(5) the advance of money under a contract to a person who is carrying on a business, and the interest of which is linked to the profits does not in itself make the lender a partner (provided the contract is in writing and signed by the parties).

Since a partnership agreement is normally based on a contract, it is open to the parties to include express provisions governing the operation of the partnership.[4] Rights and obligations of the parties may also be implied into the partnership agreement by a court in appropriate circumstances.[5]

A partnership cannot include more than 20 partners.[6] This restriction can be avoided by the incorporation of a company that is to fulfil the role of partner, which can itself have an unlimited number of members. The advantage of this is that the liability of the corporate members will be limited.

2.17.1 Limited partnership

A limited partnership created under LPA 1907 must be registered with the companies registrar. LPA 1907 requires that various particulars be given to the registrar.[7] The particulars must state the firm's name, type and place of business, name of the partners, that the partnership is limited together with a description of the limited partners, and the capital sums contributed by each of them. The particulars must also state whether the capital is paid in cash or in kind.[8]

---

1 LPA 1907, s 1(1).
2 *Dungate v Lee* [1967] 1 All ER 241.
3 PA 1890, s 2.
4 LPA 1907, s 24.
5 Ibid.
6 CA 1985, s 716.
7 LPA 1908, s 8.
8 Ibid, s 8.

2.18 PARTNERSHIP CAPITAL

There are no minimum capital requirements in respect of a partnership. The capital of a partnership can be provided from two sources: these are from general partners and limited partners. The provision of capital by a person as a general partner results in a liability for all debts and obligations incurred by the partnership. Where a person contributes capital as a limited partner this results in a liability which corresponds to the amount of the capital contribution.[1] A person who provides capital and wishes to limit his liability must comply with the terms of LPA 1907.

For a limited partnership to exist, there must be two or more persons, one of whom is classified as a general partner. Such a person is liable for all debts and obligations of the firm.[2] A limited partner must not receive any part of his contribution, because if this occurs the person will become liable for the debts and obligations of the partnership that corresponds to the amount received. A limited partner may be a company, however, the number of partners must not exceed 20.[3]

A limited partnership must be registered with the registrar of companies otherwise it will be treated as a normal partnership.[4] The reduction in financial risk offered by LPA 1907 comes at a cost because a limited partner is prohibited from participating in the management of the partnership business. Where participation in the business occurs, a limited partner becomes liable for all the debts and obligations of the firm incurred whilst he takes part in the management.[5]

Table 2 provides a comparison of the nature, advantages and disadvantages of using a company or partnership for the purposes of business.

1 LPA 1907, s 4.
2 Ibid.
3 Ibid.
4 Ibid, s 5.
5 PA 1907, s 6.

Table 2: Advantages and disadvantages of a company and partnership as business vehicles

Partnership	*Company*
Nature	
Association of two or more persons carrying on a business in common with a view to profit	Incorporated body created under the Companies Act 1985
Creature of contract	Company cannot be a partnership
Legal Personality	
No legal personality separate from that of the partners	Possesses separate legal personality from members with the result that a company can enter into contracts on its own account, sue and be sued
Limited Liability	
Each partner bound by obligations incurred by fellow partners in the course of partnership business	A company can be limited in liability in respect of its members
Creditors are entitled to seek judgment against the partnership property and the assets of each and every partner	A shareholder is only liable up to the nominal value of his shareholding
Some partners can have limited liability but not all. See the Limited Liability Act 1907	The debts of the company cannot be imputed to its membership, unless the company is created with unlimited liability
Profits	
Each partner has a right to share in the profits	Shareholders are only entitled to a share in the profits if the company management chooses to distribute the profits
Profile	
Tend to have less of a profile in the general consciousness of the public	A company tends to have a higher profile which is reflected on the management. This is because relevant management personnel are referred to as holding specific posts such as 'Managing Director', 'Finance Director', 'Non-Executive Director'

Partnership	*Company*
Regulation	
PA 1890 tends to be a voluntary code. The rights and duties of partners vis-à-vis each other can be varied by consent (express or implied), or by a course of dealing	Running a company is onerous. The Companies Act makes a number of demands, such as the requirement for meetings to be called in a particular way, an audit is required, annual shareholders' meetings must take place, although private companies can elect to dispense with certain requirements
Finance	
Potentially difficult to raise finance. A partnership is limited to 20 members	Finance can be raised more easily. Membership is potentially without limitation
Dissolution	
Automatically dissolved on death or bankruptcy of any partner in the absence of express agreement to the contrary	Capable of perpetual existence. Company is only dissolved on winding up which generally occurs where debts cannot be paid
Transferability of Shares	
A partner may transfer his share in the partnership. However the assignee cannot interfere in the management. He is only entitled to receive the partner's share of the profits	Shares in a company which is listed on the Official Stock Exchange or the AIM are generally much easier to transfer than partnership interests. Broadly a larger market exists for the shares of a publicly quoted company. The assignee of shares usually obtains the full right to participate in the management of the company via the shareholders' general meeting. The market for shares in a private company may be more limited
Taxation	
Partnership profits determined by reference to corporation tax principles if a partner is a company. The profits of the partners, divided according to their profits sharing ratios, are then subject to the relevant tax rate	Corporation tax applies to company. Income tax applies to salaries of directors and employees, and dividends distributed to shareholders

Partnership	*Company*
Property Partnership property is owned by the partners, and not by the partnership	Property vested in a company belongs to the company and not its members
Contracts Every partner in a firm may act for the purposes of the firm's business, and bind fellow partners	No member of the company as a member has any authority to bind the company contractually

2.19 JOINT VENTURES

In some situations, it is thought desirable to collaborate with other people. One way of facilitating such collaboration in a business context is by creating a company in which both collaborators hold a specific proportion of the shareholding. The amount of shares held usually reflects the extent of that party's contribution to the collaboration. The 'joint venture' is not a person, although the vehicle through which the collaboration is carried on may possess legal personality.

Example 6

Internet Technologies Ltd ('IT Ltd') and Internet Access Provider Ltd ('IAP Ltd') decide that they wish to develop technology to meet a specific problem experienced in the transfer of information between Internet access providers. IT Ltd is to provide the use of technologies developed in-house, while IAP Ltd is to contribute the use of personnel, technologies and facilities for the purposes of the collaborative project. The parties agree that the joint venture should be carried on through the medium of a company to be called 'Joint Venture Technologies Ltd'. The parties transfer their respective contributions to the joint venture company in exchange for the issue of shares which are held in equal numbers. The parties enter into a shareholder agreement which defines how the parties are to vote on specific issues in controlling the company, such as appointment of management. Additionally, the shareholders' agreement specifies that the venture is to terminate after six years unless agreement to the contrary is reached. The termination is to be effected by seeking voluntary liquidation.

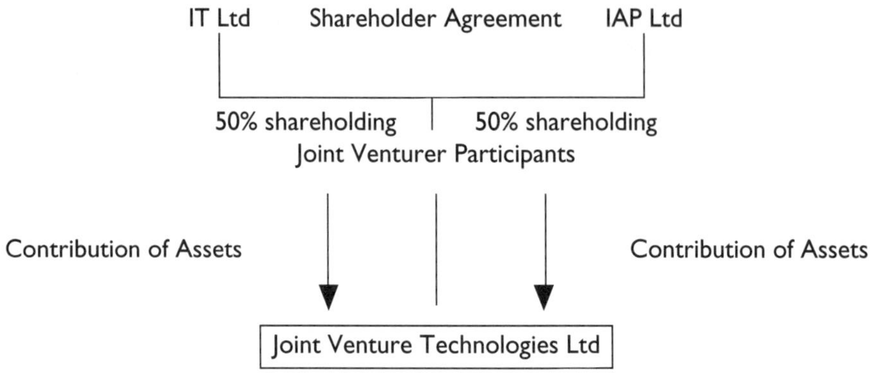

Joint Venture Vehicle

In the UK, there are many ways in which a collaborative venture can be implemented. A joint venture vehicle may take one of the following forms:

- corporate venture;
- general partnership;
- limited partnership;
- European Economic Interest Grouping;
- contractual joint ventures.

The nature of an EEIG and a contractual joint venture is explored below.

2.20 EUROPEAN ECONOMIC INTEREST GROUPING ('EEIG')

The EEIG is designed to assist cross-border business ventures within the European Union ('EU'). An EEIG is formed by a contract typically entered into between two or more persons from various EU Member States. An EEIG registered in the UK may be managed by a legal person such as a company.[1] At least one or more natural persons must be appointed to represent the legal person. Any natural person is subject to the same liabilities as if he were manager.[2] The name registered for an EEIG is prohibited from including any reference to 'Limited', 'unlimited' or 'public limited company'.[3] This is because an EEIG does not possess such characteristics.

Example 7

Internet Technologies Ltd ('IT Ltd'), a UK based company and Internet Access Provider Gmbh ('IAP Gmbh'), a company based in Germany, decide that they wish to develop technology to meet a specific problem experienced in the transfer of information between Internet access providers. IT Ltd is to provide the use of technologies developed in-house, while IAP Gmbh is to contribute the use of

1 Article 5(1) of the European Economic Interest Grouping Regulation (EEC) 2137/85 (OJ 1985 L199/1).
2 Ibid, Art 6.
3 Ibid, Art 10(1).

personnel, technologies and facilities for the purposes of the collaborative project. The parties agree that the joint venture should be carried on through the medium of an EEIG. The parties enter into a written contract which is registered in the UK.

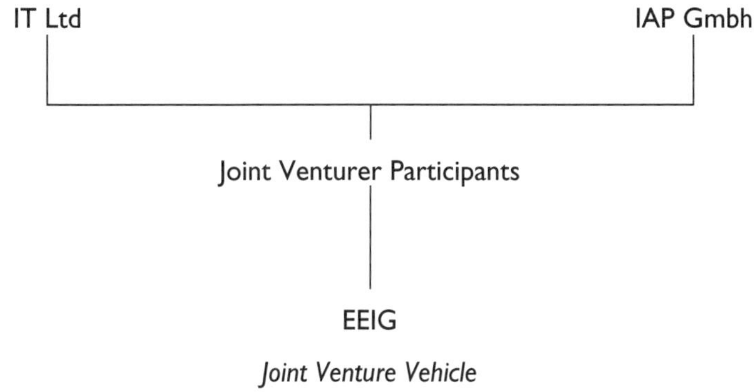

The EEIG has legal personality if the EEIG has registered its official address in the UK.[1] The effect of this is that it acquires legal personality with the power to enter into contracts, borrow money etc, in its own name. Although the EEIG has legal personality, the liability of members for the obligations of an EEIG are joint and several.[2] For the purposes of UK taxation, it is fiscally transparent, ie profits and losses arising from its activities are only taxable in the hands of the members.[3]

For the purposes of registration in the UK, the registrar of companies is the EEIG registrar.[4] The contract forming the EEIG must be delivered to the registrar, together with Form EEIG 1. This contains the names and particulars specified in Art 5 of the EC Regulation.[5] Upon registration, a certificate is issued stating the date of registration.[6] The issue of a certificate is conclusive evidence that the requirements of the EC Regulation have been met.[7] The EEIG can itself be wound up under Part V of the Insolvency Act 1986 as an unregistered company.

---

1 See the Department of Trade and Industry Regulations European Economic Interest Grouping Regulations 1989, SI 1989/638. See also Inland Revenue guidance manual *European Economic Interest Groupings* 'General Introduction', Section 2.

2 Regulation (EEC) 2137/85 (OJ 1985 L199/1), Art 24.

3 ICTA 1988, s 510A. Transparency is achieved by making the EEIG agent of its members.

4 Regulation (EEC) 2137/85 (OJ 1985 L199/1), Art 9(1).

5 Ibid, Art 9(2).

6 Ibid, Art 9(5).

7 Ibid, Art 9(7).

Chapter 3

COMMERCIAL INTERMEDIARIES

3.1 INTRODUCTION

The appointment of a commercial intermediary for the purposes of carrying on e-commerce is an option available to those who want to develop an export trade. One of the advantages of appointing a commercial intermediary is that it can be used for tax effective purposes. The insertion of an introduction agent in a foreign jurisdiction can legitimately be used to minimise profits. This is achieved because the economic function of an introduction agent is generally minimal compared to the functions and risks undertaken by fully fledged agents and distributors. For this reason more 'receipts' can be allocated to another jurisdiction. There are many forms of commercial intermediary which are considered below.

Example 8

Alpha US Inc appoint Beta UK Ltd as its introduction agent for the purposes of soliciting orders for products made by Alpha US Inc. The agent fulfils this function by operating an Internet trading site within the UK. The agent is paid a commission for each order accepted by Alpha US Inc. Beta UK Ltd effectively operates an advertising window for Alpha US Inc within the UK. Orders are placed with Beta UK Ltd, but these are transferred to a computer server operated by Alpha US Inc. It is via the US company that the order is processed, accepted and delivered.

In this way the economic function performed by the introduction agent is minimised. The agent will only be entitled to a commission which will be small in contrast to the receipts which must be allocated to the US company because of the functions performed by it. In other words, the processing, acceptance, and delivery of the product justifies higher profits being allocated to the US company on each and every transaction.

Alternatively, a commercial intermediary might be appointed to act in its own name and to conclude contracts with third parties via the medium of e-commerce trading sites. The effect of this is that arrangements will typically exist under which the agent passes onto the principal (for example, Alpha US Inc) orders which are then delivered in accordance with a scheme laid down by the principal. If, as in the above example, Alpha US Inc delivers the products, bears all risks as to loss of products in transit to the customer, and the risk of any default by a customer in payment then these risks should justify a high profit margin being retained by Alpha US Inc. Although the UK company in this scenario has power to conclude contracts with customers upon which it will be liable, it is none the less possible to minimise the profits which are to be attributed to the UK company. If the US company is to compensate the UK company for any liability it incurs as a result of the contracts this should minimise the profit margin of the UK company. This should be the case where the US company bears the risks of delivery, and retains title to the goods until delivery to the UK customers.

It may be the case that the agent is granted power to consign goods once it has concluded contracts with third parties. Possession of physical goods for onward transmission carries risk which must be reflected in the commission rate of the agent.

3.2 LEGAL CONTROL OF COMMERCIAL INTERMEDIARIES

The relationship between commercial intermediaries and their appointing parties is generally governed by a written contract. Additionally, local jurisdictions may have specific legislation which regulates the operation of particular commercial intermediaries. An example of such legislation is the Dutch Civil Code, which deals specifically with the regulation of commercial intermediaries. Within the EU, regulations may also exist which deal with particular commercial relationships. For example, the Commercial Agents (Council Directive) Regulations 1993, SI 1993/3053 contains rules governing the form and content of agreements in respect of commercial agents.

Generally, the main source of rules governing the relationship is the written contract. It is of paramount importance that the arrangement is carefully planned and drafted with precision.

3.3 BENEFITS OF APPOINTING A COMMERCIAL INTERMEDIARY

Some of the benefits of appointing a commercial intermediary are summarised below.

(1) An intermediary knows the local market, and so can operate efficiently with knowledge of the competition.
(2) An intermediary is close to designated local markets, which is important in the context of e-commerce because this facilitates quicker and more efficient access times for customers to Internet trading sites.
(3) An intermediary can use its presence to develop knowledge of that market and implement appropriate advertising.
(4) Appointment of an intermediary in a local market may result in quicker and more efficient delivery of products.
(5) An intermediary can generally be used to create a permanent presence within a jurisdiction to create brand awareness of products. Title to a brand is typically held by the principal, which generally means the creation of brand awareness by the intermediary is for the benefit of the principal.
(6) A commercial intermediary bears the burden of start-up costs and generally the appointing party will only need to pay for the services of the intermediary and/or supply of the products.

(7) If the commercial intermediary is an associated person, it may have tax advantages for the appointing party. For example, if the intermediary is a subsidiary and located in a low tax jurisdiction the relationship can be injected with sufficient risk and obligation to justify retention by the intermediary of a larger slice of the receipts received. In this way, more of the receipts in respect of transactions can be retained in the low tax jurisdiction.
(8) A commercial intermediary assumes the risks of everyday business.
(9) Appointment of an entity local to a particular jurisdiction is sometimes the first step towards takeover, and thus acquisition of an interest in the jurisdiction.
(10) Use of a commercial intermediary is sometimes effective in establishing a low cost presence within a jurisdiction.
(11) Appointment of a commercial intermediary may also be effective because it may undertake responsibility/liability to the third party within the jurisdiction for the products, or alternatively the intermediary may limit the risk of the foreign exporter by guaranteeing the performance by the third party of its obligations such as payment of the price.

3.4 THE FAMILY OF COMMERCIAL INTERMEDIARIES

Many varieties of commercial intermediary exist. Table 3 highlights the type of intermediary which may be chosen for the purposes of carrying on an export trade outside the UK, or a trade in the UK by an overseas trader. Some commercial entities are, as a matter of law, only able to do certain things, or incur specific responsibilities because of the attributes which are associated with that entity. Because of either the inherent limitation on function, or undertakings assumed by an intermediary, a 'sliding scale' operates in respect of the payments a commercial intermediary is entitled to expect.

Table 3: Commercial intermediaries

Intermediary	***Description***
Mere Representation Agent	Commonly known as an introduction agent. Under this arrangement the agent has authority to solicit orders which are passed on to the principal. The principal then determines whether or not to accept the order, and usually makes arrangements for delivery of merchandise to the third party 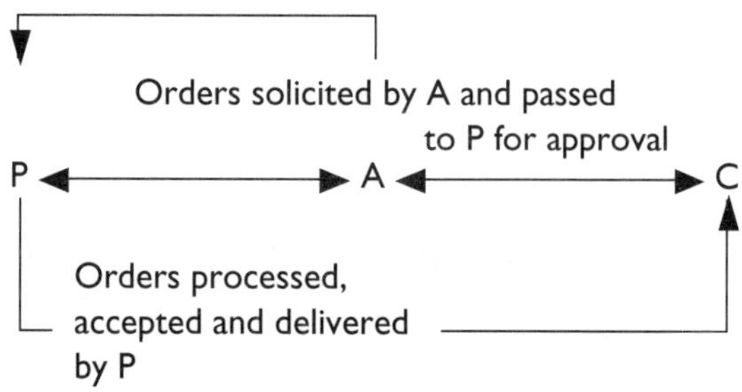
Agent Acting for Disclosed Principal	This is an agent who discloses that he is working on behalf of another. Generally, the work of such an agent results in the formation of a contract directly between the principal and third party. The precise way in which the agent is to conduct business, for example, in terms of the parameters for accepting orders placed via Internet trading sites will be governed by the contract between principal and agent 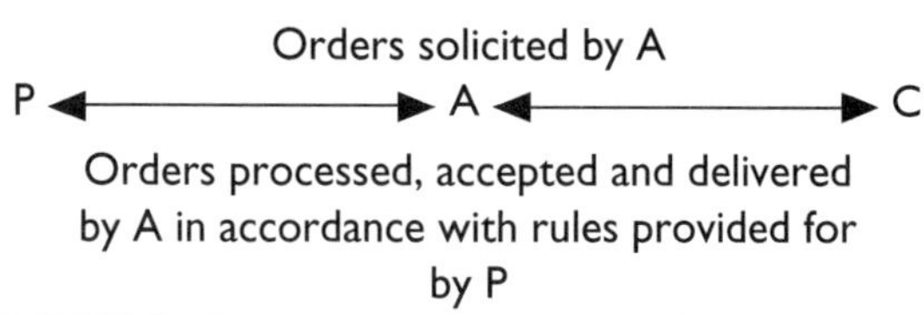
Agent Acting for Undisclosed Principal	This type of agent deals with the outside world apparently for its own account. The UK undisclosed principal is potentially liable on the contracts entered into by the agent. This is because once the third party discovers that the agent is operating for an undisclosed principal it can elect to sue the principal. Under this type of arrangement the agent would appear to be for example a sole Internet trader concluding contracts directly with consumers

Intermediary	*Description*
	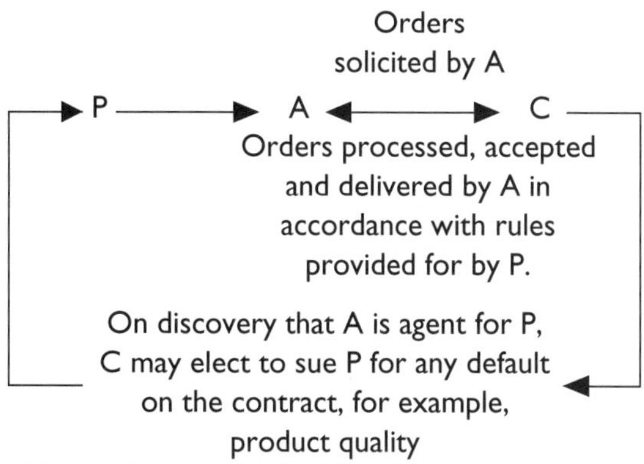
Del Credere Agent	Under this form of arrangement the agent guarantees that the buyer will pay the price of the goods. Because he undertakes the risk of bearing the cost of the product(s) the agent is entitled to what is known as the del credere commission.
Broker	A broker generally operates as a negotiator, and has no possession of products. For example, a broker may negotiate a price for products not in his possession via the use of e-commerce
Mercantile Agent	Under this arrangement the agent has possession of merchandise owned by the principal. The agent consigns products to third parties on the direction of the principal, or alternatively is given authority to supply third parties directly with merchandise from stock held by it A mercantile agent usually has authority to conclude contracts directly with third parties on behalf of its principal. Because a mercantile agent assumes more risk than say an introduction agent it is entitled to a higher commission. This is because the agent has possession of the goods and will generally be responsible for their safety in the absence of specific agreement The Factors Act 1889 defines under s 1(1) a mercantile agent as an agent who in the customary course of business has authority to sell goods, or to consign goods for sale, or to buy goods or to raise money on the security of goods

Intermediary	***Description***
	In the context of Internet trade an agent of this type would be appointed to sell goods via the medium of an Internet trading site, with power to consign goods from stock held by it once orders have been accepted
Distribution Arrangement	A distributor is a person appointed by a manufacturer to sell products within a specific territory The distributor buys goods at wholesale prices from the manufacturer/supplier. The distributor is in business on his own account and sells the goods to third parties at a resale price. The difference between the resale price and wholesale price generally represents the profit of the distributor on individual transactions
Franchise Arrangement	A franchise is the grant of a right to exploit a business format. A franchisee is a person in business for his own account who pays money to make use of the business format idea. A franchise could be granted in respect of a business format idea for the operation of an electronic commerce business site Under a franchise arrangement the franchisee pays for the right to use commercial know-how, registered trade marks and other associated copyright which relate to how a business in a particular sector is to be operated A franchise agreement may also include a number of other mixed elements, such as the grant of a commercial lease to property from which to run the business format. Additionally, the franchise could provide for the provision of goods to the franchisee for use in the business

The risks, rights and responsibilities attaching to the commercial intermediaries identified in Table 3 vary. For instance, the responsibilities and risks of an introduction agent are significantly less than the risks of a del credere agent. Thus, if an associated intermediary is appointed as an introduction agent it will only be entitled to a limited commission on the customers it introduces to its principal. Such an arrangement could be of use where the introduction agent is located in a high tax jurisdiction, and works on behalf of a principal in a low tax jurisdiction. The limited risk of an introduction agent justifies higher payments to the principal. It must be emphasised that the use of specific intermediaries with limited legal risks etc, is no substitute for having in existence economic transactions which support the choice of intermediary. In other words, what actually happens at 'ground level' must be reflected in the choice of vehicle for transactions. Tax authorities are not fooled by the use of mere labels.

3.5 AGENCY

In *Customs and Excise Commissioners v Johnson*,[1] Woolf J cited with approval the definition of agency in *Bowstead on Agency*[2] which states:

> 'Agency is the relationship between two persons, one of whom expressly or impliedly consents that the other should represent him or act on his behalf and the other of whom similarly consents to represent the former or so to act.'

A commercial agent is defined under the Commercial Agents (Council Directive) Regulations 1993 as:

> 'a self-employed intermediary who has continuing authority to negotiate the sale or purchase of goods on behalf of another person (the "principal"), or to negotiate and conclude the sale or purchase of goods on behalf of and in the name of that principal.'[3]

Agency is based on the relationship of three persons. These are the principal, agent and third party.

An agent is appointed to represent the commercial interests of the appointing party, known as the principal. An agent is sometimes provided with authority to contractually bind its principal to transactions with a third party. As the lines on Diagram 2 show, it is possible for rights and duties to exist between all three parties. The nature of these rights and duties varies according to the type of agency agreement which exists. As Diagram 2 illustrates, for the purposes of e-commerce, a commercial intermediary such as an agent can be appointed to solicit orders, or accept orders.

3.5.1 Agency classifications

Broadly, agency falls into two categories. Agents either act for disclosed or undisclosed principals. The nature of the relationship differs significantly. For example, an agent acting for an undisclosed principal generally incurs more risk as a result of the legal rule that the agent is liable on the contract concluded with third parties.[4] Because of variations in the type of risks injected into different agency agreements, it is possible to choose a relationship which will support the chosen pricing arrangements between associated parties. For example, if the parties want to limit the commission of an agent and maximise the returns to a principal located in a low tax jurisdiction, it is desirable to establish an agency arrangement under which the

1 [1980] STC 624 at 629.
2 (Sweet & Maxwell, 15th edn, 1986), p 1.
3 SI 1993/3053, reg 2(1).
4 This is because the contract is between the agent and third party.

Diagram 2

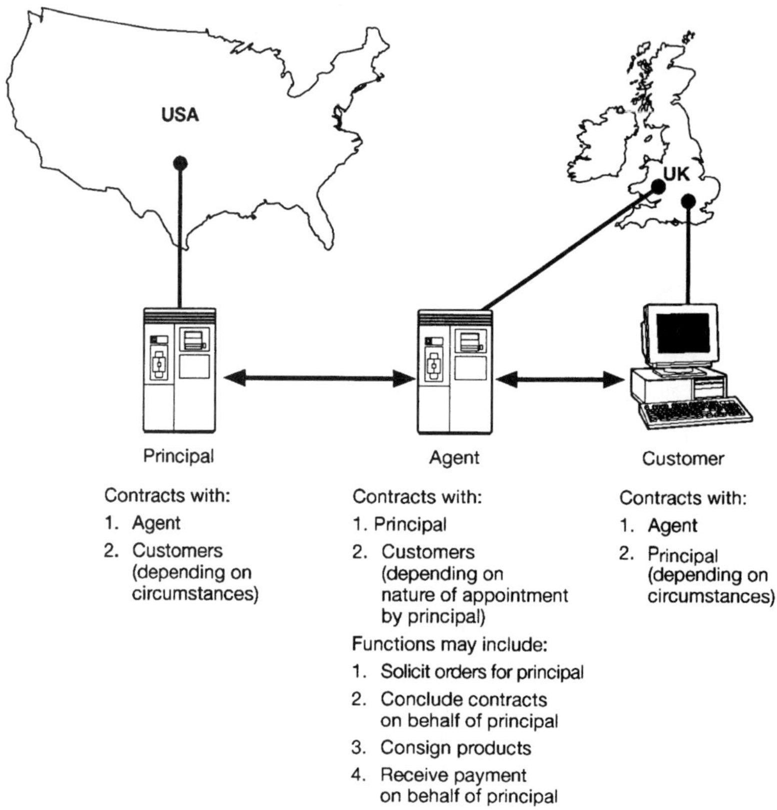

agent incurs minimal risk. An arrangement which might meet this objective is the use of a disclosed agency whereby any contract concluded with a third party is with the principal and not the agent. Alternatively, the parties may use a simple introduction agent arrangement. The benefit is that these parties generally assume minimal risk.

It is important to realise that agency is generally the product of a contractual agreement. The parties to the agreement can decide precisely how the agency is to operate, for example, the extent of the powers available to the agent in concluding contracts with third parties on behalf of the principal.

Table 4 summarises the nature of the distinction between a disclosed and undisclosed agent.

Table 4: Agency categories

Type	*Nature of relationship*
Disclosed Agency	Principal liable on contracts entered into with consumers by agent. Actions of the agent creates contractual responsibilities between principal and third party Agent not generally liable on contract concluded on behalf of principal with consumers See *Montgomerie v United Kingdom Mutual Steamship Association* [1891] 1 QB 370 Agent may undertake personal liability on contract
Undisclosed Agency	Generally, the agent initially becomes liable to the consumer on the contract which has been concluded between the two. In other words the agent incurs contractual responsibilities Principal only incurs contractual liability where the consumer discovers the existence of the principal and elects to sue the principal for any breach of responsibilities in respect of the contract The principal cannot be sued, or intervene on the contract if the consumer specifically intends to contract with the agent because of the agent's personal skill, or solvency

It is important to appreciate that because of the consensual nature of agency, it is possible to inject risk into the arrangement over and above what the law would otherwise imply into the agency relationship. For example, in the case of a disclosed agency arrangement the agent is not generally liable on the concluded contract with the third party. Instead, a binding legal contract exists between the principal and third party.

However, the risks of the agent can be increased, and accordingly its right to a higher commission can be justified by the agent entering into what are known as collateral warranties with the third party. For example, the agent might undertake that the goods supplied under the contract are of satisfactory quality, or perhaps that the consignment of goods will comply with their description, or that the goods are fit for their intended purpose.

3.5.2 Commission

The UK has no specific legal rules on the rate of commission which an agent should receive, or guidance upon how the commission should be determined. This issue is of critical importance where the appointment of a commercial intermediary is made by a related person on a cross jurisdiction basis. Such pricing issues need clarification by the assistance of transfer pricing advisors.

It has been judicially recognised that the work of an agent is precarious and subject to risk. Any commission should reflect the commercial risk of an agent's business activities. In *Alpha Trading Ltd v Dunnshaw-Patten Ltd*,[1] Lawton LJ commented:

> 'The life of an agent in commerce is a precarious one. He is like the groom who takes a horse to the water-trough. He may get his principal to the negotiating table but when he gets him there he can do nothing to make him sign, any more than the groom can make a horse drink ...'.

3.5.3 Agency, distribution and franchise arrangements

A distributor is generally classified as a reseller of products and is consequentially entitled to make a reseller's profit on transactions. A distributor does not act on behalf of another person and is not accountable to another person, as an agent is to his principal. A distributor has no power to bind the supplier of the products to a contract with consumers.

A franchisee like a distributor is in business for his own account with no power to bind the franchisor, ie the person permitting exploitation of the business format idea. A franchisee is like a distributor in that he operates rather like a reseller, but is also an exploiter of an idea.

By contrast, a simple commission agent is generally entitled only to a percentage of each transaction it concludes between its principal and a third party. This is because an agent is not an independent reseller.

Any documentation appointing a commercial intermediary should be structured so as to ensure that the risks, duties and obligations are in place which justify an arrangement being labelled as either a specific type of agency, distribution or franchise agreement. However, such documentation is no substitute for real, sustainable economic transactions.

3.6 IDENTIFYING AND CLASSIFYING COMMERCIAL INTERMEDIARIES

The UK has no form of legislation which precisely identifies the material characteristics of each and every type of commercial intermediary. Sometimes this distinction is of importance for tax and transfer pricing[2] purposes. The distinction is sometimes necessary to determine because many arrangements between associated parties are not the subject of proper documentation. It is possible to draw a number of conclusions as to the nature of a commercial intermediary by what that party is required to do. For example, the following points are useful indicators.

---

1 [1981] QB 290 at 308.

2 This is the examination of pricing structures adopted between associated people for the supply of either goods or services. The function of transfer pricing is to ensure as far as practicable that an arm's length price is paid for transactions between associated parties. The obligation to ensure an arm's length price arises only between connected parties dealing on a cross-border basis.

- The fact that an agreement permits an entity to sell goods to third parties at any price it chooses, with payment of a fixed amount for the goods to a supplier points to a resale arrangement.
- The fact that a person is required to provide details of customers, and accounts of moneys received and paid out is a clear pointer that the entity is selling as an agent. An entity which pays wholesale prices as opposed to being required to account for the whole proceeds of a sale received from a third party to another is likely to be classified as a reseller (distributor).

3.7 LEGAL DOCUMENTATION

One of the problems with the use of the term 'agency' is that it has become used in a number of circumstances to describe situations which are not proper agency relationships. A contract which merely places a 'principal' and an 'agent' tag on parties in an agreement does not succeed in automatically creating an agency relationship. The labels used in agreements cannot be relied upon as creating the relationship desired to be brought into existence.[1] The courts of England and Wales have held on several occasions that the description of a relationship as being one of agency has in fact been as a matter of commercial reality a relationship of manufacturer and reseller.[2] By contrast the courts have equally held an agency relationship to exist despite the fact that the contract between the parties excluded such a possibility.

The important point to remember is that documentation creating arrangements must reflect the risks and obligations which are common to that specific relationship. The mere use of labels does not necessarily create a relationship of that type. Legal documentation for any arrangement should reflect the economic role performed by the participants.

3.8 ADVANTAGES OF AGENCY CATEGORIES FOR TRANSFER PRICING PURPOSES

Agency takes many different forms which attract a range of risks to the role of principal and agent. This range of differences can be used to support the pricing structure chosen by parties. For example, an agent working as a representative for a disclosed principal does not incur the same risks as an agent working for an undisclosed principal. An agent working for an undisclosed principal enters directly into contractual relations with the third party, ie the consumer. A third party in this context has the choice of suing the agent or alternatively electing to sue the principal. In this scenario the agent would justifiably be entitled to a higher fee for the provision of its services.

---

1 See *Fenston v Johnstone* (1940) 23 TC 29.

2 See, for example, *WT Lamb & Sons v Goring Brick Co Ltd* [1932] 1 KB 710; or *International Harvester Co of Australia Pty Ltd v Currigans Hazeldene Pastoral* (1958) 100 CLR 644.

Example 9

Alpha Inc appoints Beta UK Ltd to sell goods manufactured by it within the UK. Both companies are associated. Alpha Inc holds the majority of the shares in Beta UK Ltd. The appointment is solely for the sale of goods through the use of Internet trading sites. Beta UK Ltd is appointed to act as an undisclosed agent. In other words, this means that consumers in the UK will believe that they are contracting for the provision of goods from a UK company. The presence of a US company in the transaction will not be indicated in any way through the activities of the UK company. Because the UK company acts as an undisclosed agent it is initially liable on the contract for supply of the goods. This means that the consumer will in the first instance have the right to sue the UK company. The use of this type of agent justifies a higher commission to it than say a mere introduction agent. Such choice of commercial intermediary can be used to bolster the pricing structure chosen.

Other types of agent may incur more risks because of the additional services they provide to their principal. The allocation of risk to a person is one factor for justifying a higher payment to that person. For example, a del credere agent guarantees that the third party will pay for the goods it purchases. The del credere agent incurs an additional risk over and above that of a normal agent which justifies a higher commission on transactions. The creation and use of a del credere agent would be of value where a principal is located in a high tax jurisdiction. The risks undertaken by the del credere, ie responsibility for discharge of the buyer's contractual obligations to the seller, would justify the attraction of higher commission rates.

Example 10

US Internet Trading Inc appoint UK Intermediary Ltd as a del credere agent for the purposes of selling products manufactured by the US company. The point of sale will be via Internet trading sites. The UK company is appointed to market the products to two distinct categories of client. These are businesses and the general public. The UK company is appointed on the basis that it will guarantee the payment by each and every buyer of the purchase price for products.

An order for £30,000 worth of goods is placed via the Internet trading site by an authorised business entitled to access and place orders via the business section of the trading site. Under the terms of access the business buyer is entitled to delivery of the goods on order, and for payment within 60 days to be made to UK Intermediary Ltd. No payment is made within the 60 day period. Because the agent is a del credere, it is obliged to pay the £30,000 to US Internet Trading Inc. The intermediary will then be left to pursue a claim for payment against the business buyer itself. For the increase in responsibility the del credere is entitled to a higher commission.

Alternatively, the use of an introduction agent may have several advantages. From a transfer pricing perspective a disclosed introduction agent is not liable on any contract between principal and third party, ie the consumer. Neither is the agent responsible for concluding the contract. The legal risk associated with the activities of such an agent are limited. This means that the introduction agent is limited to a lower rate of return. An introduction agent is a person appointed to solicit customers, for example, through the use of Internet trading sites and who acts as a go-between for the principal and third party. The introduction agent has no power to conclude contracts between the principal and third party. The solicited orders are submitted to the principal who decides whether or not to accept the order. An introduction agent represents the interests of a person in the sense that such an agent is eager to acquire business, because he is rewarded by a commission for each order accepted. Any foreign trader must, however, be careful in appointing an agent. The arrangement should be structured so that it cannot be used as the basis for the UK tax authority claiming that a trade is being carried on in the UK through that agent for the purposes of applying a corporation tax charge, or that a trade is being exercised within the UK so that an income tax charge can be applied.

3.9 TAXATION OF UK REPRESENTATIVES OF NON-RESIDENTS TRADING IN THE UK

3.9.1 Definition of a UK representative

In certain circumstances, it is possible to assess a non-resident through his UK representative (either a branch or agent). The legislation governing the collection machinery is contained in s 126, and Sch 23 to the Finance Act 1995 ('FA 1995'). The effect of the legislation is to impose obligations and liabilities in relation to income tax, corporation tax, and capital tax on the branch or agent which is a UK representative of a non-resident.[1] A branch or agency is only a UK representative if the non-resident carries on a trade through either of those mediums.[2] A branch or agency is defined as meaning 'any factorship, agency, receivership, branch or management'.[3] The UK representative could, thus, be the person who operates a computer server in the UK for a non-resident company. Of course a branch would need to exist which was used as a centre of economic operations to produce profits for the non-resident.

If the non-resident does not carry on a trade through a branch or agency in the UK, then there can be no UK representative. In these circumstances the non-resident is responsible for complying with UK tax obligations in respect of any UK source trade.

Example 11

X Inc sets up a branch in the UK through which it operates an e-commerce business. The profits for 1998–99 are £1 million. The branch will constitute a UK representative of X Inc. Accordingly, the branch will be responsible for the assessment and payment of the UK tax attributable to the profits of the branch.

Example 12

Z SA operates a computer server in the UK. The server acts as a conduit for relaying customer orders placed via an e-commerce web site hosted by the computer server. A computer server in Spain then processes the orders, interrogates the UK

---

1 FA 1995, s 126(1).
2 Ibid, s 126(2).
3 Ibid, s 126(8); Taxes Management Act 1970, s 118.

Diagram 3

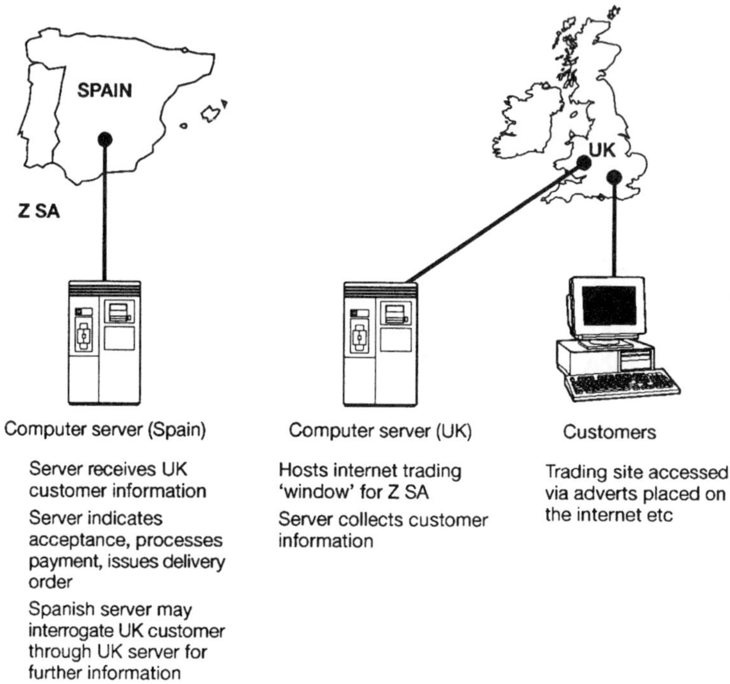

computer server for further information concerning the customer, processes the payment details, and issues the delivery order. Delivery is made from Spain. In these circumstances there is no branch or agency in the UK through which a trade is carried on. Accordingly, there is no UK representative. Any income tax liability which might arise because a trade is being carried on in the UK would be the responsibliity of Z SA. It is unlikely that a trade would be carried on in the UK because the operations from which the profits arise are not in the UK.

3.9.2 Agents prevented from being UK representatives

FA 1995 excludes certain types of agent from being a UK representative. These persons are as follows:

(1) A person who although an agent for the non-resident does not carry on a regular agency for the non-resident.[1] In other words, casual agents are excluded.
(2) Brokers, provided certain conditions are met.[2]
(3) Investment managers, provided certain conditions are met.[3]

---

1 FA 1995, s 127(1)(a).
2 Ibid, s 127(1)(b). For the conditions see generally s 127.
3 Ibid, s 127(1)(c). For conditions see generally s 127.

3.9.3 Obligations of a UK representative

Insofar as relevant to an e-commerce trade, the obligations of the UK representative are in relation to the following amounts:[1]

(1) any income from the trade which arises directly or indirectly through or from that branch or agency;
(2) any income from property or rights which are used by, or held by or for, that branch or agency;
(3) which are chargeable gains by reference to the branch or agency.

The obligations imposed on a UK representative are detailed in Sch 23 to FA 1995. The obligations include all matters relating to assessment and collection of tax. Generally, the UK representative is jointly responsible with the non-resident for all the tax obligations arising from the trade carried on through the branch or agency.[2]

1 FA 1995, s 126(2).
2 Ibid, Sch 23.

Part III

UNITED KINGDOM TAXATION: GENERAL

Chapter 4

TAX CHARGES

4.1 WHAT IS TAX, AND HOW IS IT CHARGED?

Tax is a compulsory requirement to pay money to the Government.[1] The method by which the payment is calculated varies according to the type of tax. In some cases the amount of money to be paid is fixed as a specific percentage of profits from a designated source, and the tax liability is imposed upon the person who derives money from that source, such as a trade.[2] This is known as direct taxation.[3] Tax can also be imposed on the use of various forms of supply, such as a telecommunication service. The person paying for the use of the service is required to pay tax calculated by reference to the value of that service. However, the person paying the tax is not necessarily the person who accounts for the tax to the Government. This is known as indirect taxation.[4]

Before considering the application of specific tax charges it is appropriate to recognise the fact that there is no specific territorial limitation on the right of the UK to impose a tax charge. However, in the absence of clear words it is presumed that a charging statute only applies to the UK. In other words, the operation of a charging statute would not extend to the Channel Islands or elsewhere. The Tax Acts of the UK impose their own inherent territorial limits, since tax is chargeable only on a resident in the UK or income derived from property or a trade situated in the UK.[5] There are situations whereby profits created by a company incorporated abroad are taxable in the UK.[6] The circumstances in which overseas income from e-commerce is taxed in the UK are examined later.

---

1 For a historical introduction to UK tax law see the excellent book by J.A. Kay and M.A. King *The British Tax System* (OUP, 5th edn, 1990), and for an amusing illustration of what governments have sought to tax, such as windows!, see Shipwright and Keeling *Revenue Law* (Blackstones, 1997), pp 1–2, and generally Chapter 1 for an overview of the UK tax system. See also *Simon's Direct Tax Service* (Butterworths, loose-leaf, 1997), Part A1.102.

2 See s 18 of the Income and Corporation Tax Act 1988, Case I of Schedule D.

3 Guidance on this area of taxation can be acquired from *Simon's Direct Tax Service*, *op cit*.

4 Guidance on this area of taxation can be acquired from *DeVoil's Indirect Tax Service* (Butterworths).

5 See the comments as to territorial limit made by Lord Herschell in *Colquhoun (Surveyor of Taxes) v Brooks* (1889) 14 App Cas 493 at 503; approved in *National Bank of Greece SA v Westminster Bank Exor and Trustee Co (Channel Islands) Ltd* [1971] AC 945 at 964; and *Clark v Oceanic Contractors Inc* [1983] STC 35 at 41, per Lord Scarman.

6 See, for example, s 747 of ICTA 1988 (Controlled Foreign Company Legislation).

4.2 DIRECT TAXATION

4.2.1 Corporation tax

Corporation tax[1] is applied to company profits at a rate of 31 per cent (1998–99),[2] with a lower rate of 21 per cent (1998–99)[3] applied to a small company (where the profits are below £300,000).[4] Any profits in excess of the small company rate, but not in excess of £1.5 million are subject to what is know as the marginal rate.[5] The corporation tax regime applies to profits which comprise income and chargeable gains made from the disposal of assets.[6] The profits of a company are calculated by reference to ICTA 1988.[7] Chargeable gains are calculated by reference to TCGA 1992.[8] The rules by which a company's tax liability is determined is generally through the use of those rules which apply to determine the tax liability of an individual to income and capital gains tax.[9]

The label of corporation tax is slightly misleading to the non-tax lawyer, because it applies to entities which would not be regarded as companies for the purposes of CA 1985.[10] For the purposes of corporation tax, a 'company' means 'any body corporate[11] or unincorporated association but does not include a partnership, a local authority or a local authority association'.[12] Thus, clubs which operate e-commerce sites for membership subscriptions or sale of club merchandise are potentially liable to corporation tax.

As Table 5 illustrates a company is subject to corporation tax in the UK if it is a resident.[13] Where this is the case the profits include those accruing to it on a worldwide basis.[14] In appropriate circumstances, it is possible for a non-resident company to be subject to UK corporation tax where it carries on a trade in the UK through a branch or agency.[15] One issue in this context is the extent to which an item of information technology such as a computer server carrying on an electronic trade, or a satellite

---

1 For a detailed overview see *Simon's Direct Tax Service*, *op cit*, Division D.2, and the Inland Revenue guidance manual *Company Taxation*, Vol I–VI.
2 Finance (No 2) Act 1997, s 18(1).
3 Ibid, s 18(2).
4 ICTA 1988, s 13.
5 The small company rate is calculated in accordance with the rules set out in s 13 of ICTA 1988.
6 Ibid, s 6.
7 Ibid, ss 6 and 9.
8 TCGA 1992, s 8.
9 ICTA 1988, s 9.
10 CA 1985 defines a company as 'a company formed and registered under this Act ...' (s 735(1)). The essential characteristic of a company which distinguishes it from other business entities, is that the company has a separate legal personality from those of its members (see *Salomon v Salomon & Co* [1897] AC 22). By contrast, a trust, partnership and an EEIG (unless registered in the UK) do not have separate legal personality.
11 A body corporate is defined as: 'any body politic, corporate or collegiate, and any company, fraternity, fellowship and society of persons whether corporate or not corporate' (s 832(1) of ICTA 1988).
12 Ibid, s 832(1).
13 Ibid, s 6.
14 Ibid, s 8.
15 Ibid, s 11.

earth station can constitute a branch or agency for the purposes of imposing corporation tax.

4.2.2 Income tax

Individuals – generally not companies[1] – are subject to income tax[2] within a variable band ranging from 20 per cent up to 40 per cent (1998–99)[3] in respect of profits derived from a specific source. The rules governing the application of this tax are provided by ICTA 1988. As described above, these rules are generally used for the purposes of calculating a company's chargeable profits.

An individual is subject to income tax if either resident or ordinarily resident in the UK.[4] Unlike a company the chargeable gains of an individual are subject to capital gains tax.[5]

As Table 5 illustrates a company is generally not subject to income tax, but it will nevertheless be subject to this tax where it is a non-resident which carries on a trade within the UK otherwise than through a branch or agency.[6] In this context, it is possible, in appropriate circumstances, for a company using IT to trade via the Internet to be subject to a tax charge in the UK.

4.2.3 Capital gains tax[7]

This is a tax on chargeable gains accruing from the disposal of assets. The application of this tax is limited to individuals and is regulated by TCGA 1992.[8] The tax rate is generally linked to the individual's marginal rate of taxation.[9] In other words, an individual pays capital gains tax at the rate which applies to their top slice of income. A tax charge will be imposed on gains derived from the disposal of assets situated in the UK by a UK resident or a person ordinarily resident there.[10] A non-resident individual will be subject to tax where he disposes of an asset situated in the UK and used for the purposes of a trade carried on in the UK through a branch or agency.[11]

1 ICTA 1988, s 6(2).

2 For a detailed overview see *Simon's Direct Tax Service*, *op cit*, Division A.1, B.1, and the Inland Revenue guidance manual *Inspector's Manual*, para 110.

3 Lower rate of 20 per cent on income up to £4,300 (ICTA 1988, s 1(2)(aa), Finance Act 1997 ('FA 1997'), s 54(1),(2)). Basic rate of 23 per cent on income between £4,301, to £27,100 (ICTA 1988, s 1(2)(a); FA 1997, s 54(2)). A higher rate of 40 per cent applies to income in excess of £27,100.

4 ICTA 1988, s 334.

5 TCGA 1992, s 2.

6 Ibid, s 11.

7 For a detailed overview see *Simon's Direct Tax Service*, *op cit*, Division A.1, C.1, and the Inland Revenue guidance manual *Capital Gains*.

8 TCGA 1992, s 2(1).

9 Ibid, s 4.

10 Ibid, s 2(1).

11 Ibid, s 10.

4.2.4 International double taxation agreements[1]

These are arrangements entered into between the UK and other countries. The purpose of the arrangement is to eliminate or limit the extent to which profits or chargeable gains accruing to a resident of another country can be taxed by the country in which the profit or gain arises, such as the UK. In other words, the purpose of them is to eliminate double taxation. Double taxation agreements have effect in UK law as part of the tax legislation as a result of the ICTA 1988.[2] Many of the agreements are based upon the principals of the OECD[3] Model Tax Convention on Income and Capital (the 'Model Convention') (November 1997).

The Model Convention uses the term of 'permanent establishment' as the key to determining the rights of respective countries in their ability to tax business profits. Article 7(1) of the Model Convention illustrates how the term is used for the purposes of determining taxing ability of a country.

> '1. The profits of an enterprise of a Contracting State shall be taxable only in that State unless the enterprise carries on business in the other Contracting State through a permanent establishment situated therein. If the enterprise carries on business as aforesaid, the profits of the enterprise may be taxed in the other State but only so much of them as is attributable to that permanent establishment.'

Example 13

An Italian company receives income from a trade carried on through a branch in the UK. If the UK/Italian double taxation agreement is based on Article 7 of the OECD Model, the Italian company could only be taxed by the UK Inland Revenue on profits *attributable* to a permanent establishment in the UK. The taxable profits would be those derived from the UK branch.

Careful attention should be paid to double taxation agreements since they can be of significant help in eliminating source taxation.

4.2.5 Taxation of worldwide income and chargeable gains

The UK tax scheme applies in many cases to income and chargeable gains which are derived from activities carried on by a person throughout the world. The globalisation of the market place available to people carrying on e-commerce makes it imperative for them to know the circumstances in which they will be taxed on income and gains accruing outside the UK. It is equally important that overseas traders are aware of the precise circumstances in which they will be taxed in jurisdictions with which they are trading. Table 5 summarises the circumstances in which a person will be taxed on worldwide income, or merely upon income and gains accruing within the UK. The circumstances in which a non-resident will be taxed are also identified.

---

1 For a detailed overview see *Simon's Direct Tax Service*, *op cit*, Division F.1, F.2, F3; and the Inland Revenue guidance manuals *International Tax Handbook* and *Double Taxation Relief.*

2 ICTA 1988, s 788.

3 Organisation for Economic Co-operation and Development.

Table 5: Scope of UK tax rules

Person	***Worldwide income/gains taxed***	***Only UK income/gains taxed***
Company Resident	✓ 'all profits wherever arising'. ICTA 1988, s 8(1) 'profits' include income and chargeable gains. ICTA 1988, s 6(4)(a) Plus any income/gains attributed to a resident under the controlled foreign company rules. ICTA 1988, s 747(1), TCGA 1992, s 13	✗
Non-resident	✗	✓ (a) Trading income directly or indirectly accruing from a branch or agency in the UK used to carry on a trade, and (b) Any income from property used/held by the branch or agency, and (c) Any chargeable gains accruing from the disposal of assets situated in the UK used for the purposes of the trade, and (d) Chargeable gains accruing from the disposal of assets situated in the UK which were used or held for the purposes of the branch or agency. ICTA 1988, s 11, TCGA 1992, s 10(3) Plus income from a trade carried on in the UK

Person	**Worldwide income/gains taxed**	**Only UK income/gains taxed**
Individual's		
Income		
Resident	✓ (a) Taxed on profits or gains accruing from any type of property whether situated in the UK or elsewhere. ICTA 1988, s 18(1)(a)(i) (b) Taxed on profits or gains accruing from any trade, profession or vocation whether carried on in the UK or elsewhere. ICTA 1988, s 18(1)(a)(ii) Plus any income attributed under the controlled foreign company legislation. ICTA 1988, s 747	✗
Non-resident	✗	✓ (a) Taxed on any profits or gains from any property situated in the UK; (b) Taxed on any profits or gains from any trade, profession or vocation exercised within the UK. ICTA 1988, s 18(1)(a)(iii)
Non-domiciled, or a Commonwealth/Republic of Ireland citizen who is not ordinarily resident	✗	✓ Income subject to tax under Cases IV or V, Schedule D are subject to tax only on those amounts received in the UK. ICTA 1988, s 65(4), (5)
Gains		
Foreign domiciled but resident or ordinarily resident	✗	✓ Cannot be taxed on gains accruing from the disposal of assets situated outside the UK. Tax is only charged where the gain is received in UK. TCGA 1992, s 12(1)

Person	Worldwide income/gains taxed	Only UK income/gains taxed
Non-resident	✗	✓ Where a non-resident is carrying on a trade in the UK through a branch or agency, it is taxed on chargeable gains acruing from the disposal of assets situated in the UK: (a) used for the purposes of a trade carried on through a branch or agency in the UK; or (b) used or held for the purposes of the branch or agency. TCGA 1992, s 10(1)
Resident or ordinarily resident	✓ Taxed on all chargeable gains which accrue. TCGA 1992, s 2(1) Plus any gains attributed under the controlled foreign company legislation. TCGA 1992, s 13	✗

4.3 INDIRECT TAXATION

4.3.1 Value added tax[1]

Tax is imposed in the UK, and throughout the EU on expenditure in respect of supplies through the system of value added tax ('VAT'). The scheme of tax is governed in the UK by the Sixth VAT Directive[2] and Value Added Tax Act 1994 ('VATA 1994'). VAT is charged on taxable supplies made in the UK by a taxable person in the course or furtherance of business.[3] In appropriate circumstances, it is possible for a supplier to recover VAT paid by it against VAT received on supplies made in the course of its business.[4] VAT applies to intra-EC trade, and to trade with other countries outside of the EU. The scope of these charges is examined in later chapters.

The rate of tax depends upon how the transaction, known as supplies, are classified. A transaction can be classified in one of three ways. Those which are designated as

1 For a detailed overview see *DeVoil's Indirect Tax Service*, *op cit*, Part VI; HM Customs and Excise internal guidance manual, Vol 1 (published by Butterworths).

2 Directive 77/388 (OJ 1977 L145/1).

3 VATA 1994, s 4.

4 Ibid, ss 8–16.

standard rated are subject to a tax of 17.5 per cent (1998–99)[1] of the value of the supply. Some supplies are classified as exempt[2] or zero-rated,[3] of which more later.[4] For example, in appropriate circumstances the export of goods are zero-rated. This effectively means that the rate of VAT is nil. One key question in this area is the extent to which the supply of computer software via the Internet can be classified as the supply of goods.

Example 14

If a computer manufacturer purchases 10,000 microchips for installation in hardware at a price of £500,000 it would pay an additional £87,500 in VAT.

The liability to account for VAT is imposed upon persons who are required to be registered as a taxable person under VATA 1994. The requirement to register depends upon a person having a turnover of £50,000 or more.[5] A service is supplied in the UK if the supplier belongs in the UK.[6] Whether a supplier belongs in the UK is determined under VATA 1994.[7] Generally, a supplier is based in the UK if it has a place of business, or a fixed establishment in the UK. In some circumstances, supplies are deemed to take place in the UK, such as data-processing services.[8]

A particularly grey area for the purposes of VAT is the extent to which IT can constitute a fixed establishment. The possibility exists for a person to use a piece of IT as a fixed establishment, with the result that it is possible to locate a supply outside the charge to UK VAT.

VAT may also apply to transactions involving the supply of goods in pursuance of an order placed via an electronic trading site. The obligations imposed upon traders within Europe are complex. Traders are required to monitor the place of supply of goods, and the type of person receiving the supply. For example, in some instances, a UK trader must apply UK VAT to the supply of goods to another Member State of the EU, while in some circumstances a UK trader is required to apply VAT of the EU Member State to which the supply is made. In some circumstances, VAT must be accounted for on the acquisition of goods from other Member States of the EU. This complexity undoubtedly causes serious compliance problems for suppliers within the EU.

---

1 VATA 1994, s 1
2 Ibid, s 31 and Sch 9.
3 Ibid, s 30 and Sch 8.
4 Ibid, s 25.
5 Ibid, s 3 and Schs 1–3.
6 Ibid, s 7.
7 Ibid, s 9.
8 Ibid, s 8. Value Added Tax (Place of Supply of Services) Order 1992, SI 1992/3121.

Chapter 5

CORPORATION TAX

5.1 INTRODUCTION

The code of taxation applicable to companies is governed by ICTA 1988,[1] and TCGA 1992.[2] The scheme of taxation referred to in ICTA 1988 and TCGA 1992 specifically applies to individuals, but the same scheme also applies to corporations, with some modifications.[3] As Table 5, in Chapter 4, illustrates, a UK resident corporation is subject to corporation tax on profits wherever arising,[4] while a non-resident corporation is subject to tax on trading profits arising through a branch or agency in the UK.[5] The purpose of this chapter is to explain the framework of corporation tax in the UK, providing practical examples of how corporation tax interacts with IT and e-commerce based business.

Detailed analysis of UK tax law is beyond the scope of this book, and as far as possible the reader is directed to practitioner, academic and Inland Revenue literature.[6] For example, the tax related issues to the finance of a company is the same irrespective of whether it is carrying on a business as a watch, food or computer manufacturer.

5.2 MEASUREMENT OF PROFITS[7]

5.2.1 Accountancy rules

The function of accountancy rules is the accurate measurement of economic value. In other words, the profit and loss accounts of a company are concerned with reflecting accurately its economic performance. CA 1985 imposes upon directors the obligation to ensure that the balance sheet, and the profit and loss accounts give a 'true and fair' view of the company for that financial year.[8] In ascertaining profits for tax purposes,

---

1 ICTA 1988, ss 6 and 9.

2 Ibid, ss 1(2) and 8.

3 Ibid, s 9.

4 Ibid, s 8.

5 Ibid, s 11.

6 The following are of significant value dealing with the taxation of companies: *Simon's Direct Tax Service* (Butterworths, loose-leaf, 1997) Part D.2; Bramwell *The Taxation of Companies* (Sweet & Maxwell, 6th edn, 1994); *Tolley's Corporation Tax* (published annually). Useful guidance is also provided by the Inland Revenue guidance manuals *Company Taxation* (4 volumes).

7 See *Simon's Direct Tax Service, op cit*, Part D2; Inland Revenue guidance manual *Company Taxation*, Part 1, para 12.

8 CA 1985, s 226.

the courts have emphasised that accountancy practice represents the most appropriate way to answer such questions.

Accountancy concepts are of assistance in determining whether expenditure is to be classified as revenue or capital as occurred, for example, in *Heather v P-E Consulting Group Ltd*,[1] or when expenditure or receipts are to be recognised in a company's accounts, as in *Gallagher v Jones (Inspector of Taxes)*[2] (time of lease payment recognition in accounts).

5.2.2 Tax rules

Accountancy practice forms the bedrock of information relating to the economic performance of a company. This ideal source of financial information is drawn upon for the purposes of determining taxable profits. Subject to any express or implied rule to the contrary in a tax statute profits are ascertained by applying the generally accepted principles of commercial accountancy. In *Gallagher v Jones*, Sir Christopher Slade in the Court of Appeal commented:

> '... the reason why the courts rightly attach such importance to accepted principles of commercial accounting in this context is, of course, that these principles will normally afford the surest means of ascertaining the *true* profits or losses of a trader as the case may be.'[3]

The chief source of corporation tax revenues is from profits of a trade. Profits are calculated by reference to the accounting period of the company.[4] A distinction is drawn between revenue and capital in respect of both receipts and expenditure for the purposes of computing profits. The computation process is achieved by reference to generally accepted accounting principles ('GAAP').[5] A detailed examination of UK GAAP policies can be obtained elsewhere.[6] Profits are the excess of revenue receipts over expenditure incurred in earning those receipts. The approach to the computation of profits for tax purposes has been outlined by the courts.[7] In *Odeon Associated Theatres*[8] the judge stated that the profits of a company must first be calculated by reference to GAAP. These profits must then be adjusted in light of any prohibited deduction of expenditure under the tax legislation.[9]

---

1 [1973] 1 All ER 8.

2 [1993] STC 537.

3 Ibid, at 189.

4 ICTA 1988, s 12. For a short summary of the importance of accounts see Davies *Principles of Tax Law* (Sweet & Maxwell, 1996), pp 75–77 for more detailed guidance see the series of articles 'Accounting Standards and Taxable Profits' (1995) BTR 433–524.

5 See *Odeon Associated Theatres v Jones* (1971) 48 TC 257. In *Gallagher v Jones (Inspector of Taxes)* [1993] STC 537 at 560, Nolan LJ said: 'the law does not enable or require us to ascertain profits of a trade on a basis divorced from the principles of commercial accountancy'.

6 See Davies, Paterson and Wilson *UK GAAP* (Macmillan, 4th edn, 1995).

7 See particularly *Odeon Associated Theatres v Jones* [1971] 1 WLR 442 at 454, per Sir John Pennycuick V-C; *Gallagher v Jones* [1993] STC 537 (judgment of Sir Thomas Bingham MR); *Johnstons (Inspector of Taxes) v Britannia Airways Ltd* [1994] STC 763; *R v Inland Revenue Commissioners ex parte S G Warbourg & Co Ltd* [1994] STC 518.

8 (1971) 48 TC 257.

9 *Odeon Associated Theatres v Jones* (1971) 48 TC 257 at 272–273; [1971] 1 WLR 442 at 453–454, per Sir John Pennycuick V-C.

5.3 ACCOUNTANCY: THE BASIS OF COMPUTING PROFITS

Revenue receipts are classified as income which arise from the day-to-day activity of an enterprise, such as sales, and royalties from the licensing of copyright or patents.[1] By contrast, revenue expenditure is the cost of earning those receipts, for example, the cost of employing staff, the cost of buying merchandise to sell on to customers via Internet trading sites etc. The tax year of a company runs from 1 April to 31 March each year. It is therefore necessary to apportion a company's accounting period within the time frame of the tax year.[2] The time at which revenue receipts or expenditure is to be recognised in the accounts, depends upon accounting practice. Although a person may pay a lump sum for the right to use technology, such as software, or an invention used for the purposes of providing a telecommunications service, it does not necessarily follow that the receipt of the lump sum will be brought into account at the time it is paid. One firmly established principle of accountancy is that revenue is recognised in accounts when it is earned. Correspondingly, expenditure is recognised when it is incurred, which is not necessarily when the expenditure is paid.[3]

The basis upon which accounts are drawn up is governed by CA 1985.

5.4 SOURCE TAXATION[4]

Corporation tax is calculated according to the source of the receipts. The current scheme of corporation tax is based on legislation originally enacted in 1965 and 1972.[5] The legislation refers to a number of sources which are classified as Schedules and Cases.[6] Each Case contains a set of rules by which tax is to be calculated.[7] The Schedules referred to in ICTA 1988 are shown below.

Schedule A[8] – annual profits or gains from land.

Schedule D[9]

Case I – annual profits or gains from a trade.
Case II – annual profits or gains from a profession.
Case III – (a) annual profits or gains arising from loan relationships;
(b) any annuity or annual payment.
Case V – annual profits or gains in respect of foreign possessions.
Case VI – annual profits or gains in respect of miscellaneous income.

Schedule E[10] – emoluments from an office or employment.

---

1 See Davies, Paterson and Wilson, *op cit*, p 137.
2 ICTA 1988, s 12.
3 See Davies, Paterson and Wilson, *op cit*, pp 57 and 121–165.
4 See *Simon's Direct Tax Service*, *op cit*, Part A1 and Part B1; Inland Revenue guidance manual *Inspector's Manual*, para 110 *et seq*.
5 See Shipwright and Keeling *Revenue Law* (Blackstone Press, 1997), pp 548–549.
6 See generally ICTA 1988, s 18.
7 The Schedular form of taxation was first introduced in 1803. See generally Kirkbridge and Olowofoyeku *Revenue Law, Principles and Practice* (Tudor, 1993), Chapter 1.
8 ICTA 1988, s 15.
9 Ibid, s 18.
10 Ibid, s 19.

The scheme of taxation relevant to IT and Internet activities is Schedule D.[1] As described above, tax is typically charged on profits (receipts less expenditure). This right of set-off is inherent in the language of the legislation because tax is typically charged on 'profits'. The Scheduler system described above is applied for the purposes of calculating corporation tax.

5.4.1 Resident and non-resident corporations[2]

The charge to corporation tax applies to a company which is a resident of the UK,[3] and to a non-resident company which carries on a trade in the UK through a branch or agency.[4] Where a non-resident company has no branch or agency it will be subject to income tax on any income which can be sourced to Schedule D.[5] Unless an Internet business activity is within a specific charge, there is no right to impose UK tax.[6]

Example 15

If a microchip manufacturer is based in the UK it will be required to pay corporation tax on profits derived from that trade. If a non-resident company manufactures computers in the USA and then sells those through a branch based in the UK it will also be required to account for corporation tax. By contrast a non-resident which locates an Internet shopping centre program on computers based in the UK, which accepts orders and then relays these to the non-resident who in turn gives delivery instructions to a distributor in the UK, may be subject to income tax, rather than corporation tax on the basis that it is exercising a trade within the UK. Whether a person is trading within the UK is partly determined by the location of the contract.[7]

A company is resident in the UK if it satisfies one of the following conditions:[8]

(1) it is incorporated in the UK;[9] or
(2) the central management and control of the company is located in the UK.[10]

---

1 ICTA 1988, s 18.

2 See *Simon's Direct Tax Service*, *op cit*, Part D2.104; the Inland Revenue guidance manuals *Company Taxation*, paras 3365–3379, 3389, 3405; and *Capital Gains*, para 42300. See also the Inland Revenue Statement of Practice, SP1/90.

3 ICTA 1988, s 6.

4 Ibid, s 11(2).

5 Ibid, s 6(2). See Whitehouse, *Revenue Law* (Butterworths, 14th edn, 1996), Chapter 28.146.

6 Tax can only be charged on a taxpayer if the charging statute clearly and unambiguously applies. Otherwise the Inland Revenue has no right to charge tax. This is a fundamental principle of UK tax law. In *Partington v Attorney-General* (1869) LR 4 100 at 122, HL. Lord Cairns made the following observations which are applicable in the UK today.

> 'If the person sought to be taxed comes within the letter of the law he must be taxed, however great the hardship may appear to the judicial mind to be. On the other hand, if the Crown, seeking to recover the tax, cannot bring the subject within the letter of the law, the subject is free, however apparently within the spirit of the law the case might otherwise appear to be.'

7 This point is analysed in Chapter 14 dealing with e-commerce.

8 A company which is regarded as resident in the UK for the purposes of the Tax Acts is excluded from residence where under a double taxation agreement the company is regarded as resident outside the UK and not resident in the UK; Finance Act 1994, s 249.

9 Finance Act 1994, s 66 (with effect from 15 March 1988).

10 *De Beers Consolidated Mines Ltd v Howe* 5 TC 198 at 213 per Lord Loreburn LC). In that case Lord Loreburn LC said: 'a company resides, for the purposes of income tax, where its real business is carried on ... I regard that as the true rule; and the real business is carried on where the

The first test is easily satisfied by reference to the register of incorporated companies maintained at Companies House.[1] However, the second test is a creature of the common law. The test is influenced by physical considerations, such as the location of where directors' meetings are held. The quest for determining the place of residence on this basis is a question of fact.[2] The Inland Revenue has issued a Statement of Practice[3] which is their view of the factors relevant to determining residence under the common law test. In the Statement of Practice, the Inland Revenue draws attention to some of the factors which have been regarded as relevant in the case-law.

Relevant factors include the location of directors' meetings, the location of where the controlling individual of a company, such as a managing director, exercises powers conferred upon him by the company, and the location of the directors who actively carry on the running of the business. It is to be observed that these factors depend upon a physical location of the directors. Where the residence of a company cannot be established under the common law test in the UK, tax cannot be charged on worldwide profits.[4] In these circumstances, tax will be limited to the profits of a trade carried on through a branch or agency in the UK. In the absence of a branch or agency, income tax may be charged on profits if the company is trading within the UK.[5]

Example 16

Internet Consultancy (Web Site) Services Inc, based in the USA establish an office in London. The office is used to operate a web site design service for UK companies. The profits of the main business in the USA are the sterling equivalent of £25 million, whilst the profits of the branch are only £500,000. The right to charge corporation tax in the UK is limited to the profits of the branch.

Problems in the application of the central management and control test will be particularly acute where a business can be actively controlled from other continents by the use of instantaneous methods of communication, and virtual reality conferencing. This problem is recognised in the Statement of Practice which describes it in the following terms:

> 'The case-law test examined in this Statement is not always easy to apply. The courts have recognised that there may be difficulties where it is not possible to identify one country as

---

central management and control actually abides'. In *Unit Construction Co Ltd v Bullock (Inspector of Taxes)* [1959] All ER 831 at 836, HL, Lord Radcliffe said that this principle was firmly enshrined into the tax law. See also *American Thread Co v Joyce* 6 TC 163 at 165; *New Zealand Shipping Co Ltd v Thew* 8 TC 208; and *Bradbury v English Sewing Cotton Co* 8 TC 481. The test was re-formulated in *American Thread Co v Joyce* 6 TC 163 at 165 in the following terms: '... the real test ... and that which has been accepted as a test, is where what we should call the head office in popular language is, and where the business of the company is really directed and carried on in that sense.'

1 The Registrar is under a duty to retain all information required to be delivered to the Registrar under the Companies Acts. See ss 707A and 709 of the Companies Act 1985.

2 *De Beers Consolidated Mines Ltd v Howe* 5 TC 198 at 213, per Lord Loreburn LC: 'This is a pure question of fact, to be determined, not according to the construction of this or that regulation or bye-law, but upon scrutiny of the course of business and trading.'

3 SP1/90 (9 January 1990).

4 See ss 11, 18 and 70 of ICTA 1988.

5 The nature of a branch or agency, and trading within the UK are examined in Chapter 14 on e-commerce.

> the seat of central management and control. The principles to apply in those circumstances have not been fully developed in case-law. In addition, the last relevant case was decided almost 30 years ago, and there have been many developments in communications since then, which in particular may enable a company to be controlled from a place far distant from where the day-to-day management is carried on.'[1]

Under the common law test, it is possible for a company to have more than one place of residence.[2] A company may be regarded as resident in country X because it is incorporated in that State, but it may also be regarded as a resident of the UK because its real place of business, ie its central management and control is based in the UK. The Inland Revenue holds the view that the residence of a company can be established in the UK if a dominant person within a company, for example, a managing director exercises powers bestowed upon him in UK, or if an influential shareholder exercises voting rights in the UK.[3] In this context the efficiencies represented by IT must be watched, as the example below illustrates. The effect of IT is to facilitate the diversification of management control of businesses.

Example 17

Zoltan Associates SA, a family business is incorporated in Spain, and the majority shareholder is a resident of the UK. The business of Zoltan Associates SA is guided by Mr Zoltan, the family patriarch. He controls the financial strings of the business, and appoints its directors. Mr Zoltan 'attends' the general meeting of the company, at which crucial decisions are usually made, through the medium of a video-conferencing facility. Mr Zoltan also guides the operation of the business by sending instructions to his co-directors via an electronic messaging service. Is Zoltan Associates SA resident in the UK for the purposes of corporation tax?

In this type of scenario the ultimate control of the company is within the UK, and based on the principles described in the Inland Revenue's Statement of Practice, it is likely that the view would be taken that profits of the company were assessable to UK tax. However, if the facts are changed slightly it is possible to ensure that the company is only resident in Spain.

The facts are as above, except that the business is owned by Mr Zoltan in equal shares with his two brothers. The business is operated in Spain by the employees. However, the three brothers live in three different jurisdictions, the USA, France and the UK. All directors' meetings take place via virtual reality video-conferencing facilities. Each director has an equal voice in the company, as one-third shareholders.

5.4.2 'Branch or agency' of a non-resident

As discussed previously, a non-resident company is subject to corporation tax if it carries on a trade through a branch or agency within the UK.[4] The level of profits subject to corporation tax are limited to those derived from the branch or agency, and

1 Inland Revenue Statement of Practice SP1/90, para 19 (9 January 1990).

2 See *Swedish Central Ry Co Ltd v Thompson* (1925) 9 TC 342 at 352, per Rowlatt; and *Unit Construction Co Ltd v Bullock (Inspector of Taxes)* [1959] All ER 831 at 833, HL, per Viscount Simonds.

3 Inland Revenue Statement of Practice, SP1/90, para 13 (9 January 1990).

4 ICTA 1988, s 11(1).

also those profits derived from property used by the branch or agency.[1] The tax legislation defines a 'branch or agency' as 'any factorship, agency, receivership, branch or management'.[2] These key words, all except branch, refer to legal relationships which can arise through contractual agreements,[3] or by operation of law.[4] This is one way in which the UK tax authority may successfully impose tax on an Internet business activity, even though the company carrying on the trade is otherwise a non-resident.

Example 18

Alpha Technologies Inc based in the USA, is the developer and manufacturer of a secure payments mechanism ('SPM') for e-commerce. A UK based company called Spectrum Technologies Ltd, is appointed the sole agent of Alpha Technologies Inc. The UK company on receiving an order for a SPM, relays the order to Alpha Technologies Inc. Upon confirmation from the US company, Spectrum Technologies Ltd supplies the SPM to the customer. In the first year Spectrum Technologies Ltd, is paid £900,000 for supplying the SPM in the UK. The profits can potentially be assessed to corporation tax if the non-resident carries on a trade in the UK via its agency.

The simplest commercial agency arrangement could potentially bring an Internet business activity within the charge to UK corporation tax. Careful tax planning is needed to ensure that agency relationships do not attract UK tax charges.

By contrast, the term 'branch' is a reference to a physical presence, such as the existence of offices rather than to a legal relationship.[5] Either concept of branch or agency can be used as a force of attraction in respect of subjecting Internet business to UK corporation tax. It cannot be overlooked that a second condition must be satisfied, which is that a trade is carried on within the UK through the branch or agency. In this respect, a distinction must be drawn between trading with the UK and exercising a trade within it.[6]

Although a non-resident company may have no 'branch or agency' which operates to attract corporation tax, it may none the less be possible to impose income tax where the company receives annual profits or gains from a trade exercised within the UK, or from property in the UK.[7] A company can be subject to income tax in the absence of a branch or agency.[8] This charge to tax may be particularly important, as the example below illustrates, to the Inland Revenue as a means of capturing e-commerce across the Internet.

---

1 ICTA 1988, s 11(2).

2 Ibid, s 834(1).

3 See *Bowstead on Agency* (Sweet & Maxwell, 1985), Chapter 2.

4 Ibid.

5 In *Hughes (HM Inspector of Taxes) v Bank of New Zealand* [1938] 1 All ER 778, the bank was subject to tax in the UK because it derived profits from offices opened in London.

6 See *Grainger v Gough* [1896] AC 325 at 335, per Lord Herschell. The issue of trading with and trading within the UK is examined in Chapter 14 on e-commerce.

7 ICTA 1988, s 18(1). See also C. Whitehouse *Revenue Law: Principles and Practice* (Butterworths, 1996), p 559.

8 ICTA 1988, s 6(2).

Example 19

USA Shopping Mall Inc operate an Internet site for their clothing merchandise, which can be accessed solely by wholesale distributors authorised by the company. The wholesalers purchase the merchandise by accessing the web site, through which orders are placed, and payment can be made by credit card. A UK wholesaler places an order for merchandise worth $150,000. Is USA Shopping Mall Inc assessable to UK tax? It is likely that the US company would not be subject to any form of UK tax. However, everything will turn upon the precise facts of each case, and an identification of where the contract is entered into with the UK consumer and location of the operations which create the profits for USA Shopping Mall Inc.[1]

5.5 COMPUTATION OF THE TAX CHARGE[2]

5.5.1 Introduction

Corporation tax is charged on profits which are computed by reference to a designated source. The profits are calculated by reference to the accounting period of the company.[3] Income is calculated under ICTA 1988 and chargeable gains under TCGA 1992.

5.5.2 Chargeable income

The typical relevant sources of chargeable income identified in Schedule D for the purposes of IT and Internet business activity are those derived from a trade (Case I), an investment (Case III) and foreign possessions (Case V). Income derived from a trade is particularly important because it entitles the trader to deduct all expenditure of a revenue nature incurred in earning revenue receipts arising from that trade.[4] A person who carries on a trade is entitled to a number of tax reliefs (known as allowances) which are not available in respect of income derived under other Cases, such as investment income.[5] The tax legislation permits, under different circumstances, revenue and capital expenditure to be deducted.

Revenue expenditure is that which has a recurrent quality and represents the day-to-day cost of carrying on a trade, for example, the salary of employees, the rent of office accommodation or the acquisition of raw materials to manufacture goods that the trader sells.[6] Capital expenditure may also be deducted from receipts derived from a trade where it qualifies for relief under what is known as the capital allowances

1 The application of tax law in this area is fully examined in Chapter 14 on e-commerce.

2 See *Simon's Direct Tax Service*, *op cit*, Part B; Inland Revenue guidance manual *Company Taxation*.

3 ICTA 1988, s 12.

4 The right to deduct expenditure arises because only 'profits' from a trade are subject to a tax charge.

5 A person who receives income from an investment is not entitled to deduct any expenditure. See ICTA 1988, s 64.

6 See *International Accounting Standards* (1998) published by the International Accounting Standards Committee explanation number 18, (IAS 18).

system governed by the Capital Allowances Act 1990 ('CAA 1990').[1] The profits of a company are initially calculated by reference to accountancy principles. These principles will determine when revenue and capital expenditure or receipts are to be recognised in the taxpayer's accounts. The time of recognition may not necessarily be when a payment is received or expenditure incurred. The principles applied in the calculation must be generally accepted principles of commercial accountancy.[2] Once this calculation has been undertaken adjustments must then be made for any expenditure which is prohibited from being deducted by the tax legislation. This sum will then represent the profits of the Internet business. In certain circumstances, it may be possible for a company which has incurred a loss to off-set this against the taxable profits.[3]

Before corporation tax can be imposed, the company is entitled to deduct any payments made to another person which are regarded as a 'charge on profits'.[4] The following paragraphs will focus on the particular elements identified here in the computation of chargeable profits. Once the corporation tax liability of the company has been assessed, it will then be entitled to off-set any income tax deducted at source on payments received by it.[5]

5.5.3 Chargeable gains

Once chargeable income has been computed, it is also necessary for any chargeable gains to be calculated by reference to TCGA 1992.[6] The combination of this and the chargeable income produces the company's chargeable profits.[7]

5.5.4 Expenditure within the UK tax system

Many of the tax rules apply tax only to 'profits'. This section examines expenditure in the context of its use for determining taxable profits under Schedule D, Case I. The concept of income implies the deduction of expenditure from receipts and the time at which revenues and expenditure are recognised will determine the income in any particular accounting period. Generally, the matching of expenditure against revenues as adopted by accounting practice is recognised for tax purposes, but capital expenditure is specifically dealt with in that it is first not allowed as a deduction,[8] but may, secondly be afforded some relief under the capital allowances system.

The rate at which these allowances are given clearly affects the tax liability in that earlier reliefs are more valuable than later reliefs. Thus, whether expenditure is treated

---

1 For a detailed analysis of the application of CAA 1990, see *Simon's Direct Tax Service*, *op cit*, Part B2; and Inland Revenue guidance manual *Capital Allowances*.

2 *Odeon Associated Theatres v Jones* [1971] 1 WLR 422.

3 ICTA 1988, ss 393 and 393A. See *Simon's Direct Tax Service*, *op cit*; Davies *Principles of Tax Law* (Sweet & Maxwell, 1996), pp 156–161. Shipwright and Keeling, *Revenue Law* (Blackstone Press, 1997), Chapter 28.

4 See ICTA 1988, s 338. Charges on income include annuities, annual payments and patent royalties.

5 Ibid, s 7, eg tax deducted in respect of payments for the user of a patent by the licensee. See ss 348 and 349.

6 TCGA 1992, s 8.

7 ICTA 1988, s 6(4)(a).

8 Ibid, s 74(1)(f).

as capital expenditure, or not, and the rate at which relief is given for capital expenditure, is an instrument of policy which can be used to encourage a particular type of economic activity. For example, in the first budget of the present Labour Government, the Chancellor of the Exchequer, Gordon Brown introduced changes which enabled small businesses investing in machinery or plant to deduct the cost of that plant at the rate of 50 per cent of the cost per tax year (for 1997–98).[1] As the Chancellor explained in his budget, the purpose of this change was to encourage investment in business. The Chancellor said of this: 'at this point in the economic cycle an investment incentive should encourage companies considering future investments to bring those investments forward'. These changes were made in the overall context of the Government seeking as the Chancellor put it 'to encourage more long-term investment'.

ICTA 1988 provides detailed rules on the type of revenue expenditure that can be deducted, and adjustments must accordingly be made for any expenditure permitted under accountancy principles, but prohibited under the tax legislation.[2] For example, expenditure of a revenue nature cannot be deducted unless incurred wholly and exclusively for the purposes of a trade.[3]

As noted above, expenditure which is classified as of a capital nature is generally not a permitted deduction, unless it falls within the capital allowances system governed by CAA 1990. Under this Act, classes of capital expenditure can be deducted in calculating profits. The indicia of capital expenditure is that it is usually incurred once and for all for the purposes of a business, and involves the acquisition of an asset with an enduring benefit to the business.[4] The scope of the capital allowances system and the rate of deduction is a matter of Government policy. For our purposes the most significant capital allowances are those dealing with:

(1) 'machinery and plant', which includes expenditure on copyright in respect of the right to deal with computer software;[5]
(2) patent rights;[6] and
(3) know-how.[7]

The rate of deduction where capital expenditure is incurred on these things is set at a rate of 25 per cent of the value of the asset, on a reducing balance basis.

The capital allowances legislation provides relief for capital expenditure on a 'reducing balance basis', otherwise than where a first year allowance ('FYA') is available. The operation of this relief is shown below.

Example 20

Internet Associates Ltd, acquire computer software for £100,000. The taxpayer qualifies for relief under the CAA 1990 on the basis that the expenditure is on plant

1 CAA 1990, s 22, as amended by the Finance (No 2) Act 1997, s 42.
2 *Odeon Associated Theatres Ltd v Jones* [1971] 1 WLR 442.
3 ICTA 1988, s 74.
4 *Atherton v British Insulated & Helsby Cables Ltd* (1925) 10 TC 155.
5 CAA 1990, s 67A.
6 ICTA 1988, s 520.
7 Ibid, s 530.

and machinery. The way in which the expenditure is off-set against the receipts of the trade is shown below:

		1997–98
	£	£
Plant Expenditure	100,000	
less WDA[1] @ 25%	(25,000)	
WDA c/f	75,000	
Trading Income		100,000
Taxable Profits		75,000
		1998–99
WDA pool c/f	75,000	
WDA @ 25%	(18,750)	
WDA c/f	56,250	
Trading Income		250,000
Taxable Profits etc		231,250

If the taxpayer had disposed of some of the rights to the computer software in the 1998–99 tax year for £50,000 this would represent disposal value that is deducted against the pool of expenditure. In this case, the expenditure pool would be reduced to £25,000. It is to be observed that the allowance is weighted towards giving large amounts of relief in the earlier years than the later years.

PART III UK TAXATION

5.6 SCHEDULE D, CASE I: PROFITS OF A TRADE

5.6.1 What is a trade?[2]

As described above the existence of a trade is of fundamental importance because it entitles the trader to a very wide range of tax reliefs, such as:

(1) the right to deduct expenditure;
(2) the right to make a claim for the transfer of a trading loss against trading profits.

Despite the importance of this concept to the tax legislation, it is defined in only ambulatory terms.[3] The characteristics of a trade is a question of law which is determined by the courts. Whether a trade exists is a question of fact.[4] A trade has been described as a commercial transaction whereby a person supplies goods or services for reward to another person.[5] For a trade to exist there must be a bilateral transaction with another person. It is not possible to carry on a trade with oneself.[6] For a trade to exist there is no requirement of continuity. The legislation specifically provides that a

1 Ie Writing Down Allowance.

2 See *Simon's Direct Tax Service*, *op cit*, Part B3.2; Inland Revenue guidance manual *Company Taxation* paras 120a–120g; Shipwright and Keeling *Principles of Tax Law* (Sweet & Maxwell, 1996), pp 72–74; Davies *Revenue Law* (Blackstone Press, 1997), pp 259–276.

3 ICTA 1988, s 832(1) defines trade as including 'every trade, manufacture, adventure or concern in the nature of trade'.

4 *Edwards v Bairstow and Harrison* [1956] AC 14; [1955] 3 All ER 48, HL.

5 See *Ransom v Higgs* [1974] 3 All ER 949, HL.

6 Ibid.

trade includes 'an adventure or concern in the nature of a trade'.[1] A trade can exist although the activity is unlawful.[2] If a person sold prohibited handguns through the medium of the Internet in the UK, this would not prevent the activity being classified as a trade, and the Inland Revenue would be entitled to raise an assessment to tax.

5.7 EXPENDITURE DEDUCTIONS

The distinction between revenue and capital expenditure is not a particularly easy area of tax law.[3] It is however of critical importance because the timing of relief differs. Revenue expenditure is relieved immediately while capital expenditure is relieved over a period of time. In *British Insulated Cables v Helsby*,[4] capital expenditure was described in the following terms:

> 'When an expenditure is made, not only once and for all, but with a view to bringing into existence an asset or an advantage for the enduring benefit of a trade, I find that there is a very good reason [...] for treating such an expenditure as properly attributable not to revenue but to capital.'

The classification of expenditure is concerned not only with that on tangible products, but also with intangible property such as contracts which establish rights within a market. For example, contracts establishing the scope of a distributor's market for the sale of computers. Problems may be experienced in the application of this distinction where the technology acquired by an IT or Internet business has a short economic lifespan.

Example 21

Chip Computers Ltd are manufacturers of micro-processors. The company manufactures the chip under licence from the developer, and incurs expenditure in the acquisition of a master program, which is used to guide the robotic arms that etch the circuit for the operation of the processor. The company would not be able to manufacture the processors without the computer program, and in every sense the business is dependant upon using this master program. The processors are developed very quickly with the result that expenditure of £100,000 is incurred every four months on new computer programs. How is this expenditure to be classified?[5]

---

1 ICTA 1988, s 832(1).

2 *IRC v Aken* [1988] 69 QBD, affirmed [1990] 497, CA.

3 See *Simon's Direct Tax Service*, *op cit*, Part A1.123 and A1.2; Davies, *Principles of Tax Law* (Sweet & Maxwell, 1996) pp 85–87; Shipwright and Keeling *Revenue Law* (Blackstone Press, 1997), pp 316–320.

4 [1926] AC 205.

5 The distinction between revenue and capital expenditure is diminishing to a vanishing point in the area of IT. This is because the rate of technology growth is exceptionally high, with the result that expenditure, although of an enduring benefit to many trades is being incurred at regular intervals. The regularity of these transactions, is a characteristic which is usually associated with revenue expenditure.

5.7.1 Revenue expenditure

Pre-trade expenditure

The tax legislation allows revenue expenditure incurred prior to a trade to be deducted from revenue receipts derived from that trade once it has commenced.[1] This relief is available where expenditure is incurred no more than seven years before the trade is started.[2] However, a deduction is permitted only if it would be allowed for the purposes of computing profits from a trade.[3]

Trade related expenditure

Revenue expenditure which is brought into account on the basis of generally accepted accountancy principles must be adjusted for any prohibited expenditure contained in the tax legislation. Of principal importance is the rule that no deduction can be made unless the expenditure is incurred wholly and exclusively for the purposes of a trade.[4] Expenditure would not, for example, be capable of deduction where a computer manufacturer pays rent for office space which also accommodates its distribution and marketing companies. Expenditure such as royalty payments incurred, for example, on the use of intellectual property rights for the purposes of securing access to technology for the manufacture of components may be deducted.

Under UK law, interest payments on loans are a deductible expense. Interest deductions are governed by the Finance Act 1996 ('FA 1996'). The Act applies to 'loan relationships'. This is the situation where a company is a debtor in respect of a money debt and that debt exists because of a transaction arising from the lending of money.[5] Finance expenditure incurred prior to trading is deductible as a pre-trading expense. Where this occurs the expenditure is brought into account as a trade expense in the period in which the company begins to trade.[6]

There are many more detailed rules under the tax legislation dealing with prohibited revenue deductions.[7]

5.7.2 Capital expenditure

Relief for 'plant and machinery'[8]

The typical head of relief for IT and Internet business will usually be that in respect of 'plant or machinery'.[9] Where a company incurs capital expenditure on plant or machinery for the purposes of a trade which belongs to that person as a result of the

---

1 ICTA 1988, s 401(1).
2 Ibid.
3 Ibid.
4 Ibid, s 74(1). See also *Mallalieu v Drummond* [1983] STC 665.
5 FA 1996, s 86(1).
6 ICTA 1988, s 401(1AA)–(1AC).
7 The principal restrictions are contained in s 74 of ICTA 1988. See Shipwright and Keeling *Revenue Law* (Blackstone Press, 1997), pp 311–330.
8 See *Simon's Direct Tax Service, op cit*, Davies *Principles of Tax Law* (Sweet & Maxwell, 1996), pp 148–154; Shipwright and Keeling *Revenue Law* (Blackstone Press, 1997), pp 349–360.
9 Relief under this head is given by s 24 of CAA 1990.

expenditure, the company is entitled to an allowance.[1] The allowance is worth 25 per cent of the capital expenditure incurred, on a reducing balance basis.[2] This is set against income receipts arising from the trade in the same period.

In certain circumstances the expenditure against which the relief is allowed must be reduced before the allowance is given, because an event has occurred which requires the expenditure to be reduced. The deduction which must be made is typically referred to as 'disposal value'. Such value must be brought into account where, for example, the plant ceases to belong to the trader.[3]

Example 22

Alpha Associates Ltd, acquire plant and machinery of an e-commerce business for £100,000. The taxpayer qualifies for relief under CAA 1990. The way in which the expenditure is off-set against the receipts of the trade is shown below:

		1997–98
	£	£
Plant Expenditure	100,000	
less WDA @ 25%		25,000
WDA c/f		(75,000)
Trading Income		100,000
Taxable Profits		75,000
		1998–99
	£	£
Plant Expenditure		
WDA pool c/f	75,000	
WDA @ 25%		18,750
WDA c/f		(56,250)
Trading Income		250,000
Taxable Profits		231,250
etc		

If the taxpayer had disposed of some of the business assets in the 1998–99 tax year for £50,000 this would represent disposal value which is deducted against the pool of expenditure. In this case the expenditure pool would be reduced to £25,000. It is to be observed that the allowance is weighted towards giving large amounts of relief in the earlier years than the later years.

The term plant was described in *Yarmouth v France*[4] in the following way:

> '... in its ordinary sense ... [it] ... includes whatever apparatus is used by a business man for carrying on his business – not his stock-in-trade which he buys or makes for sale; but all goods and chattels, fixed or moveable, live or dead, which he keeps for permanent employment in his business.'

---

1 CAA 1990, s 24(1). See **7.2.1**.

2 Under the Finance Act (No 2) 1997, s 42 a small company can qualify for a 50 per cent allowance where the expenditure is incurred between 2 July 1997 and 1 July 1998.

3 CAA 1990, s 24(6).

4 (1887) 19 QBD 647 at 658.

It is clear from this definition of plant that a number of pre-conditions exist in order for something to qualify as plant.[1] These are that:

(1) it must not be stock-in-trade;
(2) it does not include items which are not used for carrying on a business;
(3) excluded are things which are not 'apparatus ... goods and chattels'.

It is also established that premises do not qualify as plant. However, it is possible for apparatus to be either plant or premises depending upon the circumstances of each case.[2] In distinguishing what category apparatus falls into the central question will be whether it is the means by which the business activity is carried on, or whether it is the place from which the activity is carried on.[3] Apparatus within the former classification is plant and that in the latter are premises. An interesting problem may arise in the context of e-commerce, as the example below illustrates.

In some situations, a taxpayer will have things specifically designed in order to meet the purposes of a trade. A telecommunications operator may have specialist sub-stations which house junctions, and contain specialist equipment. In these situations, it does not automatically follow that what is created will be treated as plant. The Inland Revenue is entitled to examine the thing for which relief is claimed and disallow expenditure in respect of specific parts, because some qualify as plant, others as premises.[4] In each case, it is necessary to examine what the function of the thing is within the context of the taxpayer's business.[5]

The fact that certain things are attached to land does not prevent them from being classified as plant. In *Schofield (Inspector of Taxes) v R & H Hall Ltd*,[6] the Court of Appeal upholding the decision of the commissioners held that a concrete grain silo erected at a dockside was plant because it was necessary to the way in which the taxpayer's trade of grain importing, was carried on. The silo was designed for the purpose of ensuring an efficient process of unloading and distribution and so facilitating bulk unloading of grain. The silo was an important part in the reception and distribution of grain. This case is potentially of relevance in supporting claims for technology, such as satellite receivers which distribute information. In other words, sending stations built on land within buildings are an integral instrument of a satellite communication business.

Example 23

Intranet Telecommunication Services plc establish a hub-station for the purposes of carrying communications between their corporate users. The station operates as a central hub for the reception and distribution of information passing between its users. The structure of the hub-station and equipment housed in it were designed together. It is argued by the Inland Revenue that the structure is to be treated as a

---

1 See *Wimpey International Ltd v Warland (Inspector of Taxes)* [1988] STC 149 at 170–171, per Hoffmann J, and cited with approval by Fox LJ in the Court of Appeal [1989] STC 273 at 275.
2 In *CIR v Barclay, Curle & Co Ltd* [1969] 4 STC 221 it was held that a dry-dock was plant.
3 *Gray (Inspector of Taxes) v Seymour Garden Centre (Horticulture) (a firm)* [1995] STC 706, and *Attwood (Inspector of Taxes) v Anduff Car Wash Ltd* [1997] STC 1167.
4 *Bradley v London Electricity plc* [1996] STC 1054.
5 *IRC v Barclay, Curle & Co Ltd* [1969] 4 STC 221, per Lord Reid.
6 [1975] STC 353.

building from which the taxpayer's trade is carried on and the equipment housed within it is to be treated as plant. In situations such as this, it is clear that an apportionment must be made between expenditure incurred on plant and premises.

The relief available in respect of plant expressly extends to capital expenditure incurred by a trader on the right to use or otherwise deal with computer software.[1] The term 'computer software' is not defined in the legislation. For software to be treated as plant, the expenditure must be incurred for the purposes of a trade.[2] Computer software is also treated as plant for the purposes of the legislation where it would not be classified as plant, but a trader incurs capital expenditure in the acquisition of computer software for the purposes of a trade, which as a result of that expenditure belongs to him.[3] Some guidance on the application of the plant allowance is contained in the Inland Revenue internal manuals of interpretation. In the Inland Revenue's *Capital Allowances*, it is provided that all computer programs and data of any type should be treated as computer software.[4] The manual also states that where software is transferred by 'electronic means', in circumstances where there is no physical asset, the legislation will none the less apply.[5] No doubt this means that software delivered via the Internet will qualify for the plant capital allowance. The Inland Revenue has issued one interpretation dealing with the application of a capital allowance to computer software.[6]

In various prescribed circumstances a taxpayer is required to deduct disposal value of an asset from qualifying expenditure incurred in acquiring that asset. The disposal value which must be brought into account is set out in s 24(6) of CAA 1990. This section provides that disposal value must be brought into account when one of the following events occur:

1 CAA 1990, s 67A. The legislation applies to expenditure incurred after 9 March 1992 (Finance (No 2) Act 1992, s 68(1), (8)). See Inland Revenue guidance manual *Capital Allowances*, para 1601 (Machinery and Plant).
2 Ibid.
3 CAA 1990, s 67A(2).
4 Inland Revenue guidance manual *Capital Allowances*, para 1600 (Machinery and Plant).
5 Ibid, para 1602.
6 The guidance is contained in *Revenue Interpretation* RI 56 (issued November 1993). This provides that where software is acquired under licence the treatment of expenditure depends upon the form of consideration. Regular payments akin to a rental are revenue. The deduction of such payments are governed by accounting practice. In respect of a lump sum payment the first issue in determining tax treatment is to identify whether the licence is a capital asset. In general terms a licence is a capital asset if it has a 'sufficiently enduring nature.' Where the software has a useful economic life of less than two years the inspectors will accept that the expenditure is revenue. The interpretation also deals with equipment acquired as a package and software owned outright.

Table 6: Events triggering disposal value

	Event
(1)	the plant ceases to belong to the trader
(2)	the trader loses possession of the plant in circumstances where it is reasonable to assume that the loss is permanent
(3)	the plant ceases to exist as such (as a result of destruction, dismantling or otherwise)
(4)	the trade is permanently discontinued

The amount and method of valuation of disposal value which must be brought into account is set out in s 26 of CAA 1990, which provides that the amount of disposal value shall be:

Table 7: Amount of disposal value

	Prescribed event	*Disposal value*
(a)	Sale	Net proceeds of the sale + insurance received because of any event affecting the sale price + any other capital sum in respect of compensation of any description
(b)	Sale at a price below the market value	The price which would have been fetched if sold in the open market (except where the buyer's expenditure is taken into account in making an allowance for plant. The buyer must not be a dual resident investing company connected with the seller: see ICTA 1988, s 839 or there is a tax charge under Schedule E)
(c)	Demolition or destruction of the plant	Net proceeds received by the person for the remains of the plant + any insurance money received in respect of the demolition + capital sums received as compensation
(d)	Permanent loss of the plant	Insurance money received for the loss + capital sums received as compensation

	Prescribed event	*Disposal value*
(e)	Permanent discontinuance of the trade	If this event occurs before any mentioned in (a) to (d) the disposal value for the last mentioned event must be brought into account
(ea)	Grant to use or otherwise deal with computer software for non-monetary, or not wholly monetary consideration	Consideration in money which would have been obtained in the open market
(eb)	Where (ea) does not apply, and there is a grant of a right to use or otherwise deal with computer software for no consideration, or for a consideration in money lower than that which would have been given in the open market	The consideration which would have been fetched if sold in the open market (except where the grantee's expenditure is taken into account in making an allowance for plant. The grantee must not be a dual resident investing company connected with the seller: see ICTA 1988, s 839 or there is a tax charge under Schedule E)
(ec)	Where (ea) and (eb) do not apply and there is the grant of a right to use or otherwise deal with computer software	Net consideration in money received by the grantor for the grant + any insurance money received by the grantor in respect of the computer software by reason of any event affecting the consideration obtainable on the grant + any capital sum which represents compensation
(f)	Any other event	Open market price which the plant would have fetched if sold

CAA 1990 prohibits disposal value being brought into account insofar as it exceeds the capital expenditure incurred by the taxpayer.[1] Thus, if a computer software company incurred capital expenditure of £50,000 in the acquisition of a computer server which is subsequently destroyed in a fire, and receives insurance money of £60,000 to buy a replacement, the taxpayer cannot bring into account disposal value in excess of £50,000. The Act provides that disposal value must be increased by any capital sum (or where there is no consideration in money, would so constitute a capital sum) received for the grant to another person of the right to use or otherwise deal with the whole or part of the computer software.[2]

1 CAA 1990, s 26(2). Special rules apply where the person who acquires the plant is as a result of a transaction between connected persons (s 26(3); and see s 839 of ICTA 1988).

2 CAA 1990, ss 26(2AA) and 24(6A).

Relief for scientific research[1]

CAA 1990 provides that expenditure of a capital nature incurred in the pursuit of scientific research may be relieved against trading income.[2] The relief is subject to a number of strict pre-conditions which must be satisfied. These are:

- the taxpayer while carrying on a trade incurs capital expenditure on scientific research related to that trade;[3] and
- that the scientific research is directly undertaken by the taxpayer or on its behalf.[4]

Relief is available for expenditure incurred on scientific research which is started before any trade is commenced. This form of relief is available where:

- the taxpayer incurs expenditure of a capital nature on scientific research; and
- the research is directly undertaken by the taxpayer or on its behalf; and
- the taxpayer thereafter sets up and commences a trade connected with that research.[5]

The rate of the allowance is equal to 100 per cent of the expenditure incurred by the taxpayer.[6] The time at which the expenditure must be brought into account is the 'relevant chargeable period'.[7] The legislation provides that this is the time when either:

(a) the expenditure is incurred; or
(b) when the trade resulting from the scientific research is commenced, in respect of pre-trade expenditure.[8]

Scientific research is defined in the legislation as meaning 'any activities in the fields of natural or applied science for the extension of knowledge'.[9] The relief does not extend to expenditure incurred in the acquisition of rights in, or arising out of, the scientific research.[10] The legislation does provide that the term otherwise includes 'all expenditure incurred for the prosecution of, or the provision of facilities for the prosecution of scientific research'.[11]

Example 24

Alpha Enterprises Ltd, incurs expenditure of £2 million on scientific research relating to various technologies associated with virtual reality video-conferencing. The taxpayer carries on a trade in the sale of video-conferencing equipment, and in the tax

1 See *Simon's Direct Tax Service*, *op cit*.
2 CAA 1990, s 137.
3 The legislation provides that expenditure is related to a trade if the scientific research may lead to, or facilitate an extension of the trade (s 139(1)(d)(i) of CAA 1990).
4 Ibid, s 137(1)(a).
5 Ibid, s 137(1)(b).
6 Ibid, s 137(1).
7 Ibid.
8 Ibid, s 137(5).
9 Ibid, s 139(1)(a).
10 Ibid, s 139(1)(c).
11 Ibid.

year 1998–99 it receives trading income of £10 million. By use of the allowance taxable profits are £8 million.

The application of this relief is restricted to those taxpayers who directly carry on the scientific research, or which is directly undertaken by another person on the taxpayer's behalf. The case of *Gaspet Ltd v Ellis (Inspector of Taxes)*[1] illustrates the ambit of the relief which is available to those who incur expenditure on scientific research. The case illustrates that the finance of scientific research must be appropriately structured, because in the absence of a very tight link akin to agency between the financier and the person carrying on the research and development, no allowance will be allowed.

The legislation permits an allowance only in respect of capital expenditure incurred in the prosecution of scientific research by a trader related to that trade, or arising out of which research a trade will be carried on. In addition to these general limitations, CAA 1990 expressly excludes expenditure incurred on the acquisition of, or of rights in or over any land.[2] This limitation does not apply in so far as the expenditure is, on a just apportionment, referable to the acquisition of, or of rights in or over, or of machinery or plant which forms part of, a building or other structure already constructed on the land.[3] The example below illustrates the operation of this relief.

Example 25

Alpha Services Ltd, carries on trade in the distribution of data throughout the world. The company undertakes scientific research into how it can achieve a greater flow of data through satellite transmission units. For this purpose the company acquires such a unit for £1 million in the 1998–99 tax year. The equipment and building in which it is housed is worth £750,000. The company is not entitled to any relief for the purposes of a scientific research allowance in respect of £250,000 (the value of the land) because this is not referable to the building or plant.

Disposal value must also be brought into account in respect of assets which qualify for a scientific research allowance.[4]

The amount of the disposal value is shown in Table 8.

1 [1985] STC 572, ChD, affirmed [1987] STC 362, CA.
2 Ibid.
3 CAA 1990, s 137(2).
4 Ibid, s 138.

Table 8: Disposal value: SRA

	Event	Disposal value
(a)	Sale of the asset	Price not less than that which would have been fetched on the open market
(b)	Deemed sale of the asset:	Deemed proceeds of sale
	(i) where the asset is destroyed	any insurance moneys + other compensation of any description received by the person carrying on the trade in respect of the destruction + any money received for the remains of the asset
	(ii) demolition of the asset	cost of demolition + expenditure represented by the asset
(c)	Any other event	Price asset would have fetched if sold in the open market

An asset ceases to belong to a trader in the case of a sale from the time of completion or at the time when possession is given of the asset.[1] The time the asset ceases to belong to a trader will be whichever is the earlier.

Short-life assets[2]

The depreciation allowance of 25 per cent on a reducing balance basis, can cause problems where the economic life of the plant or machinery is less than the time it takes for the value to be written-off in the tax accounts. In order to ameliorate this problem, relief is available which accelerates the rate of depreciation on what are known as short-life assets (assets with a life of less than five years). To qualify for relief, an election must be made to the Inspector.[3] The election must be made within two years from the end of the accounting period in which the expenditure is incurred.[4] Although strictly the company should specifically mention *each* type of asset in respect of which an election is claimed, this is not adhered to by the Inland Revenue.[5] Relief is available only where a trader has incurred capital expenditure upon plant or machinery, which is not excluded from the short-life asset relief.[6]

1 CAA 1990, s 139(4) in respect of a sale which is effected, or a contract of sale which is entered into after 26 July 1989.

2 See *Simon's Direct Tax Service*, *op cit*, Part B2.326; Inland Revenue guidance manual *Capital Allowances*, paras 2350–2357, 2365–2368 and 2376; Shipwright and Keeling *Revenue Law* (Blackstone Press, 1997), pp 358–359.

3 CAA 1990, s 37(2).

4 Ibid, s 37(2A).

5 Inland Revenue guidance manual *Capital Allowances*, paras 2376–2378. See also Inland Revenue Statement of Practice SP1/1986. Paragraph 6 states that a claimant can aggregate the cost of a large number of similar short-life assets, and show in the election that one sum. This statement of practice provides a series of useful illustrations in how the relief is to be operated.

6 CAA 1990, s 37(1). Assets excluded from these provisions are set out in s 38. Assets excluded include various types of leased plant or machinery.

Example 26

A telecommunication provider incurs expenditure on micro-processors for incorporation in various exchanges within its network. In the 1997–98 tax year, it purchases 500,000 processors at a cost of £25 million. The micro-processors have an economic life of three years.

	1997–98	*1998–99*	*1999–2000*	*2000–01*
Short-life pool	£25m	£18.75m	£14,062,500	nil
WDA @ 25%	£6.25m	£4,687,500m	£3,515,625	£10,546,875
WDA c/f	£18.75m	£14,062,500	£10,546,875	nil

The relief is given by treating the short-life asset as part of a different writing down allowance pool from the pool which exists generally for plant or machinery.[1] When the asset ceases to be used for the purposes of the trade, it is deemed that for the purposes of the short-life asset the trade is permanently discontinued. The result of this is that the rate of depreciation is accelerated to the whole of the short-life pool representing that asset.[2] The relief must be used within four years of the expenditure being incurred. Otherwise the asset is placed back in the general plant or machinery expenditure pool.[3]

Long-life assets[4]
Where capital expenditure is incurred on or after 26 November 1996,[5] for the purposes of a trade, and it is expenditure on plant or machinery with a useful economic life of 25 years or more, then it will be treated as a long-life asset.[6] The effect of this scheme is to limit the rate of depreciation to 6 per cent rather than 25 per cent.[7] Certain assets are not subject to the long-life asset provisions, for example, expenditure on a motor car.[8] None of the exclusions apply to IT. The provisions do not apply unless the expenditure within a chargeable period is in excess of £100,000.[9]

Where the scheme applies the expenditure on long-life assets is placed in a pool separate from that incurred on plant or machinery generally. The allowance which is permitted in respect of a long-life asset is given against the trading receipts of the trade carried on by the taxpayer.[10] Where expenditure is incurred on other long-life assets, the expenditure is pooled together.[11]

1 CAA 1990, s 37(3).
2 Ibid, s 37(3)(b).
3 Ibid, s 37(5).
4 See Shipwright and Keeling *Revenue Law* (Blackstone Press, 1997), pp 358–359.
5 CAA 1990, s 38H. The long-life asset provisions were inserted by FA 1997.
6 Ibid, s 38A.
7 Ibid, s 38F(1),(2).
8 Ibid, s 38B.
9 Ibid, s 38D.
10 Ibid, s 38E(3).
11 Ibid, s 38E(5).

Example 27

A cable television/Internet access provider incurs expenditure of £10million in the acquisition of a cable network, in the 1997–98 tax year. The network has a useful economic life of 28 years.

	1997–98	*1998–99*	*1999–2000*	*2000–01*	
Long-life pool	£10m	£9,400,000	£8,836,000	£8,305,840	
WDA @ 6%	£600,000	£564,000	£530,160		
WDA c/f	£9,400,000	£8,836,000	£8,305,840	£7,807,489.60	etc

5.7.3 Patent rights: capital allowance

The capital allowances granted in respect of a patent fall into two distinct categories. Capital expenditure incurred for the purposes of a trade is set-off against receipts derived from the trade.[1] In addition, the legislation permits capital expenditure to be set-off against income from a patent that is generated otherwise than in the course of a trade.[2] Table 9 below summarises the effect of the provisions dealing with the application of allowances. Like the capital allowance given for plant and machinery, disposal value must be brought into account in relation to patent rights.

Table 9: Allowances

Activity	*Method of Allowance*	*Conditions for allowance*
Trade s 528(1)	Allowance in taxing trade s 528(1)	Carrying on a trade, the profits of which are, or would be if any chargeable under Case I Schedule D, and at any time within the chargeable period the patent rights, or rights out of which they are granted were or were to be used for the purposes of that trade s 528(1)
No Trade s 528(3)	Allowance deducted from company's income from patents of the accounting period (s 528(3)(a)) Where the allowance cannot be given effect by reason of deficiency of income from patents the unallowed amount is carried forward to the succeeding accounting period (but the company must remain within the charge to CT) s 528(3)(b)	An allowance falls to be made under, either, s 520 s 522 s 523 s 526 (s 528(3))

1 ICTA 1988, s 520.
2 Ibid, s 528.

PART III UK TAXATION

5.7.4 Patent rights: revenue expenditure

The tax legislation contains specific relief provisions in respect of professional fees incurred on patent rights, which are classified as revenue expenditure.[1] Table 10 below summarises the circumstances in which each relief will be granted.

Table 10: Revenue expenditure

Type of revenue expenditure	*Fees paid, expenses incurred obtaining grant of a patent*	*Fees paid, expenses incurred on maintenance of patent*	*Fees paid, expenses incurred for extension of a patent*	*Fees paid, expenses incurred on rejected application for a patent*	*Fees paid, expenses incurred on abandoned application*
Expenditure incurred for purposes of a trade	✓ (ICTA 1988, s 83)	✓	✓ (ICTA 1988, s 83)	✓ (ICTA 1988, s 83)	✓ (ICTA 1988, s 83)
Expenditure incurred otherwise than for purposes of a trade	✓ (ICTA 1988, s 526)	✓	✓ (ICTA 1988, s 526)	✓ (ICTA 1988, s 526)	✓ (ICTA 1988, s 526)

5.7.5 Royalty expenditure

Royalty expenditure incurred in the use of patent rights is not absorbed in the same way within a company's tax accounts as other royalty payments such as those for use of copyright. Royalty expenditure on a patent by a company is a prohibited deduction in the payer's accounts in computing taxable profits, but such a royalty is regarded as a charge on the payer's profits which can be deducted in appropriate circumstances.[2]

5.7.6 Know-how: capital allowance

A capital allowance is available for capital expenditure incurred upon industrial know-how. This is a key area of relief since many IT and e-commerce businesses use industrial techniques. Know-how is defined in ICTA 1988 as:

> 'any industrial information and techniques likely to assist in the manufacture or processing of goods or materials, or in the working of a mine, oil-well or other source of mineral deposits (including the searching for, discovery or testing of deposits or the winning of access thereto), or in the carrying out of any agricultural, forestry or fishing operations.'[3]

The Inland Revenue has adopted the position that this definition does not apply to commercial know-how.[4] Thus, expenditure of £100,000 on know-how which assists in the manufacture of goods would qualify for relief. However, similar expenditure on

1 ICTA 1988, s 84.
2 Ibid, s 338.
3 Ibid, s 533(7).
4 See *Revenue Interpretation*, IRInt 46 (August 1993).

marketing data relating to consumer preferences for the efficient running of an e-commerce business would not qualify for relief provided under s 533 of the Act.

Although receipts from the exploitation of know-how cannot normally qualify as capital,[1] except where disposed of with part of a business, it is possible for expenditure upon know-how to qualify as capital. In *Atherton (HM Inspector of Taxes) v British Insulated and Helsby Cables, Limited*,[2] Viscount Cave commented:

> '... when an expenditure is made, not only once and for all, but with a view to bringing into existence an asset or an advantage for the enduring benefit of a trade, I think that there is very good reason (in the absence of special circumstances leading to an opposite conclusion) for treating such an expenditure as properly attributable not to revenue but to capital.'[3]

Lord Atkinson felt that references to an 'asset' could not be confined to something material.[4]

The approach is given particular support by *Vodafone Cellular Ltd v Shaw (Inspector of Taxes)*[5] where the taxpayer acquired know-how and technical support for £2 million. This agreement was not in dispute. As Millett LJ commented in respect of the agreement: 'The initial know-how was admittedly a capital asset, and the payment by which it was obtained was admittedly a capital payment ...'[6]

Where capital expenditure is incurred by a person upon know-how for use in a trade carried on by him, a capital allowance is provided under ICTA 1988.[7] The allowance also applies where the expenditure was incurred prior to a trade being commenced which is subsequently started.[8] The rate of allowance is 25 per cent of the acquisition cost, after adjustments, on a reducing balance basis.[9] The adjustment which must be made to acquisition cost before any allowance is given is in respect of any disposal value. The allowance under s 530 of ICTA 1988 is given solely on a reducing balance basis until all the expenditure is written-off even though the know-how may have ceased being used.

The tax rules require disposal value to be brought into account so that a taxpayer cannot retain the advantage of a capital allowance after sale of the asset. The disposal value to be brought into account is that arising when 'a person sells any know-how' in respect of which capital expenditure was incurred and qualified for a capital allowance.[10] The amount to be brought into account is that which is 'equal to the net proceeds ... of that sale'.[11]

---

1 This is because no proprietary right exists in know-how.
2 (1925) 10 TC 155.
3 Ibid, at 188–189.
4 Ibid, at 195.
5 [1997] STC 734.
6 The strange anomaly implicitly arising from the comments of the judge is that know-how is referred to as a 'capital asset'. The 'disposal' of know-how itself can never generate a chargeable gain for the reason that it is not regarded as an 'asset' independent of a business. Thus, why do some commentators regard know-how as a capital asset?
7 ICTA 1988, s 530(1)(a).
8 Ibid, s 530(1)(b).
9 Ibid, s 530(2).
10 Ibid, s 530(5).
11 Ibid.

5.7.7 Disposal of a trade including know-how

Under ICTA 1988, where a person disposes of a trade or part of a trade after 19 March 1968 together with know-how used in it, the consideration for the know-how is to be treated as a payment of goodwill.[1] The know-how is thus treated as goodwill for all purposes from the perspective of both the 'seller' and 'buyer'.[2]

However, it is open to the parties to elect jointly for the know-how not to be treated as a payment of goodwill.[3] Such an election must be given by notice within two years of the disposal. Treating know-how as goodwill in these circumstances has one important tax advantage: all chargeable gains accruing on the disposal of goodwill can be postponed under the rollover relief provisions in TCGA 1992.[4]

5.7.8 Restrictive covenants

Under ICTA 1988, where a person disposes of know-how and also gives an undertaking which is to restrict its, or another's, activities in any way, any consideration received in respect of the undertaking is treated as consideration received for the disposal of know-how.[5]

5.8 TRADING LOSSES[6]

5.8.1 Transfer of losses against trading income of subsequent accounting periods[7]

Once allowable expenditure has been offset against revenue receipts the resulting computation may establish a loss. Under the tax legislation, it is possible for this loss to be used in a number of ways so as to reduce the level of taxable profits in subsequent or earlier accounting periods of the company. Under s 393 of ICTA 1988, a company which incurs a trading loss can set-off the loss against trading income from the same trade in subsequent accounting periods.[8] Where the loss is only partially absorbed by trading income of a subsequent period, this is carried forward to trading income arising in later accounting periods.[9] In this way, the trading loss is absorbed throughout subsequent accounting periods.

---

1 'Goodwill' has been described as 'the benefit and advantage of the good name, reputation, and connection of a business. It is the attractive force which brings in custom', per Lord Macnaghten in *IRC v Muller & Co Margarine Ltd* [1901] AC 217 at 223, HL.

2 ICTA 1988, s 531(2).

3 Ibid, s 531(3)(a).

4 TCGA 1992, s 150 *et seq*.

5 ICTA 1988, s 531(8).

6 See *Simon's Direct Tax Service, op cit*; Shipwright and Keeling *Revenue Law* (Blackstone Press, 1997), pp 605–614; Davies *Principles of Tax Law* (Sweet & Maxwell, 1996), pp 156–161.

7 See *Simon's Direct Tax Service, op cit*.

8 ICTA 1988, s 393(1).

9 Ibid.

Example 28

Galaxy Associates Ltd incur a trading loss of £80,000 (1997–98) from the licensing of its Internet web browser. Trading income in subsequent accounting periods is £25,000 (1998–99), £45,000 (1999–2000), £250,000 (2000–01). The trading loss will be absorbed in the following way:

	1997–98	*1998–99*	*1999–2000*	*2000–01*
Trading Income		£25,000	£45,000	£250,000
Trading Loss	£80,000	£55,000 c/f	£10,000 c/f	–
Taxable Profit	–	–	–	£240,000

A trading loss is determined by precisely the same principles as the computation of trading income.[1] In various circumstances where trading income is insufficient to absorb the trading loss, it is possible to use the loss against income arising in respect of interest or dividends on investments.[2] Relief will not be given unless the company carrying on a trade is within the charge to UK corporation tax.[3]

5.8.2 Transfer of losses against preceding accounting periods

Where a company incurs a trading loss, on or after 1 April 1991, a claim[4] may be made for that loss to be offset against profits of any kind arising in the same accounting period.[5] It is also possible for a company to off set the loss against profits of earlier accounting periods.[6] The legislation permits the loss to be transferred against profits of the preceding period. This effectively means that a trading loss can only be carried back a maximum of 12 months.[7] Relief is denied where the trade in which the loss arises is not carried out on a commercial basis.[8]

Example 29

Alpha Computer Component Manufacturers Ltd, achieve profits of £60,000, £80,000 and £100,000 for the 1994–95, 1995–96 and 1996–97 tax years respectively. A trading loss of £180,000 is incurred in the 1997–98 tax period. The taxpayer may elect to off set the loss against profits of earlier accounting periods in the following way. For the purposes of this example it is assumed that the tax rate throughout these years is fixed at 24 per cent.

1 ICTA 1988, s 393(7).
2 Ibid, s 393(8).
3 Ibid, s 393(10).
4 A claim for relief must be made within two years from the accounting period in which the loss is incurred, s 393A(10) of ICTA 1988.
5 Ibid, s 393A(1)(a).
6 Ibid, s 393A(1)(b).
7 See Finance (No 2) Act 1997.
8 ICTA 1988, s 393A(3)(b).

	1994–95	1995-96	1996–97	1997-98
Taxable profits Tax payable Trading loss	£60,000 £14,400 –	£80,000 £19,200	£100,000 £24,000 £100,000 (carried back)	– £180,000 (carry back under s 393A ICTA 1988)
Tax repayment	No	No	Yes	–

A trading loss is calculated in precisely the same way as trading income[1] would be computed. In other words, revenue expenditure and any capital allowance is offset against revenue receipts for an accounting period.[2] The loss relief is available only to a company carrying on a trade so as to be within the charge to UK corporation tax.[3]

The carry-back of a trading loss does not apply to trades which are within Case V of Schedule D.[4] Where a company incurs a loss under Case VI, the loss is set-off against income arising under Case VI in the same or any subsequent accounting period.[5]

Example 30

Zoltan Electronic Commerce Ltd, carries on a trade in the UK, and from the USA in selling computer software via the Internet. In the 1997–98 tax year a loss is incurred of £40,000 under Case I of Sch D, which is carried back against profits of the preceding accounting period under ICTA 1988, s 393A. A trading loss of £70,000 is incurred in respect of a trade which is assessed under Case V of Schedule D. Profits of preceding accounting periods under Case V for 1996–97 and 1995–96, were £110,000, and £60,000 respectively. The loss under Case V cannot be carried back under ICTA 1988, s 393A, although the loss can be carried forward under ICTA 1988, s 393. However, the loss of £40,000 can be carried back against the profits of the preceding accounting periods (including those under Case V) under ICTA 1988, s 393A (this is limited to the preceding 12 months).

5.8.3 Schedule D, Case V

Schedule D, Case V is used to impose tax on receipts derived from foreign possessions.[6] Receipts sourced to Case V are also assessed to tax on 'profits'.[7] The precise nature of the receipts brought within this Case is 'income arising from possessions out of the UK not being income consisting of emoluments of any office or employment'.[8] The tax legislation does not define the word 'possessions'. In

1 Defined in s 393A(9)(b) of ICTA 1988.
2 ICTA 1988, s 393A(9).
3 Ibid, s 393A(9)(c).
4 Ibid, s 393A(3).
5 Ibid, s 396(1).
6 Ibid, s 18.
7 Ibid, s 70(2).
8 Ibid, s 18(3).

Colquhoun (Surveyor of Taxes) v Brooks,[1] Lord Herschell delivered the following opinion on the nature of the word 'possessions' within the context of this charging provision:

> 'When, therefore, the term "possessions" is employed it seems to indicate an intention to cover by it something more than "property". And it is difficult to see why, unless the intention were to embrace something more, the latter word was not used. "Possessions" is a wide expression; it is not a word with any technical meaning; the Act supplies no interpretation of it. And I cannot see why it may not fitly be interpreted as relating to all that is possessed in Her Majesty's dominions out of the United Kingdom, or in foreign countries. And if so, I do not think any violence would be done to the language if it were held to include the interest which a person in this country possesses in a business carried on elsewhere.'

Lord Macnaghten said in the course of delivering his opinion that: 'The word "possessions" is not a technical word. It seems to me that it is the widest and most comprehensive word that could be used.' Where a trade is carried on wholly outside of the UK, it has been decided that the receipts derived from such a trade will be taxable under Case V. This is the implication of the charge which encompasses 'income arising from possessions out of the United Kingdom'.

If part of a business is carried on outside of the UK and also partly within the UK, any income is taxed under Case I of Schedule D. Receipts arising under Case V are taxed in accordance with the same principles as those applicable to receipts derived from a trade under Case I.[2] It is important to appreciate that receipts arising in respect of foreign possessions will be taxed in the hands of a company whether or not those receipts are received in or transmitted to the UK.[3] For example, if a UK company operated an e-commerce site via a branch in the USA the receipts would be taxable under this Case.

5.8.4 Schedule D, Case VI

This is a 'sweeper up' Case that encompasses income that does not fall within any other Case of Schedule D. It is usually the source of a tax charge for casual profits derived from isolated transactions.

5.9 CHARGEABLE GAINS

5.9.1 Introduction: basis of charge on gains

A company is subject to corporation tax on any chargeable gains arising from the disposal of assets.[4] This tax charge is important because it can potentially touch upon all assets used within the world of IT and e-commerce. A chargeable gain is calculated using the principles which are applied for the purposes of computing an individual's liability to capital gains tax.[5] A chargeable gain is calculated by reference to the

1 [1886–90] All ER Rep 1063, 2 TC 490.
2 ICTA 1988, s 70(2).
3 Ibid, s 70(1). Relief is available in terms of deferring tax liability on unremittable overseas income. See ICTA 1988, s 584.
4 TCGA 1992, s 1(2).
5 Ibid, s 8(3).

company's accounting period.[1] In order for a chargeable gain to exist the following criteria must be satisfied:

(1) existence of an asset;
(2) disposal of an asset;
(3) disposal proceeds;
(4) deduction of allowable costs; and
(5) apportionment of cost where there is a partial disposal.

Example 31

Alpha Business Park Ltd operates an Internet business park site, whereby other companies purchase a site on an Internet map. The Internet business park has built up considerable goodwill with the result that it is valued at £250,000. The company disposes of the Internet business park at market value. The transfer involves the disposal of computer software, trade marks and goodwill. Circumstances such as these will trigger a tax charge on the disposal of assets.

A non-resident company is subject to corporation tax on chargeable gains, where it carries on a trade through a branch or agency[2] within the UK.[3] The tax charge arises in respect of the disposal of assets which are situated in the UK and are used for the purposes of a trade.[4] Alternatively, a tax charge will apply on gains from the disposal of assets situated in the UK which are used or held for the purposes of a branch or agency.[5] No tax can be imposed in respect of this charge unless the company is carrying on a trade through a branch or agency in the UK.[6]

5.9.2 Assets

An asset is broadly defined within TCGA 1992. It includes all forms of property,[7] and specifically any form of property created by the company disposing of it.[8] All tangible and intangible property used by IT or e-commerce businesses will therefore potentially be subject to TCGA 1992.

Example 32

(1) A company has the benefit of an exclusive agreement with Internet access providers for the distribution of electronic mail. The agreement is capable of assignment with the unanimous consent of the Internet providers. Another company is interested in acquiring an interest in the distribution agreement for a payment of £5 million. The overall value of the agreement is £12 million. In this situation the transfer of the right to participate within the agreement is potentially a taxable disposal under TCGA 1992.

---

1 TCGA 1992, s 8(1).
2 The definition of 'branch or agency' is explained in Chapter 14 on e-commerce.
3 TCGA 1992, s 10(3).
4 Ibid, s 10(1)(a).
5 Ibid, s 10(1)(b).
6 Ibid, s 10(2).
7 Ibid, s 21(1).
8 Ibid, s 21(1)(c).

(2) Web Consultancy Ltd specialises in the creation and maintenance of web sites for companies throughout the world. The company maintains web sites for a diverse range of business entities, including supermarket retailers, pharmaceutical manufacturers and for some university faculties. The company is approached, and offered £250,000 for the contractual rights which it has acquired.

In both these examples the contractual rights are assets, the transfer of which are disposals capable of giving rise to chargeable gains. All aspects of IT and e-commerce are capable of being subject to TCGA 1992.

Disposal

In simple terms, an asset is disposed of, where there is a conveyance of the asset, by sale or by operation of law. The time of a disposal is fixed at when the contract is entered into for the disposal and acquisition of the asset.[1] The fact that the asset is transferred at a different time from the period of entering into the contract is wholly irrelevant.[2] In addition, a disposal occurs where a capital sum[3] is derived from an asset.[4] In this situation, the time of disposal is the period when the capital sum is received.[5] TCGA 1992 makes particular reference to capital sums derived from the surrender of rights, or for refraining from exercising rights, and such sums received as consideration for the use or exploitation of assets.[6] A disposal is also deemed to occur where the asset is destroyed, irrespective of whether any capital sum is received by way of compensation for the destruction of the asset.[7] In the event that a disposal is subject to a conditional contract, such as the exercise of an option, the time of the disposal is when the contract becomes unconditional.[8]

Example 33

Alpha Internet Services Ltd processes and distributes electronic mail for an Internet access provider. The contract is exclusive to Alpha Internet Services Ltd, and is for a period of 12 years. The contract is worth £5 million to the company. The Internet access provider is acquired by a US based company which operates an Internet access service in the UK through a subsidiary. The subsidiary's electronic mail is processed by a competitor of Alpha Internet Services Ltd, called Trans E-Mail Ltd. The US company wishes to see Trans E-Mail Ltd distribute e-mail for both access providers. A payment of £3 million is made to secure the surrender by Alpha Internet Services Ltd of its contractual rights.

In this situation, the payment of £3 million would represent a capital sum derived from the surrender of an asset. It is possible that in these circumstances a chargeable gain would arise on any gain accruing to Alpha Internet Services Ltd.

---

1 TCGA 1992, s 28(1).
2 Ibid.
3 A capital sum is defined as 'any money or money's worth which is not excluded from the consideration taken into account in the computation of the gain', TCGA 1992, s 22(3).
4 Ibid, s 22.
5 Ibid, s 22(2).
6 Ibid, s 22(1)(c)(d).
7 Ibid, s 24(1).
8 Ibid, s 28(2).

Disposal consideration
Normally the Inland Revenue will not be able to interfere with the consideration agreed upon for the disposal of an asset. However, there are circumstances in which the Inland Revenue is entitled to substitute another amount as the disposal consideration. This occurs where an asset is acquired or disposed of otherwise than on an arm's length basis between connected persons.[1] Other detailed provisions may also apply for fixing the value of the disposal.[2]

5.9.3 Allowable deductions

In the computation of a chargeable gain a company is entitled to make a number of deductions. The permitted deductions are as follows:[3]

(1) the amount given wholly and exclusively for the purposes of acquiring the asset;
(2) the incidental costs of acquisition;
(3) any amount incurred wholly and exclusively for the purposes of enhancing the value of the asset;
(4) any expenditure wholly and exclusively incurred in establishing, preserving or defending title to the asset, or to a right over the asset;
(5) any incidental costs incurred in the disposal of the asset.[4]

A company is not permitted to make any deduction in respect of expenditure which has been deducted for the purposes of ascertaining the profits or gains or losses of a trade.[5]

Example 34

Alpha Electronic Merchandising Ltd (AEM) acquired in 1991, for £50,000 computer software which was used for the purposes of carrying on a trade across the Internet in supplying software in an electronic format. In 1997–98 AEM disposes of the computer software for £60,000, including the trademarks associated with the Internet business for £100,000, and copyright in the software sold via the Internet, for £200,000. The original cost of acquiring the copyright and trade marks by AEM amount to £65,000.

1997–98		
	£	£
Disposal consideration		360,000
Acquisition costs	65,000	______
Chargeable gains		295,000

5.9.4 Wasting assets

Where an asset is disposed of a chargeable gain may arise for the purposes of TCGA 1992. Where such an event occurs, a deduction must be made for the acquisition cost against the disposal proceeds to ascertain any chargeable gain.[6] The acquisition cost is

1 TCGA 1992, s 17(1).
2 Ibid, ss 18–20.
3 Ibid, s 38(1).
4 That is fees, commission or remuneration paid for professional services (s 38(2) of TCGA 1992).
5 Ibid, s 39.
6 Ibid, s 38(1)(a).

restricted where an asset is regarded as a 'wasting asset'. Expenditure on wasting assets must be written-off on a straight-line basis,[1] unless capital allowances were available.[2]

An asset will be regarded as a wasting asset where its 'predictable life [does] not exceed 50 years'.[3] No definition is given of 'predictable life' for the purposes of intangible assets. Plant and machinery is deemed to have a predictable life of less than 50 years.[4] In some cases the wasting asset provisions will not be relevant. For example, the typical duration of copyright is the author's life plus 70 years.

The wasting asset rule may, however, be particularly relevant in the case of licensing. A licence is capable of qualifying as an asset under TCGA 1992. If the terms of the licence are such that it will last for less than 50 years, it is treated as a wasting asset.[5] If a licence contains a renewal clause, the Inland Revenue takes the view that the predictable life of the asset should be based upon the initial duration. The reason for this is that there is no certainty that the licence would be renewed.[6]

Because the legal duration of registered UK trade marks is not predictable, it does not qualify as a wasting asset.[7] This is because the duration of the legal life of a trade mark is potentially unlimited. The Inland Revenue adopts the same approach in relation to foreign registered trade marks, unless it is established that a different approach should be taken, for example, because the laws of another country are different.[8]

The effect of the wasting asset rule is to restrict the amount of the acquisition cost which can be deducted against the proceeds of disposal. The reason for the operation of this rule is because the owner will have enjoyed use of the asset and as a result it is necessary to write-off the acquisition value, save for any residual value.[9]

5.9.5 Relief for gains arising on the disposal of business assets

A chargeable gain accruing on the disposal of business assets can be deferred by the acquisition of further business assets with the consideration arising on the disposal.[10] This is known as roll-over relief. Where a claim is made for this relief, it is deemed

1 TCGA 1992, s 46.
2 Ibid, s 47.
3 Ibid, s 44(1). Where a licence is acquired in respect of computer software, the capital expenditure is deemed to be on plant (CAA 1990, s 67A). As a result under TCGA 1992 it is regarded as having a predictable life of less than 50 years. Such an item will always be regarded as a wasting asset.
4 TCGA 1992, s 44(1(c).
5 See Inland Revenue guidance manual *Capital Gains*, para 76724.
6 Ibid.
7 Ibid, para 76749.
8 Ibid, para 76748.
9 TCGA 1992, s 46(1).
10 Ibid, s 152.

that the consideration received is adjusted so that neither a gain nor a loss is secured.[1] The legislation also operates to reduce the value of the acquired asset, by the excess of the amount accruing from the asset disposed of, over the adjusted value. The operation of this relief does not affect the value of the consideration paid by the person acquiring the old asset, or the other party selling the new asset.[2] The relief is not available where the new assets are not acquired for the purposes of use in a trade.[3]

Roll-over relief only operates in respect of assets specified in TCGA 1992.[4] There is no requirement for the disposal consideration accruing from an asset to be invested in exactly the same type of asset. The only requirement is that the consideration is used to acquire an asset within the specified classes which qualify for roll-over relief. The relief is excluded where the new asset is not acquired, or an unconditional contract is not entered into for the acquisition of the new asset, 12 months before the disposal of the old asset, or within three years of the disposal of the old asset.[5] Where an unconditional contract is entered into, the relief is given on a provisional basis.[6] Where the asset is not acquired under such a contract then all necessary adjustments will be made to recover the relief.[7] There are provisions which deal with the appropriation of an asset to trading stock.[8]

5.9.6 Assets qualifying for roll-over relief

The assets in which disposal consideration must be reinvested to qualify for roll-over relief are as follows:[9]

Table 11: Qualifying categories for roll-over relief

Class	***Type of asset***
Class 1	*Head A* Any building or part of a building occupied, or used only for the purposes of a trade *Head B* Fixed plant or machinery not forming part of a building
Class 2	Ships, aircraft and hovercraft

1 TCGA 1992, s 152(1)(a).
2 Ibid, s 152.
3 Ibid, s 152(5).
4 Ibid, s 152(1). For the procedure to claim relief, see TCGA 1992, s 153A.
5 Ibid, s 152(3).
6 Ibid, s 152(4).
7 Ibid.
8 Ibid, s 161.
9 Ibid, s 155.

Class	Type of asset
Class 3	Satellites, space stations and spacecraft, launch vehicles
Class 4	Goodwill
Class 5	Not relevant
Class 6	Not relevant

5.9.7 Relief where partial reinvestment

Where a company applies only part of the consideration arising from the disposal of an asset in the acquisition of a new asset, roll-over relief is not available except in specified circumstances.[1] Where the taxpayer applies all of the consideration except part of the chargeable gain arising from the disposal relief is still available.[2] In these circumstances, it is deemed that the amount of the gain corresponds to the amount applied in the acquisition of a new asset,[3] and that the acquisition cost of the new asset is reduced by the amount of the deemed gain.[4]

5.9.8 Roll-over relief and non-residents

Where a non-resident makes a chargeable disposal of an old asset, roll-over relief is only available where new assets are acquired which are chargeable assets in relation to the non-resident.[5] An asset is a chargeable asset in relation to a non-resident where if it was to be disposed of at that time, the chargeable gains would form part of chargeable profits arising from a branch or agency through which a trade is carried on in the UK.[6]

5.9.9 Other reliefs

TCGA 1992 provides a number of other reliefs from capital gains tax. The primary reliefs relate to intra-group transfers (s 171), schemes relating to reconstruction or amalgamation of a company's business (s 139), and mergers (s 181). Gifts of business assets by an individual qualify for relief (s 165) the effect of which is to hold over the gain. Disposals made by individuals are subject to taper relief (s 2A), the effect of which is to reduce the amount of the chargeable gain by a specified percentage, for instance, if a business asset has been held for 10 or more years only 25 per cent of the gain is chargeable.

5.10 DEDUCTION OF TAX AT SOURCE ON PAYMENTS

In certain circumstances, there is a requirement for a person making a payment to deduct income tax at source, known as 'withholding tax'. The obligation to deduct at

1 TCGA 1992, s 153.
2 Ibid.
3 Ibid, s 153(1)(a).
4 Ibid, s 153(1)(b).
5 Ibid, s 159.
6 Ibid, s 159(1), (4). See also s 10(3).

source, insofar as it is relevant to e-commerce, arises either in the context of:

(a) Schedule D, Case III because the payments are annual payments; or
(b) payments for the use of patent rights, copyright or design rights.

5.10.1 Schedule D, Case III

This charge applies to income which comes within the category of annual payments.[1] In other words, income which is regarded as 'pure income'. A receipt falls into the 'pure income' category if it accrues to a person without the expense of earning it. Where an 'annual payment' is made, tax must be deducted at source by the person making the payment.[2] Guidance on what is an 'annual payment' was given by Jenkins LJ in *IRC v Whitworth Park Coal Co Ltd*[3] where he said:

> '(1) To come within the rule as an "other annual payment" the payment in question must be *ejusdem generis* with the specific instances given in the shape of interest of money and annuities [...]
> (2) The payment in question must fall to be made under some binding legal obligation as distinct from being a mere voluntary payment [...]
> (3) The fact that the obligation to pay is imposed by an order of the court and does not arise by virtue of a contract does not exclude the payment [...]
> (4) The payment in question must possess the essential quality of recurrence implied by the description "annual" [...]
> (5) The payment in question must be in the nature of a "pure income" profit in the hands of the recipient.'

In relation to point (5), it follows that for income to be pure profit of a recipient he must not have incurred any revenue expenditure in return for the payment. Where such a payment is made, income tax is deducted at the basic rate.[4] The tax is collected by the payer under ICTA 1988, ss 348 and 349. Where a payee receives an annual payment it is taxed under Schedule D, Case III. The taxpayer is deemed to receive the gross value of the payment, but is given credit for the tax deducted at source. Where the obligation to make the payment is subject to UK law the charge is under Schedule D, Case III, irrespective of whether or not the recipient is resident or non-resident.[5] If the obligation is governed by foreign law, and the recipient is UK resident, then the tax charge will be under Schedule D, Case V.[6]

5.10.2 Patent rights

Any sum paid for the user of a patent not out of profits or gains brought into charge to income tax (ie all payments by a corporate licensee) must be made under deduction of income tax at source.[7] Table 12 below summarises the nature of the obligation to deduct tax at source.

---

1 ICTA 1988, s 18.
2 Ibid, ss 348 and 349.
3 (1957) 38 TC 531.
4 ICTA 1988, s 3.
5 Ibid, s 18(3).
6 Ibid, s 18.
7 Ibid, s 349.

Table 12: Deduction of tax for use of patent rights

Payments subject to withholding tax	***Rate of withholding tax***
Revenue Payments	
Payments out of profits or gain brought into charge to income tax (ICTA 1988, s 348)	23% (1998–99)
Payments not out of profits or gains brought into charge to income tax (ICTA 1988, s 349)	23% (1998–99)
Capital Payments	
Capital sum in respect of a UK patent owned by a non-resident	23% (1998–99)

5.10.3 Copyright

Under ICTA 1988, a person who makes payments of or on account of royalties in relation to the use of copyright material to the owner whose usual place of abode is abroad must be made under deduction of income tax (23 per cent, 1998–99).[1] The type of copyright in respect of which deductions must be made is restricted. It does not include copyright in a film or video recording, or the sound track accompanying such a film or video.[2] The requirement to deduct tax at source does not apply to a lump sum payment made for the outright purchase of copyright.[3] This form of withholding tax can also apply to payments in respect of computer software. The provision applies only where expenditure is incurred on the right to duplicate computer software and market it.[4] No deduction of tax is required at source where payment is made for the use of normal 'off-the-shelf' computer software.

1 ICTA 1988, s 536. An obligation to deduct tax at source also exists in relation to a right in a design (see s 537B).
2 Ibid, s 536(2).
3 See Inland Revenue guidance manual *Inspector's Manual*, para 4001.
4 Ibid.

Table 13: Summary of UK tax rules

Business vehicle	*Charge to tax*	*Method of computation*	*Source of income/capital computation*	*Rate of taxation*
Company	'Profits wherever arising' (ICTA 1988, s 8) in a 'Financial Year' (ICTA 1988, ss 8 and 10) to a UK resident company (ICTA 1988, s 11) 'Residence' see SP/1 1990 issued by the Inland Revenue 'Profits' include 'Income and Chargeable Gains' (ICTA 1988, s 6(4)) Profits *accruing* to the benefit of the company in a financial year must be brought into account. These include profits from: 1. Trust(s) 2. Partnership(s) (ICTA 1988, s 8(2)) Profits received by a company in a fiduciary or representative capacity are not to be brought into account (ICTA 1988, s 8(2))	'Income' calculated by reference to income tax principles (ICTA 1988, s 9) 'Gains' calculated by reference to capital gains tax principles (TCGA 1992, s 8) 'Profits' arising in a financial year shall be computed by reference to the company's accounting period, with apportionment between financial years where relevant (ICTA 1988, s 8(3)) Ascertainment of accounting periods (ICTA 1988, s 12) Income must be computed under Schedule D, Cases I to VI on the 'full amount of the profits or gains or income arising' in the relevant accounting period irrespective of whether the sum is received in or transmitted to the UK (ICTA 1988, s 70(1))	Income receipts Schedule A [Receipts arising from the exploitation of land] (ICTA 1988, s 15) Schedule D 1. *Case I:* Receipts from trade (includes a vocation) 2. *Case II:* Receipts from profession 3. *Case III:* Receipts from loan relationships, annuities & other annual payments 4. *Case IV:* — 5. *Case V:* Receipts from foreign possessions 6. *Case VI:* Receipts from miscellaneous sources (ICTA 1988, s 18) Capital receipts As for capital gains (TCGA 1992, s 8(3))	Company profits or gains: 31% (1998/1999) Small companies rate Applicable to: A resident company; & which is not a close investment holding company (ICTA 1988, s 13, 13A) Rate: 21% (1998/1999) A sliding scale operates in respect of 'profits' in the range: £300,000 to £1,500,000
Companies not resident trading in the UK	Only where a trade is carried on in the UK through a branch or agency will tax be levied on 'chargeable profits' (ICTA 1988, s 11(1))	'Chargeable profits' arising in the UK to be brought into account are from: trading income arising directly/indirectly through /from the branch or agency Income from property or rights used/held by or for the agency (ICTA 1988, s 11)	Application of TCGA 1992	The chargeable gain of a company is subject to corporation tax and not capital gains tax (ICTA 1988, s 6(3)) A chargeable gain can arise where there is no actual disposal of an asset. This occurs where a capital sum is derived from an asset (see TCGA 1992, s 22) 'Asset' see TCGA 1992, s 21

Schedule D	Income to be brought into account	Revenue expenses to be brought into account	Relief of capital expenditure	Loss relief
Case I (trade which includes a vocation)	Profits arising from a trade (ICTA 1988, s 18) 'Trade' (ICTA 1988, s 832) A trade includes 'vocation' and an 'office or employment' (ICTA 1988, s 6(4)(b) 'Profits' = income receipts minus allowable deductions For the badges of a trade see Royal Commission Report on the Taxation of Profits and Income (1955) (Cmnd 9474) *Case-law illustrative of a trade* 1. *Martin v Lowry* (11 TC 297) 2. *Cape Brandy Syndicate v CIR* (12 TC 358) 3. *Rutledge v CIR* (14 TC 490) 4. *Edwards v Bairstow* (36 TC 207) 5. *Wisdom v Chamberlain* (45 TC 92) *Pre-trade expenditure* Expenditure incurred no more than 7 years before a trade is commenced is treated as having been incurred on the first day it is carried on (ICTA 1988, s 401) *Loan relationships* Trading credits from a loan relationship are brought into account as receipts of the trade (FA 1996, s 82(2))	Only those incurred 'wholly and exclusively' for the purposes of trade (ICTA 1988, s 74) *Deductible expenses do not inter alia, include:* 1. Sums attributable to domestic or private purposes (ICTA 1988, s 74(1)(a)) 2. Rent for house/domestic offices unless used for part of a trade (ICTA 1988, s 74(1)(b)) 3. Any 'expenditure' over that actually incurred in repairing premises occupied for the purposes of a trade (ICTA 1988 s 74(1)(d)) 4. Loss not connected with or arising out of the trade (ICTA 1988, s 74(1)(e)) 5. Debts (except those which are bad) (ICTA 1988, s 74(1)(j)) 6. Any annuity or annual payment (not interest) payable out of profits or gains (ICTA 1988, s 74(1)(m)) 7. Interest payable to a non-resident in so far as it exceeds a reasonable commercial rate (ICTA 1988, s 74(1)(n)) 8. Royalty for use of a patent (ICTA 1988, s 74(1)(p)) Management expenses of an investment company are deductible if UK resident (ICTA 1988, s 75) *Loan relationships* Trading deficits arising from a loan relationship are brought into account as an expense of the trade (FA 1996, s 82(2))	Capital expenditure is relieved against income receipts through the system of capital allowances. See generally Capital Allowances Act 1990 Classification of a receipt as capital or income is a question of fact The test to determine the classification of expenditure is a question of law (*Tucker v Granada Motorway Services Ltd* (53 TC 92)) Guidance on the principles adopted in the classification of a sum can be acquired from the following cases: 1. *Atherton v British Insulated and Helsby Cables Ltd* (10 TC 155) 2. *Heather v P-E Consulting Group Ltd* (48 TC 293) 3. *Tucker v Granada Motorway Services Ltd* (53 TC 92) 4. *Lawson v Johnson Matthew plc* (65 TC 39)	Trading losses incurred by a company can be relieved in the following ways: *Forward set-off* Carry the loss forward against trading income of the same trade in future accounting periods (ICTA 1988, s 393) *Current/backward set-off* Alternatively a loss incurred in an accounting period from a trade may be set-off against profits arising from whatever source in that accounting period, or against profits of a preceding accounting period (restricted to 12 months) (ICTA 1988, s 393A) *Claims for relief* Relief under ICTA 1988, s 393A is carried forward automatically under the pay and file system which applies to accounting periods ending after 30 September 1993 Relief under ICTA 1988, s 393 is only relieved on a claim being made within two years from the end of the accounting period in which the loss is incurred (ICTA 1988, s 393A(10))

Schedule D	**Income to be brought into account**	**Loan relationship non-trading credits**	**Loan relationship computation**	**Annual payments**
Case III (investment)	*Receipts to be brought into account:* Non-trading profits arising from a loan relationship (Finance Act 1996, Part IV, Ch 11); Any annuity or annual payment (whether payable in or outside the UK) in respect of anything other than a loan relationship; Any discount arising otherwise than under a loan relationship (ICTA 1988, s 18(3A))	A loan relationship arises where a company stands in the position of a creditor or debtor in respect of any money debt and which arises from the lending of money (FA 1996, s 81) A credit is brought into account under Case III of Schedule D where it is a product of a non-trading relationship (ICTA 1988, s 82(4)) Credits to be brought into account (ICTA 1988, s 84)	The credit to be brought into account shall not include one which is treated as a distribution (FA 1996, s 9(1)) Distribution: for definition see (ICTA 1988, s 209)	An annual payment paid by a company is treated as a charge on the payer's profits (ICTA 1988, s 338) The definition of an annual payment was given by Jenkins LJ in *IRC v Whitworth Park Coal Co Ltd* (1958) 38 TC 531 Annual payments are taxed without deduction of any expenditure
Other Schedule D income				
Case V	Profits arising from foreign possessions (ICTA 1988, s 18) eg foreign bank interest, profits from a trade carried on abroad through a branch Losses from such a source are relievable under ICTA 1988, ss 393, 393A	*Basis of assessment* Where income arises from a trade or vocation which is assessable under this case the computation will be made in accordance with Schedule D, Case I principles (ICTA 1988, s 70(2))	*Case VI* Profits from miscellaneous sources (ICTA 1988, s 18)	Losses from such a source can be set-off against income arising in the same or subsequent accounting periods (ICTA 1988, s 396) Tax is chargeable on the profits arising in the accounting period irrespective of whether received or transmitted to the UK (ICTA 1988, s 70(1))

Intellectual property	Copyright	Know-how	Trade marks	Patents	Designs
Charge to tax on receipt	If income: Schedule D, under one of the following cases: Case I (Trade) Case II (Profession) Case III (Investment) Case V (Foreign Possession) Case VI (Miscellaneous) If capital the receipt is taxable under TCGA 1992	Only taxable as an income receipt unless the know-how is combined with the disposal of a trade: Case I (Trade) Case II (Profession) Case III (Investment) Case V (Foreign Possession) Case VI (Miscellaneous) If capital under TCGA 1992	If income: Schedule D, under one of the following cases: Case I (Trade) Case II (Profession) Case III (Investment) Case V (Foreign Possession) Case VI (Miscellaneous) If capital the receipt is taxable under TCGA 1992	Only taxable as an income receipt, under one of the following cases: Case I (Trade) Case II (Profession) Case III (Investment) Case V (Foreign Possession) Case VI (Miscellaneous)	If income: Schedule D, under one of the following cases: Case I (Trade) Case II (Profession) Case III (Investment) Case V (Foreign Possession) Case VI (Miscellaneous) If capital the receipt is taxable under TCGA 1992
Capital allowances	Only if qualifies as Plant under CAA 1990, s 24	Yes under ICTA 1988, s 530	Only if qualifies as Plant under CAA 1990, s 24	Yes under ICTA 1988, s 520	Only if qualifies as Plant under CAA 1990, s 24
Averaging provisions	Yes Limited to the author Initial exploitation: ICTA 1988, s 534 Receipts after 10 years: ICTA 1988, s 535	None	None	Yes Capital sum: ICTA 1988, s 524 Royalty: ICTA 1988, s 527	Yes Limited to the designer: ICTA 1988, s 537A
Deduction of tax on payments for use of right	Only specific provision deals with payments to a non-resident (ICTA 1988, s 536)	No specific provision but maybe an annual payment	No specific provision but maybe an annual payment	Yes ss 348 and 349	Only specific provision deals with payments to a non-resident (ICTA 1988, s 537B)
Deduction of royalty payments as an expense of carrying on the trade	Normal principles apply	Normal principles apply	Normal principles apply	No deduction in computing profits (ICTA 1988, s 74(1)(p)) Treated as a charge on profits, see ICTA 1988, s 338	Normal principles apply
Expenses of acquiring/maintaining the intellectual property	Normal principles apply	Normal principles apply	See ICTA 1988, s 83	See ICTA 1988, s 83	See ICTA 1988, s 83 (Registered Designs) and normal principles apply in respect of design rights
VAT					
Charge to tax VATA 1994	Supply of Services (VATA 1994, s 5(2)(b))	Supply of Services (VATA 1994, s 5(2)(b))	Supply of Services (VATA 1994, s 5(2)(b))	Supply of Services (VATA 1994, s 5(2)(b))	Supply of Services (VATA 1994, s 5(2)(b))

Chapter 6

TRANSFER PRICING

6.1 INTRODUCTION

E-commerce facilitates global trading in respect of products and services. The mechanisms for facilitating e-commerce such as telecom networks, Internet access points etc, are sometimes structured between associated parties, particularly companies that are members of multinational groups. Where transactions are entered into between associated parties on a cross jurisdiction basis with different tax regimes, the incentive exists to use those transactions for the purposes of taking advantage of the disparity which exists between national tax systems. For example, a trade could be structured to move receipts from a high tax country to a low tax country by imposing an above market rate on the supply of goods or services by an entity in a low tax jurisdiction to an associated party in a high tax jurisdiction. The net effect of such a policy would, assuming the application of tax to 'profits', be a reduction in taxable profits in the high tax country (and of course a corresponding increase in the low tax country).

This is because generally to calculate profits of a trade, the taxpayer is allowed to offset expenditure incurred in carrying on the trade, for example, expenditure relating to products or services, against receipts derived from the trade.

Example 35

Cayman Island Trading Ltd is the parent company of a UK subsidiary. Cayman Island Trading Ltd provides an Internet service to its UK subsidiary which in turn carries on a trade. The price of the service provided to the UK subsidiary is fixed at £150,000 per year. The true market cost of the service if provided between independent parties dealing on an arm's length basis would only be £50,000. The UK subsidiary makes a trading profit of £300,000 in 1998–99. Assuming no other adjustments, the UK subsidiary seeks to deduct the expense of £150,000 paid to its parent company. If such a deduction was permitted, taxable profits would be £150,000. If the deduction is restricted to the market cost of the service, taxable profits would be increased to £250,000.

Transactions between associated parties structured to take advantage of different tax regimes are the subject of increasing scrutiny by tax authorities throughout the world. It is particularly important to ensure that all transactions between associated parties meet the arm's length test. To determine an arm's length price, it is necessary to examine the economic functions carried on, assets deployed, and risks assumed by each of the related parties. This must be done because these factors among other things are used by unrelated parties to determine the price for transactions.

Diagram 4

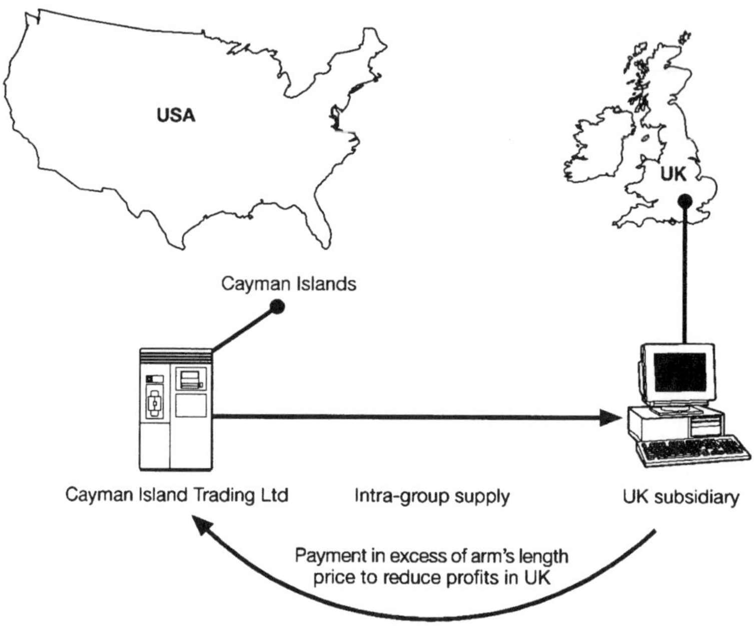

6.2 COUNTER PRICE MANIPULATION LEGISLATION

Manipulation of transaction prices between associated parties offers potentially huge rewards for multinational organisations, and a significant loss of revenue by national tax authorities. To counter such practices, many tax authorities have implemented legislation requiring taxable profits from transactions between associated parties to be calculated on the basis of arm's length prices. The theory and practice of transfer pricing (at least as it is seen by a committee of tax authorities) is contained in a loose-leaf work published by the OECD called *Transfer Pricing Guidelines For Multinational Enterprises and Tax Administrations* (1995). The source of authority to alter the pricing structure between associated parties for UK purposes is contained in the Finance Act 1998 ('FA 1998') (which introduced a new system of transfer pricing rules) and relevant double taxation agreements ('DTAs').

6.3 UK TRANSFER PRICING LEGISLATION

6.3.1 Double taxation agreements

A DTA is the result of bilateral negotiations between two sovereign jurisdictions. The purpose of a DTA is to reduce or extinguish the double taxation of profits, income or capital which is derived in a jurisdiction by a non-resident who is taxable in respect of that amount in his own jurisdiction. A DTA has force of law within the UK. Many DTAs are based upon the OECD Model Tax Convention. The Model provides under

Art 9 a right to adjust the profits of a party and to apply tax to the altered amount. The adjustment permitted is that which provides an arm's length value for a transaction between associated parties. The wide ambit of Art 9 is shown below:

> '[When] conditions are made or imposed between . . . two [associated] enterprises in their commercial or financial relations which differ from those which would be made between independent enterprises, then any profits which would, but for those conditions, have accrued to one of the enterprises, but, by reason of those conditions, have not so accrued, may be included in the profits of that enterprise and taxed accordingly.'

Example 36

UK Ltd enters into an agreement to obtain loan finance from Netherlands BV, which holds the majority of shares in UK Ltd. The interest payments agreed by UK Ltd are higher than would have been agreed between independent parties. In other words, but for the relationship interest payments would have been lower. In consequence it follows that the taxable profits of UK Ltd would have been higher, due to lower interest payment deductions. In circumstances such as these the profits of the UK company could be increased by the UK Inland Revenue because of the non-arm's length interest payments.

6.3.2 Finance Act 1998

FA 1998 introduces a new regime for transfer pricing into UK tax law.[1] The rules are focused on 'provisions' made or imposed otherwise than on arm's length basis between related parties. Broadly, if a 'provision' has:

(1) been made or imposed by means of a transaction (or series of transactions); and
(2) (a) at that time one of the parties was directly or indirectly participating in the management, control or capital of the other party; or
    (b) a third party was involved directly or indirectly in the management, control or capital of both parties to the transaction,

then the new transfer pricing rules apply.[2]

'Provision' is not defined, but it appears to be intended to be a reference to the terms of, and effects brought about by the transaction. It probably corresponds to the term 'conditions' in Art 9 of the Model Convention. It should be noted that a 'provision' can arise from a series of transactions, which need not all involve the parties that have made the provision.

The rules apply for corporation tax purposes to accounting periods ending on or after 1 July 1999. Thus, 12-month accounting periods commencing on or after 2 July 1998 will be subject to the new rules. The UK rules apply to a broad range of situations, including transactions entered into in the context of IT or an e-commerce business.

Transactions

FA 1998 defines 'transaction' as including 'arrangements, understandings and mutual practices (whether or not they are, or are intended to be, legally enforceable)'.[3] The

1 FA 1988, 108(1).
2 Schedule 28AA, para 1(1) inserted into ICTA 1988 by FA 1998.
3 Ibid, para 3(1).

term 'arrangement' is given a broad meaning of 'any scheme or arrangement of any kind (whether or not it is, or is intended to be, legally enforceable)'.[1]

Example 37

UK Internet Trading Ltd has an associated company located in the USA, called US Internet Trading Inc. Various formal written arrangements exist between the two parties, which include: (1) finance agreement; and (2) distribution agreement relating to orders placed by UK consumers via the US Internet site and US consumers via the UK Internet trading site. Various informal arrangements exist whereby when UK site access is heavy consumers are diverted to a mirror site operated by the US company in Canada. This site processes the diverted orders, and issues acceptance notices, and accepts payment for orders on behalf of the UK company. Formal and informal arrangements of this type are all potentially subject to UK transfer pricing legislation.

Participation
FA 1998 provides guidance on the concept of 'participation' which is one of the conditions for measuring whether parties are sufficiently closely associated that the transfer pricing legislation should apply. Broadly, a person participates directly in the management, control or capital of another person where:[2]

- the other person is a corporation or a partnership; and
- controlled by the first person.

Example 38

Internet Access (Corporate Intranet) Ltd is a wholly-owned subsidiary of Internet Access (World Wide) BV. In circumstances such as these The Netherlands parent company directly participates in the capital of the UK company. Any transaction between them would be subject to the UK transfer pricing rules.

There are further tests relating to what is called 'indirect participation' to prevent potential loopholes. The rules are particularly complex and are beyond the scope of this book.

6.3.3 Effect of UK transfer pricing rules

If a 'provision' exists which differs from that which would have been made between independent parties and which confers a potential advantage in respect of UK tax on one or both parties the profits or losses of the potentially advantaged party are altered for tax purposes as if the arm's length provision had been made.[3] FA 1998 provides that a potential advantage is conferred where the effect of making or imposing the actual provision, instead of the arm's length provision, would be one or both of the following:[4]

- that a smaller amount would be taken for UK tax purposes to be the amount of that person's profits (for example, by payment of an excessive expense); or

1 ICTA 1988, Sch 28AA, para 3(5).
2 Ibid, para 4(1).
3 Ibid, para 1(2).
4 Ibid, para 5(1).

– that a larger amount would be taken for UK tax purposes to be the amount of that person's losses.

Example 39

US Satellite Support Services Inc supplies data carrier services to a related party (ie one which is participating in the other), called Internet Access Ltd. The price paid is £700,000 per quarter for the carrier services. The UK company receives trading receipts of £2.7 million in 1998–99. Assuming no other deductions the profit would be £2 million. The price paid for the carrier service is in excess of an arm's length price by £200,000. This excessive pricing thus confers an advantage in respect of UK tax by decreasing the taxable profits of Internet Access Ltd. UK transfer pricing legislation would operate to adjust the deductible expense from £700,000 to £500,000 which represents the true arm's length price for the carrier service.

6.3.4 Exclusions

There are various exclusions contained in the legislation that prevent the transfer pricing rules from applying. The exclusions basically prevent most non cross-border transactions falling within the rules. No advantage is deemed to be conferred where three conditions are satisfied in the case of *each* of the two relevant persons. These conditions are:

(1) *Condition One*[1]

- the person is within the charge to income or corporation tax in respect of profits arising from the relevant activities;
- the person is not entitled to any exemption from income or corporation tax in respect of, or of a part of, the income or profits arising from all relevant activities in respect of which it is within that charge; and
- where that person is within the charge to income tax in respect of profits arising from those activities, he is resident in the UK.

(2) *Condition Two*[2]

- the person has no entitlement under any double taxation agreement, or under unilateral relief provisions, to be given credit for any foreign tax on or in respect of profits arising from the relevant activities.

(3) *Condition Three*[3]

- the amounts taken into account do not include any income which is reduced to take into account foreign tax where there is no credit allowable.

Example 40

UK Intranet Ltd uses the telecom carrier services of a related party, called UK Internet Access Ltd. The price paid for the service is £100,000, which is in excess of an arm's length price by £40,000. Both companies are UK resident, and meet the three conditions identified above.

1 ICTA 1988, Sch 28AA, para 5(3).
2 Ibid, para 5(4)(a).
3 Ibid, para 5(5).

PART III
UK TAXATION

The net result of this is that no adjustment is made. Although the excessive payment has the effect of reducing the taxable profits of UK Intranet Ltd, the payment has the effect of increasing the taxable profits of UK Intranet Access Ltd. Because both companies are UK resident, subject to corporation tax and otherwise meet the three conditions identified above no loss is suffered by the UK Revenue.

6.4 OECD TRANSFER PRICING GUIDELINES

The new transfer pricing rules introduced by FA 1998 are required to be construed in such a manner as 'best secures consistency' between UK law, which requires an arm's length provision between related parties, and 'the effect which, in accordance with the transfer pricing guidelines is to be given, in cases where DTAs incorporate the whole or any part of the OECD Model, to so much of the arrangements as does so'.[1] The term 'transfer pricing guidelines' is defined as all documents published by the OECD before 1 May 1998 as part of their *Transfer Pricing Guidelines for Multinational Enterprises and Tax Administrations*.[2]

It is clear that both FA 1998 and articles in DTAs comparable to Art 9 of the OECD Model Tax Convention require the profits for transactions between associated parties to be on an arm's length basis otherwise an adjustment will be made to achieve this objective. The OECD *Transfer Pricing Guidelines for Multinational Enterprises and Tax Administrations* provides analysis of the ways in which the arm's length price for transactions is to be ascertained. The appropriate method to adopt in determining an accurate arm's length price will depend heavily upon obtaining professional advice from transfer pricing specialists who can draw on the skills of economists, tax advisers, and corporate finance expertise. The main methods are summarised below.

6.4.1 Comparable uncontrolled price

Under comparable uncontrolled price ('CUP'), the parties identify what would have been charged between independent parties in respect of the transaction for goods or services which is entered into between the associated parties. The main requirement is that only comparable transactions between unrelated entities are used as benchmarks.[3] In other words, all the essential indicia of the supply are ascertained, and then relevant comparable transactions are identified.

6.4.2 Resale price method

This method is used where products are transferred between associated parties and then resold to an independent person. Under this method, the parties approach the arm's length issue from the starting point of the price paid for products by an independent person at the end of the supply process. This price represents the resale price. The method requires the resale price to be reduced by an arm's length 'resale

---

1 ICTA 1988, Sch 28AA, para 2(1)(b).

2 Ibid, para 2(3)(a).

3 See *Transfer Pricing Guidelines for Multinational Enterprises and Tax Administrations*, para 2.6 *et seq* which explores the issues relating to the application of CUP in determining arm's length price.

margin', which represents the costs and profits the reseller would seek to recover. Once the margin is deducted, what is left is the arm's length price for the original transfer of the product between associated parties.[1] Again, the benchmark transactions must be comparable and involve unrelated parties.

Example 41

Alpha Computer Services Inc makes a supply of computer software to Beta Software Ltd for £20,000. The UK company then makes an onward supply of the software to a business consumer for £37,000. Transactions of this nature are typical for the UK company. The Inland Revenue challenge the expenditure by saying that a true arm's length price is £15,000 for the supply from the USA. In applying the resale price method to determine the arm's length price, the parties would need to deduct a 'resale margin' from the resale price of £37,000. Once the resale margin, representing costs and a mark-up for profit, are deducted this should leave the arm's length price.

6.4.3 Cost plus method

By this approach the arm's length price is ascertained by determining the amount of the costs incurred by the supplier of products or services in their provision to an associated person. A mark-up is then added to the costs to reflect an appropriate profit to the supplier against the background of the functions performed, risks assumed by the supplier and market conditions.[2] This method is approached by determining the costs plus mark up which would be applied in a comparable uncontrolled transaction for the supply of relevant products or services.

Example 42

UK Intranet Ltd uses the telecom carrier services of a related party, called USA Access Inc. The Inland Revenue challenges the payments for the carrier services on the basis that they are in excess of an arm's length price. One method of defending the claim is for the UK company to compute an arm's length price for the same type of service. Assume the cost plus approach is the appropriate approach in this case. In other words, we must ask what would be the costs of providing a telecom carrier service, and what would be the profit, or mark-up for a comparable supplier in an uncontrolled transaction. The figure reached at the end of this process is an arm's length price.

6.4.4 Other methods

Where difficulties are experienced in applying the foregoing methods, perhaps because of inability to obtain details of comparable transactions, the OECD guidelines identify two further methods. These are the 'profit split' and 'transactional net margin' methods.[3] The profit split method[4] is useful where two associated entities enter into a collaborative venture and split the profits between themselves. The purpose of this method is to determine the appropriate profit split by reference to economic analysis of the transaction and function performed by each of the associated parties. Broadly, the party which contributes the most resources, and incurs more risk

1 *Transfer Pricing Guidelines for Multinational Enterprises and Tax Administrations* (OECD), para 2.14 *et seq*.
2 Ibid, para 2.32 *et seq*.
3 Ibid, para 3.1 *et seq*.
4 Ibid, para 3.5 *et seq*.

in the collaboration is entitled to a higher percentage of the profit split. Under the net margin method[1] the arm's length price is determined by reference to the net margin, ie the margin the party would earn on a comparable uncontrolled transaction by reference to a certain factor, such as its cost base, or its capital employed.

6.4.5 Advance pricing agreements

Ensuring that a satisfactory regime exists for the pricing of transactions in relation to goods, services, loans or intangibles between associated parties is clearly of critical importance. In some jurisdictions it is possible to enter into an advance pricing agreement ('APA') under which the tax authority gives approval to a specified pricing approach.[2] This has several advantages, the foremost of which is the relative certainty and likely absence of costly investigations and negotiations with tax authorities in respect of pricing arrangements.

The UK has an APA procedure, which is governed by s 85 of the Finance Act 1999 ('FA 1999'). Such agreements will be useful in clarifying the transfer pricing issues relating to e-commerce. It is to be emphasised, however, that the APA is designed only for clarification of complex transfer pricing issues so that UK taxpayers are able to carry out their duty to self-assess their tax liability. The effect of the APA is that the tax legislation shall be determined in accordance with the terms of the agreement.[3] The APA is a binding agreement. However, it may be revoked in certain circumstances, such as the supply by a person fraudulently or negligently of information which is false or misleading.

An APA may relate to one or more of the following matters:

> '(a) the attribution of income to a branch or agency through which the taxpayer has been carrying on a trade in the United Kingdom, or is proposing so to carry on a trade;
> (b) the attribution of income to any permanent establishment of the taxpayer (wherever situated) through which he is carrying on, or proposing to carry on, any business;
> (c) the extent to which income which has arisen or may arise to the taxpayer is to be taken for any purpose to be income arising in a country or territory outside the United Kingdom;
> (d) the treatment for tax purposes of any provision made or imposed (whether before or after the date of the agreement) as between the taxpayer and any associate of his;
> (e) the treatment for tax purposes of any provision made or imposed (whether before or after the date of the agreement) as between a ring fence trade carried on by the taxpayer and any other activities so carried on.'[4]

An APA may be requested by any UK taxpayer, including a partnership (in respect of transactions to which the provisions of s 770A of ICTA 1988 apply), any non-resident trading in the UK through a branch or agency, and any UK resident trading through an overseas branch.[5] The APA will usually last for a specified number of years.

It is important to emphasise that an APA will confirm a taxpayer's tax treatment only

---

1 *Transfer Pricing Guidelines for Multinational Enterprises and Tax Administrations* (OECD), para 3.26 *et seq*.

2 Ibid, para 4.124 *et seq*.

3 FA 1999, s 85(3).

4 Ibid, s 85(2).

5 The Inland Revenue has issued a Statement of Practice on the application of the APA legislation (1999).

within the UK. It will not determine the tax treatment within another jurisdiction. To determine the cross-border issues comprehensively the UK Inland Revenue would need to reach an agreement with the related parties' tax authority. Where a DTA is in existence, this is achieved through the mutual agreement procedure ('MAP') article.[1] The MAP article is concerned with the interpretation and handling of problems arising from the application of a DTA. This provides the Inland Revenue with authority for entering into negotiations with another DTA partner. Where conditions for the use of the MAP article are in existence, the Inland Revenue can participate in another treaty partner's APA process. This enables the Inland Revenue to agree with a treaty partner how the terms of the treaty, particularly the concept of arm's length transactions are to apply in a particular case. In this context, APA participation is limited by the MAP article.[2]

6.4.6 Documentation

Chapter V of the OECD *Transfer Pricing Guidelines for Multinational Enterprises and Tax Administrations* gives guidance on the type of documentation which a taxpayer should seek to compile for the purposes of handling transfer pricing investigations. As the guidelines rightly observe, the individual circumstances of each case vary and it is impossible to give guidance for every single scenario. However, on a general level the compilation and retention of documentation should be a matter of common sense.

In order to evaluate whether a transaction is at an arm's length price, it is necessary for both tax administrations and the taxpayer to possess full information about the particular circumstances of the associated parties and the transaction. Documentation relating to a business activity should inform the tax administration about the following matters, although this is not an exhaustive list:

- the associated parties to the transaction;
- the economic functions of each of the associated parties in the transaction, such as manufacturing, marketing, carriage and warehousing activities, training of personnel, finance provision etc;
- the risks and obligations assumed by each of the parties to the transaction;
- information concerning comparable uncontrolled transactions with independent third parties (or the lack thereof);
- market conditions within which the controlled transactions are implemented;
- nature and terms of individual transactions between associated parties, including precise identification of products and/or services supplied;
- how the transactions operate between associated parties;
- documentation of location of ownership rights in intangible assets exploited between associated parties;
- full legal documentation should ideally be maintained which records accurately the economic transactions between associated parties;
- full legal documentation of arrangements with related and unrelated commercial intermediaries which reflects the allocation of risks between the parties, for

PART III UK TAXATION

1 See Art 25 of the OECD Model Convention.
2 See *Inland Revenue Tax Bulletin*, Issue 25, October 1996, p 348.

example responsibility for damage to products, liability for defective products etc;
- pricing strategy including reasons for various margins allowed under arrangements;
- sales information such as of products, services rendered, lease of property;
- research and development ('R&D') documentation which reflects ownership of rights in R&D, as well as the finance, risks assumed, assets contributed under the R&D venture.
- market conditions such as scope of competition;

6.4.7 Intra-group services

IT is likely to be of particular use in the provision of effective channels of communication between associated parties. The parties are likely to have their own home built information superhighway. The parties could use their intranet as a means of providing technical data between a parent and subsidiary, provision of IT services (such as computer advice), financial advice, legal advice etc. In fact, it is entirely possible for a headquarters company to provide extensive management services to its subsidiaries, and other associated parties by use of IT.

Chapter 7 of the OECD *Transfer Pricing Guidelines for Multinational Enterprises and Tax Administrations* gives guidance on the issues relating to applying an arm's length standard to intra-group service provision. Generally it is desirable to identify as specifically as possible what services are provided on an intra-group basis, and the extent to which these services are charged for between the parties. The method of charge for the intra-group services should also ideally be reflected. In setting the price for intra-group services the parties should have regard to the transfer pricing methods detailed in the *Transfer Pricing Guidelines for Multinational Enterprises and Tax Administrations*.[1]

6.4.8 Impact of e-commerce and transfer pricing

The application of transfer pricing to e-commerce may not involve any particular difficulties. However, e-commerce is a new method of doing business. The experience of many advisers and tax authorities will be limited to the application of transfer pricing rules in a physical environment. E-commerce offers developers and manufacturers the opportunity of cutting out the need for commercial intermediaries and supplying direct to the consumer. Those cost savings will usually be replaced with other costs associated with e-commerce, such as investment in technology. The refocusing of expenditure must be carefully audited in order to identify the costs of making e-commerce supplies. Such audit work will assist in identifying the arm's length price.

The trading revolution caused by IT has been dematerialisation. In other words, it is now possible to deliver electronically games, books, magazines, pictures, computer software, music, video films etc without any tangible existence. One problem which

---

1 See Chapters 1, 2, and 3.

may exist for transfer pricing purposes is finding comparable data. For example, will it be possible to compare the pricing arrangements in a supply chain relating to the distribution of films for home entertainment on video, with the distribution of the same media via the Internet?

The cost of producing electronic media is very different from producing physical media. Both forms of production require plant and machinery. But the production methods are different. The costs involved are signficantly different. For instance, the cost of duplicating a film in electronic format is different from copying a film onto a video cassette. Differences such as this will create problems in finding comparable data.

In ascertaining the correct arm's length price for e-commerce, both the taxpayer and tax authority must engage in a functional analysis of how the business is operated. The allocation of cost to specific areas will vary according to the nature of the business. The significant cost of an e-commerce seller is likely to be advertising, eg via Internet search engine sites. Each e-commerce seller is competing with all the other millions of sellers for space on the individual consumer's desktop computer monitor. By contrast the costs of a developer of IT would be very different.

Functional analysis to determine the correct arm's length price is a complex operation. A number of factors must be considered in establishing and defending a price which is claimed to represent an arm's length price. These include the following.

- Determination of research and development costs.
- The legal nature of the delivery process. For example, in the transfer of electronic material is payment made for the use of copyright by the purchaser?
- The method and number of intermediaries used in the delivery process. If fewer intermediaries are used to deliver electronic products, the costs which would have existed in respect of physical media, may still be incurred in other ways because of the e-commerce delivery process. For example, the e-commerce seller may incur new costs such as payments for maintaining a dedicated delivery computer server with associated permanent Internet connections. The new costs must be identified because these will be relevant to determining an arm's length price.
- In determining the value to be allocated to a particular service it will be necessary to take into account the benefits conferred by the related party. For example, the existence of a computer server with a fast and permanent telecommunication delivery between a supplier and other parties facilitating the supplier's e-commerce business must be taken into account in ascertaining an arm's length price. In designing a transfer pricing strategy for e-commerce it is necessary to ascertain precisely where value is added by a supply. Those businesses which assist in the provision of e-commerce will need to identify precisely the nature of the value which they are providing. For instance, the value of these support services will be determined by durability, effectiveness, speed, employment of new technologies, security etc.
- The value of providing access to an infrastructure for e-commerce will turn upon the cost of plant and machinery, such as satellite earth stations, and fibre optic cables etc. It will be necessary to determine the extent to which there is any cost attributable to use of intellectual property by recipients.

– The cost of manufacturing products for electronic distribution may be minimal. However, businesses will probably find that costs will be attributed to other elements, such as research and development, advertising, and intellectual property.

Whilst e-commerce may not create unique problems in the application of transfer pricing law, it will be necessary to identify where costs are being incurred, where value is added by supplies to related parties etc.

Chapter 7

COMPUTER SOFTWARE

7.1 CHARACTERISTICS OF SOFTWARE

Computer software is information encoded upon a device: for example, information may be stored in a magnetised state on a 'floppy-disk', or recorded on a CD-ROM as a series of 'etches'. The device costs very little to manufacture. The value of the software resides in the information, and the intellectual property which protects the owner of the information from unlawful copying. The type of intellectual property that exists in software is varied. It is necessary to identify the constituent elements of software, and how it is classified for the purposes of taxation, for example, if software is classified as goods it will be subject to VAT as a supply of goods, whilst software classified as services will be subject to VAT as a supply of services. The difference is of critical importance because the application of VAT differs for goods and services.

7.1.1 Intellectual property

The value of software from a development and manufacturing perspective lies in the proprietary rights which can be used to prohibit the reproduction of the software by competitors. Computer software is essentially pure information recorded on a physical device as a series of zeros and ones (ie as a binary code). In itself, this information is subject to no proprietary right.[1] Computer software is protected by copyright to the extent that it is a literary work.[2] This is the primary method by which computer software is exploited. Payment for use of software always involves the grant of a licence, which can be express or implied.

7.1.2 Multi-media

Multi-media is computer software which produces multiple types of media, such as text, images and sound. The intellectual property which exists in this type of media, is potentially very wide. Copyright is capable of existing in computer software as a literary work. It may also be possible for multi-media to be protected as a film. The Copyright, Designs and Patents Act 1988 ('CDPA 1988') defines a film as 'a recording on any medium from which a moving image may by any means be produced'.[3] In *Information Technology and the Law*,[4] Lloyd states that this 'form of

---

1 *Oxford v Moss* (1978) 68 Cr App R 183. See also C. Reed *Computer Law* (Blackstone Press, 3rd edn, 1996), p 55.
2 Copyright, Designs and Patents Act 1988, s 2(1).
3 VATA 1994, s 5(1).
4 Lloyd *Information Technology and the Law* (Butterworths, 1994).

words used in the 1988 Act appears wide enough to cover storage of moving images on a computer disc or tape'.[1] The same view is put forward by the author of *Computer Law*.[2]

7.1.3 Off-the-shelf software/standardised software

Many forms of software can be acquired by customers directly through retail outlets or by mail order. This off-the-shelf/standardised software is characterised by the fact that it is mass-produced, and readily available to the general public, for example, Windows 98 or IBM O/S2 Warp. If the product is examined, a sticker is usually to be found stating that the opening of the package is deemed to be acceptance of the manufacturer's licence of the computer software. For tax purposes, this is important. The payment of money for off-the-shelf software could be categorised into two things. Payment is made for the device upon which the information is stored, and for the licence to use the computer software.

The fact that payment can be categorised in this way raises the question of how the purchase of this type of software is to be classified. Does it represent the sale of goods, or the supply of services for the purposes of VAT?

7.1.4 Bespoke software

Bespoke software is software which is custom-made by a computer developer for a specific client. It is characterised by the fact that it is not mass-produced and is not readily available to the general public. Procuring the services of a person to develop software raises the issue of whether the contract is one for the supply of goods, or for the supply of services. This classification is important for tax purposes.

7.1.5 Internet-provided software

Internet-provided software is computer software which a consumer obtains through the medium of the Internet. It can be acquired either from retailers for payment of a fee, or free of charge. The characteristic of this type of software is that its acquisition lacks any type of physical existence. The consumer acquires software which is transferred as a binary code from the retailer's computer network and installed directly onto the recipient's hard disk in their computer. The classification of this type of supply has important tax consequences. Is the supply of electronic software a supply of goods or services?

7.1.6 Software incorporated on hardware

Hardware such as a micro-processor, graphics card, or a hard disk in a computer are supplied with pre-encoded software. When the hardware is purchased the consumer acquires not only the device, but also a licence for use of the software encoded on the device. These classifications have different tax consequences.

---

1 Lloyd *Information Technology and the Law* (Butterworths, 1994), p 245, para 24.30.
2 C. Reed (Blackstone Press, 3rd edn, 1996), pp 108–109.

7.2 TAX POINTS AND RELIEFS

The tax legislation of the UK can apply in a number of different situations to transactions in respect of computer software. The following explains the nature of the tax charges and reliefs that may arise.

7.2.1 Expenditure on computer software

Revenue expenditure

A person is entitled to deduct revenue expenditure incurred in earning the revenue receipts derived from a trade. Accordingly, a person who makes royalty payments for a licence to use computer software will be entitled to a deduction of that expenditure.[1] Where that payment represents a royalty for the use of copyright, and the payment is made to an owner who lives abroad, he will be required to deduct tax at source.[2] The amount of the deduction is linked to the basic rate of income tax. This is currently a deduction of 23 per cent (1998–99) from the payment at source by the licensee.

Capital expenditure

Accountancy depreciation

In *Financial Reporting Standard 10* ('FRS 10') on *Goodwill and Intangible Assets*,[3] it states that there is a rebuttable presumption that the useful economic life of intangible assets is less than 20 years.[4] In these circumstances, their value should be amortised on a systematic basis over those lives against the profit and loss account of a trader.[5] The standard applies to computer software because it defines intangible assets as 'Non-financial fixed assets that do not have physical substance but are identifiable and are controlled [...] through custody or legal rights' (paragraph 2 of FRS 10). Computer software is controlled through the law of copyright.

Tax depreciation

A person is not normally entitled to deduct any sum which is classified as capital expenditure in computing the profits of a trade. A deduction is only permitted to the extent CAA 1990 applies. By s 67A of CAA 1990, a capital allowance is available for specific types of expenditure incurred on computer software.

Computer software

The legislation does not define 'computer software'. One expert in the field of computer law has described software as:

> 'the instructions which cause the hardware to work in a particular way: for example, to process a company's payroll. Looked at in this way, software is intangible, and difficult to classify in legal terms. It appears to be pure information, enjoying no physical form except that of magnetic notation on a tape or disc.'[6]

PART III
UK TAXATION

1 ICTA 1988, s 74. Subject to being 'wholly and exclusively' incurred.
2 Ibid, s 536.
3 Approved by the Accounting Standards Board.
4 FRS 10, para 19.
5 Ibid, para 15.
6 C. Reed *Computer Law* (Blackstone Press, 3rd edn, 1996), p 55.

Other definitions provided are of a similar nature.[1] The classification of software is an important question in the context of computer law, because it determines the extent to which the consumer protection legislation applies: for example, the Sale of Goods Act 1979. The Inland Revenue, in a guidance note,[2] has said that computer software although not defined for the purposes of CAA 1990 is to be given its normal meaning 'which is wide and covers both programs and data (for example, books stored in digital form)'.

Where a person incurs capital expenditure on computer software, it will be relieved against the profits of the trade, in the following circumstances.[3]

Relief condition 1
(1) expenditure is incurred for the purposes of a trade;
(2) in acquiring the right to use or otherwise deal with computer software.

Once these are satisfied the computer software is treated as though it was expenditure on plant or machinery.[4] The software is also deemed to belong to the person for as long as he is entitled to the right to use it. The result of this is that the provisions dealing with plant or machinery in CAA 1990 apply.[5] It also follows that computer software qualifies for short-life asset relief.

Relief condition 2
Expenditure on computer software can also qualify for relief as plant or machinery if it is of a capital nature, where it is made for the purposes of a trade, and in consequence of which the computer software belongs to the person.[6] This relief is available where the computer software is not otherwise machinery or plant.[7]

Revenue interpretation
In November 1993, the Inland Revenue issued guidance on how it approaches the interpretation of s 67A of CAA 1990.[8] The guidance deals with a number of different ways in which computer software can be acquired. The following paragraphs explain the Inland Revenue's position under the headings adopted by it.

7.2.2 Software acquired under licence

Software acquired under licence is where a person acquires a device such as a floppy disk or CD-ROM, but also a licence for the right to use the software encoded upon the device. The Inland Revenue adopts the view that the operation of s 67A of CAA 1990

1 Lloyd *Information Technology and the Law* (Butterworths, 1994), where a computer program is described in the following terms: 'A computer program is a series of coded instructions intended to bring about a particular result, which may be as simple as adding a series of figures or as complex as processing graphical images' Chapter 26, p 251, para 26.2.
2 See *Revenue Interpretation*, RI 56 (November 1993). The nature of this guidance is explored in subsequent paragraphs.
3 CAA 1990, s 67A(1).
4 Ibid, s 67A(1)(a).
5 See Chapter 4.
6 CAA 1990, s 67A(2).
7 Ibid, s 67A(2).
8 *Revenue Interpretation*, RI 56 (November 1993).

depends upon the nature of the payment for the licence. In other words, the method of payment, such as a royalty or lump sum will be important. It is necessary to remember that for the purposes of this relief the Inland Revenue is not concerned with the way in which the software is provided: for example, whether by floppy disk, CD-ROM, or by transfer across the medium of the Internet.

Regular payments akin to rental

Regular payments akin to rental is where a business acquires the right to use software, such as an operating system on its computers, for the payment of, for example, a quarterly amount. The amount paid is usually by reference to the number of user licences: for example, if a company pays £10,000 per quarter for 15 user licences this would represent a regular payment akin to a rental. In these circumstances the guidance provides that expenditure of this nature will be classified as revenue. Expenditure of a revenue nature is not within the terms of s 67A of CAA 1990, and will therefore be brought into account according to the general scheme of taxation. Such expenditure is first brought into account in accordance with the generally accepted principles of commercial accountancy. The Inland Revenue indicates in the guidance that this will be in accordance with the accruals concept explained in *Statement of Standard Accounting Practice Number Two*. The accruals concept requires the payments to be spread over the useful life of the software.

Once the time of recognition in respect of such expenditure is calculated the figures must be adjusted in accordance with the provisions of the tax legislation. If the expenditure has not been incurred wholly and exclusively for the purposes of a trade carried on by the taxpayer it will be prohibited expenditure.[1] For example, if a taxpayer incurs rental payments for itself and another company within a group context, which makes use of the software, this may represent expenditure for an unallowable dual purpose.[2]

Lump sum payments

Inland Revenue guidance indicates that where a lump sum is paid for the use of software, its treatment for tax purposes will depend upon the nature of the software licence. If it can be said that the licence represents a capital asset, this will result in the expenditure being classified as capital. The guidance indicates that a licence will generally be a capital asset where it is of an enduring nature. Whether the licence is of an enduring nature can be identified by the function or operation of the software in the context of the licensee's trade. Software acquired by a video games developer is of an enduring nature, because without software to use as tools it would not be able to carry on a trade of developing video games.

As the guidance points out, if the licence is for an indefinite period, but the operation or importance of the software is of a transitory nature, this will tend to lead them to the view that the expenditure is of a revenue nature.

The Inland Revenue, as a rule of thumb, adopts the following classifications, although it accepts that it is not possible to cover every type of transaction. The rule of thumb for classifying expenditure is as follows:

1 ICTA 1988, s 74(1).
2 But see *Vodafone v Shaw* [1997] STC 734.

Economic life	Classification of expenditure
Less than 2 years	Revenue
More than 2 years	Revenue/Capital depending on the circumstances

Form of software delivery

The Inland Revenue accepts that where a licence is classified as capital expenditure it will qualify for a capital allowance under s 67A of CAA 1990 even though the software does not come in a separate corporeal medium: for example, on a floppy disk, but is pre-installed on computer hardware.

Where a capital allowance is provided it is expressly recognised in the guidance that the licensee can elect for the software to be treated as a short-life asset.[1]

The following example illustrates how the relief operates in respect of computer software. The short-life relief provisions must be triggered by an election in respect of specific assets. A global figure can be placed upon the assets where there are many in existence: for example, expenditure on 100 software user licences.

Example 43

System Developers Ltd incur expenditure of £60,000 for 100 software user licences in 1997–98. The expenditure is of a capital nature. The useful economic life of the software is three years. The allowance will be given in the following way.

	1997–98	***1998–99***	***1999–2000***	***2000–01***
Expenditure	60,000	45,000	33,750	25,312.50
WDA @ 25%	15,000	11,250	8,437.50	25,312.50
WDA pool c/f	45,000	33,750	25,312.50	nil

7.2.3 Equipment acquired as a package

The guidance expressly recognises that some types of computer hardware are purchased with software as a package for a single payment. The single payment includes the acquisition of a licence to use the software. In these circumstances, an apportionment is required of the payment in respect of the computer hardware, and the software. The guidance does not define the meaning of 'computer hardware', and no definition is given in the tax legislation. Hardware can take many forms, such as a hard drive, micro-processors or a graphics card, all of which have software encoded on them. The software is usually separately licensed. On the basis of this guidance, it is suggested that 'computer hardware' like 'computer software' should be given its natural meaning, which is wide enough to include components within the shell of the computer.

1 The nature of the short-life asset provisions were examined in Chapter 5.

Where an apportionment is made, the expenditure on the computer hardware will be treated as ordinary plant and machinery for the purposes of the tax legislation. The treatment of the expenditure attributable to the licence will depend upon whether it is revenue or capital expenditure. The guidelines described above will apply in this situation. The Inland Revenue indicates in the guidance that where expenditure on software and hardware is made on 'capital account', the expenditure will be placed in the general machinery and plant 'pool', and apportionment will not be necessary.

7.2.4 Software owned outright: 'bespoke software'

The Inland Revenue adopts the same approach in respect of software which is owned outright, ie bespoke software, as software in respect of which a licence is acquired. The guidance particularly states that the economic function of the software will be important in ascertaining how the expenditure is to be classified, ie as revenue or capital. Expenditure for the purposes of bespoke software includes the salaries of in-house computer professionals who develop the software, as well as the profit made by the developer in the creation of the software.[1]

7.2.5 Deduction of tax at source on licence payments[2]

This obligation is imposed in the following circumstances.

Payments abroad for use of software

The first is where a payment of, or on account of, royalties or other revenue sums are paid periodically for copyright.[3] The amount which must be deducted is linked to the basic rate of income tax.[4] The obligation in this situation arises only where the payment is made to the owner of copyright whose usual place of abode is abroad.[5] The owner of copyright includes any person who is entitled to receive periodical payments in respect of copyright, notwithstanding the fact that the copyright has been assigned.[6] This latter requirement is to be contrasted with the operation of withholding tax in respect of patent rights, where there is no comparable provision. For the purposes of this obligation to deduct tax, the provision does not extend to copyright which subsists in a cinematograph film or video recording, or the soundtrack of such a film or recording.[7] But this is only insofar as the latter are not separately exploited.[8] Other provisions also exist where payment is made through an agent.[9] Any agreement which requires any payment in respect of copyright, to which a deduction must be made, to be paid in full without any deduction is void.

---

1 See *McVeigh v Arthur Sanderson & Sons Ltd* [1969] 2 All ER 771, 45 TC 273 where the wages bill for the creation of designs was capitalised.
2 See Chapter 5.
3 ICTA 1988, s 536(1).
4 Ibid, ss 536(1), 349(1) and 4(1).
5 Ibid, s 536(1).
6 Ibid, s 536(2).
7 Ibid, s 536(2).
8 Ibid.
9 Ibid, s 536(3),(4).

Example 44

Uniform Century Games Ltd acquires the right to use computer software from a company based in the USA. The software will enable it to produce virtual reality game software. The company makes periodical payments for the licence, granted for a five year period, of £35,000. The US company has no representation in the UK and the payment is made abroad. In these circumstances the UK user is obliged by ICTA 1988, s 536 to deduct tax of £8,050 from the periodical payment (ie £35,000 × 23 per cent) subject to any relevant DTA.

Annual payments

The second situation in which a licensee is required to deduct tax at source is where the payment represents an annual payment within Schedule D, Case III. This is where the licensor holds the copyright as an investment. The obligation does not arise where, for example, the licensor is carrying on a trade. The obligation to make the deduction is mandatory in respect of a corporate licensee, where the payment is classified as annual.[1]

7.2.6 Chargeable gains

Rights in computer software are assets for the purposes of TCGA 1992. This is indicated in the context of the Inland Revenue guidance on the application of s 67A of CAA 1990 to computer software. In the guidance, reference is made to the fact that a computer software licence is capable of being a capital asset if it has a sufficiently enduring nature.[2] The pure information itself (ie represented by binary codes) is not capable of being a chargeable asset because no property exists within it. 'Asset' is defined under TCGA 1992 as being all 'forms of property' (s 21(1)). In *Kirby v Thorn EMI*,[3] the Court of Appeal held that for TCGA 1992 to apply there must be property. Nicholls LJ said:

> ' "Property" is not a term of art, but takes its meaning from its context [...] The context in the instant case is a Taxing Act which is concerned with assets and with disposals and acquisitions, gains and losses. I can see no reason to doubt that in s 22 "property" bears the meaning of that which is capable of being owned, in the normal legal sense[...]'.

It is important to bear in mind that copyright normally protects computer software. Any capital sum received for the exploitation of copyright will usually create a taxable disposal.

7.2.7 Value added tax

Although VAT is charged at a standard rate of 17.5 per cent (other than those which are zero-rated or exempt) a distinction must none the less be made between the supply of goods and services. This is an important distinction to make because different rules apply in determining when and where a supply is deemed to take place in the UK. The purpose of this section is to concentrate on the issues which arise particularly in respect of computer software.

---

1 ICTA 1988, s 349(1).

2 See *Revenue Interpretation*, RI 56 (November 1993), under 'Lump sum'.

3 [1987] STC 621 at 627d–e.

The charge to VAT
A VAT charge arises on the supply of goods or services made by a taxable person in UK in the course or furtherance of business. A supply which is classified as exempt is not a taxable supply.[1]

Classifying computer software
The Inland Revenue expressly recognises in *Revenue Interpretation* RI 56[2] (dealing with the application of CAA 1990, s 67A) that 'software' is distinct from the device upon which it is recorded. In other words, 'software' is synonymous with the information or binary code.

For the purposes of determining whether a supply is one of goods or services HM Customs and Excise ('Customs and Excise') classifies computer software into the following:[3]

(1) normalised ('off-the-shelf') software; and
(2) specific (custom made or bespoke) software.

Where normalised software is supplied, this is said to be a supply of goods, and bespoke software is classified as either a supply of goods or services, depending on the nature of the contract.

7.2.8 Definition of goods and services

HM Customs and Excise Notice No 702[4] defines goods for the purposes of computer software as the physical device upon which information is recorded.[5] Examples of these physical carriers of information include, magnetic tapes, disks, diskettes, compact discs, and 'read only' CD videos.[6] By contrast, services are defined as comprising data, programs or instruction.[7] The notice specifically provides that 'data or instruction' does not include sound, cinematographic or video recordings. The application of VAT to each of these categories depends upon whether it is classified as normalised or specific software.

7.2.9 Normalised or specific software

In ascertaining how the goods or services are to be classified for VAT purposes, it is necessary to go a step further than solely analysing the physical carrier, and the information borne. The next step is to determine whether the product and/or software is normalised or specific. The following paragraphs explain, by reference to the Customs and Excise Notice, how the distinction is to be made, and the consequences which flow from it.

---

1 See Chapter 8.
2 *Revenue Interpretation*, RI 56 (November 1993).
3 HM Customs and Excise Notice No 702/4/94, para 2.1.
4 Ibid.
5 Ibid, para 2.1.
6 Ibid.
7 Ibid, para 2.2.

Normalised software

Normalised software is defined by Customs and Excise as mass-produced products which are freely available to the public: for example, personal computer software, and games packages, as well as any accompanying support material such as instruction manuals.[1] In the view of Customs and Excise, this definition also includes software which are 'standard packages' but are adjusted in some way at the supplier's instigation:[2] for example, to include security features, sophisticated password programs etc.

Tax treatment of normalised software

(i) Domestic supplies

The Customs and Excise Notice dealing with the classification of computer software is concerned with the importation of software. However, there is no indication that the advice given in the notice is not to be applied in a domestic context. For this reason, it is suggested that the views of Customs and Excise on the importation of computer software, insofar as it concerns the classification, and apportionment of cost to the software applies *mutis mutandis* to domestic supplies. A summary of how the principles behind the classification of supplies would apply in a domestic context is provided.

Classification	Supply for VAT purposes
Goods and services not separately identified	Supply of goods
Goods and services separately identified	Supply of goods and services

(ii) Imported supplies from outside a Member State of the EU

HM Customs and Excise Notice No 702 provides that where the goods (ie the physical carrier such as a CD-ROM) and services (ie the information) are not separately identified the import is to be treated as an importation of goods.[3] If the value of the supply of goods and services are separately identified, VAT is paid on the importation of the goods.[4] VAT is charged on the cost or value of the carrier medium.[5] In relation to the separately identified services VAT must be accounted for in respect of those services which are specified in VATA 1994, Sch 5, on the basis of the reverse charge.[6] This will normally be the case where the recipient receives the supply for business purposes. The service element of the supply is the information on the carrier, and the licence for use of the information which is subject to copyright protection. Both these services are subject to the reverse charge.[7] If a supply is made to a non-business consumer, import VAT is payable solely upon the physical carrier.

1 HM Customs and Excise Notice No 702/4/94.
2 Ibid, para 3.1.
3 Ibid, para 3.2.
4 Ibid, para 3.2.
5 Ibid.
6 Ibid, see also VATA 1994, s 8, Sch 5. The nature of the reverse charge is explained in Chapter 8.
7 Ibid, Sch 5, paras 1 and 3.

(iii) Exported supplies

Since normalised software is typically regarded as a supply of goods, this will mean that supplies to countries outside of the Member States of the EU, will typically be zero-rated.[1] The supplier will in these circumstances be entitled to recover all its VAT incurred on the components in making the supply.

Electronically delivered computer software

HM Customs and Excise Notice No 702/4/94 which deals with the importation of computer software specifically states that the transmission of information by satellite, telephone, telex etc is a supply of services.[2]

Customs and Excise holds the view that software transmitted by telephone or by any other type of data network (ie Internet supplies) will not qualify for zero-rating.[3] This is because the supply of electronic data is regarded as a supply of services. If a service is supplied abroad to a business within the EU, no UK VAT is applied. This is because of the reverse charge.[4]

However, the Customs and Excise manual contained, prior to October 1997, an important statement which conflicted with the Notice issued. Appendix G of the manual dealing with the reverse charge, and Sch 5 to VATA 1994 provided that the 'supply of standard "off-the-shelf" packages of software are regarded as supplies of goods, even where they are purchased by downloading from a computer network, and are therefore subject to the rules on place of supply of goods'.[5] It also appeared from the manual prior to October 1997 that a record of an electronic transmission coupled with confirmation of electronic delivery overseas was acceptable evidence to enable Customs and Excise to categorise a supply as an export and thus zero-rate it. This practice has been reversed.

Specific or bespoke software

Customs and Excise defines 'specific' products as items made on the specific instructions of a customer: for example, creation of unique programs or the adaptation of standard programs.[6] The Notice also provides that the following are specific products:[7]

- inter-company information data and accounts;
- enhancements and updates of existing 'specific' programs;
- enhancements and updates of existing 'normalised' programs supplied under contractual obligation to customers who have bought the original program.

This type of software is wholly different from 'normalised' software, because it is not mass-produced, and is not readily available to the general consumer. The type of

---

1 VATA 1994, s 30.
2 See HM Customs and Excise Notice No 703, para 6.6.
3 Ibid.
4 See Chapter 8.
5 HM Customs Excise internal guidance manual *Value Added Tax, Place of Supply*, Part 4, Appendix G – 'Services supplied through Computer Networks'.
6 HM Customs and Excise Notice No 702/4/94.
7 Ibid, para 4.1.

software with which we are concerned here is that customised to a particular business activity, such as control of robotic arms for the mass production and installation of motor components. For the purposes of applying the VAT legislation, Customs and Excise takes the view that specific software, involves the supply of both goods (ie the physical carrier), and services (ie the information).[1] However, because the major element of the supply is of services, ie the work of a developer, VAT is charged on the basis of a supply of services.

Tax treatment of bespoke software

(i) Domestic supplies
Because the major element of the supply is the work performed by software developers, VAT will be charged on the basis of a supply of services.

(ii) Imported supplies
Customs and Excise identifies the nature of the supply, and categorises it into a supply of goods and services.[2] In the case of an import, VAT is applied to the physical carrier which holds the information. The information is subject to VAT as a supply of services, under the reverse charge provisions.[3] It is, however, likely that Customs and Excise will ignore the trivial cost of the device upon which the software is recorded.

(iii) Exported supplies
A supply of goods is zero-rated if Customs and Excise is satisfied that the person supplying the goods has exported them to a place outside the Member States of the EU.[4] Where this is the case, a person will be able to claim all the input tax incurred in making the supply. However, the supply of bespoke software is rarely regarded as the supply of goods because the major aspect of the supply is the provision of work by computer software writers.

The classification of computer software, described above, means that the supply of specific software will never qualify for zero-rating insofar as the service is concerned (ie the information, as distinct from the physical carrier).[5] A supply of services in the case of bespoke software will be charged to VAT according to where the place of supply is for the purposes of the legislation. The place of supply of services, such as information, and copyright licensing is generally where the customer belongs.[6] Thus, effectively no VAT is paid on the 'export' of services outside the Member States of the EU since the place of supply is outside the UK.

7.2.10 Zero-rated supplies of computer software

Where a supply is classified as zero-rated, the supply is a taxable supply but the rate of VAT is zero and not the standard rate, which is currently 17.5 per cent (1998–99). VATA 1994 provides that the following supplies of computer software are zero-rated:

---

1 HM Customs and Excise Notice No 702/4/94, para. 4.2.
2 Ibid.
3 Ibid, para 4.4.
4 VATA 1994, s 30(6)(a).
5 HM Customs and Excise Notice No 703, para 6.6.
6 Sixth VAT Directive, Directive 77/338.

'Supply of computer software to an eligible body which pays for it with funds from a charity or by voluntary contributions, or a supply to an eligible body which is a charitable institution providing care for handicapped people.'[1]

The zero-rating extends to the hire of computer software, and the provision of computer services.[2] The computer services must be by way of the provision of computer software solely for use in medical research, diagnosis or treatment.[3] This would include bespoke software'.

7.3 BUSINESS VEHICLES FOR DEVELOPMENT OF SOFTWARE: TAX INCENTIVE-RELATED SCHEMES

7.3.1 Enterprise investment scheme

The purpose of this section is to focus on how the EIS is used for attracting investment into software-related business activities. The general nature of EIS was examined in Chapter 2.

7.3.2 Qualifying company

One requirement for attracting the EIS label is that a qualifying company is to be the business vehicle.[4] This is a company which, among other things, does not carry on a prohibited activity.[5] Particularly relevant to a software business is that it is necessary that none of the business nor a substantial part[6] of it consists in receiving royalties or licence fees.[7]

A company carrying on a trade which consists to a substantial extent of receiving royalties may none the less qualify where it is carrying on R&D, and the licence fees received are attributable to R&D carried on by it.[8] The legislation specifically provides that R&D *means* 'any activity intended to result in a patentable invention or in a computer program'.[9]

---

1 VATA 1994, Sch 8, Group 15, Item 5, Notes 9 and 10. An eligible body, means eg a research institution or hospital whose activities are not carried on for profit (see Note 4 to Group 15). See also *De Voil's Indirect Tax Service* (Butterworths) Division V4.266.

2 VATA 1994, Sch 8, Group 15, Item 5, Note 9.

3 Ibid, Note 10. Note that the computer software does not qualify unless it is 'solely for use' in the specified circumstances. The relief does not extend to medical or veterinary training. See HM Customs and Excise internal guidance manuals, Part 9, Chapter 2, Section 9, para 9.6.

4 ICTA 1988, s 289(1).

5 Ibid, s 293(1).

6 'Substantial' means, as a rule of thumb, about 20 per cent of the trade (Hansard, 9 May 1988, col 42).

7 ICTA 1988, ss 293(3B) and 297(2)(e).

8 Ibid, s 297(5).

9 Ibid, s 312(1).

Part IV

VALUE ADDED TAX

Chapter 8

VALUE ADDED TAX

8.1 INTRODUCTION[1]

VATA 1994 and the Sixth VAT Directive govern the application of VAT in the UK. VAT is a product of European law. At the European level, VAT is governed by a series of Directives and Regulations.[2] The former are instructions by the European Council of Ministers to national governments requiring them to implement laws within domestic legislation. Directives can be relied upon directly by nationals of each Member State of the EU. By contrast, a Regulation takes effect in domestic legislation like an Act of Parliament. Where there is inconsistency between VATA 1994 and the Sixth VAT Directive the taxpayer is entitled to rely upon the Directive.

The operation of VAT in domestic legislation through VATA 1994 is supplemented by Statutory Instruments made under order by HM Treasury. The administration of VAT is through HM Commissioners of Customs and Excise. To assist in the application of VAT, Customs and Excise has published an extensive series of Notices. In addition, Customs and Excise has published their own internal guidance manuals. These are guidelines of how the law is interpreted and applied by Customs and Excise. These Notices and internal manuals do not have any legal force.[3]

1 A detailed examination of VAT law as a whole is beyond the scope of this book. Guidance can be obtained from *De Voil's Indirect Tax Service* (a loose-leaf publication by Butterworths) which is regularly updated. It is important to check the update volume in all circumstances. General guidance on the nature of VAT can be obtained from the following material: Davies *Principles of Tax Law* (Sweet & Maxwell, 1996), pp 411–443; *De Voil's Indirect Tax Service, op cit*, Part VI; HM Customs and Excise internal guidance manual, Vol 1, Part 1, Chapter 1; HM Customs and Excise Notices 'The VAT Guide' No 700, 'The Ins and Outs of VAT' No 700/15/95, 'Keeping Records and Accounts', No 700/21/95,' Filling In Your VAT Return', No 700/12/95.

2 For the interaction between domestic and EC law see generally, Weatherill and Beaumont *EC Law* (Penguin, 1995); and at the VAT level see *De Voil's Indirect Tax Service*; *op cit*, Division V1.3, HM Customs and Excise internal guidance manual, Vol 1, Chapter 1, Section 3. See also Farmer and Lyal *EC Tax Law* (Clarendon Press, 1994).

3 The Notices can be obtained free of charge from a local VAT Business Centre. Relevant references to IT and Internet business in those notices are referred to in this Part.

8.2 PRINCIPLE OF VAT AND ITS APPLICATION TO IT AND E-COMMERCE

The tax charge is based on the sale of goods or services. The VAT net has in general terms been cast widely to include all forms of consumption which are made for consideration. The principle of VAT is stated in Art 2 of the First VAT Directive[1] in the following terms:

> 'The principle of the common system of value added tax involves the application to goods and services of a general tax on consumption exactly proportional to the price of the goods and services, whatever the number of transactions which take place in the production and distribution process before the stage at which tax is charged.
>
> On each transaction, value added tax, calculated on the price of the goods or services at the rate applicable to such goods or services, shall be chargeable after deduction of the amount of value added tax borne directly by the various cost components.
>
> The common system of value added tax shall be applied up to and including the retail trade stage.'

The main principle of VAT is that it will be borne by the final consumer. This is the reason why a person who incurs VAT on components used for the purposes of making a supply, is entitled to deduct this 'input tax' from the tax charged on supplies made by him, known as 'output tax'. As a sales tax, VAT is capable of being applied in many areas of IT and e-commerce. Consider the following situations:

(1) Communication services, whether satellite or earth-based to an Internet access provider.
(2) A licence permitting the use of a search engine database by a mirror-site.
(3) Sale of computer software 'off-the-shelf'.
(4) Sale of computer software devised specifically for a business ('bespoke software').
(5) Sale of micro-processors.
(6) Sale of computer software through the medium of an Internet transaction.
(7) Grant of an exclusive distribution agreement.
(8) Financial services accessed by subscribers via the Internet.
(9) Purchase of computer hardware, with pre-installed computer software, licensed for use by the end user.
(10) Exchange of IT between competitors.

Each of the situations noted above has the potential to fall within the VAT legislation. The application of VAT law in the area of IT and e-commerce falls to be mainly determined by the general framework of VAT under VATA 1994. To understand how VAT is applied in this area, it is first necessary to understand the general ingredients of the VAT charge.

1 Directive 67/227/EEC (OJ 1967 1301).

8.3 INGREDIENTS OF THE VAT CHARGE

The overall framework of VATA 1994 is summarised in Table 17. The key to the application of the tax charge is s 4 of VATA 1994. By s 4 a VAT charge will apply in the following circumstances:

- a supply of goods or services;
- the place of supply of which is in the UK;
- which is a taxable supply;
- made by a taxable person;
- in the course or furtherance of business[1] carried on by the supplier; and
- the supply is not an exempt supply.

Where VAT applies to a supply there are, for the purposes of an IT or Internet business, two types of rate. A VAT charge of 17.5 per cent applies on standard rated supplies,[2] while the charge is nil for zero-rated supplies.[3] The taxable person who charges VAT on supplies made by it, known as 'output tax', is required to account for that amount to Customs and Excise.[4] In accounting for this amount the taxable person is entitled to subtract the amount of VAT incurred by him in making those supplies, known as 'input tax'.[5] The right of set-off only exists where a person makes taxable supplies. Where a person makes exempt supplies there is no right of set-off.[6]

8.4 WHAT IS A SUPPLY?[7]

A supply is defined in VATA 1994 in circular terms as including 'all forms of supply, but not anything done otherwise than for consideration'.[8] The meaning of supply has been considered in a number of contexts outside of the VAT legislation. It has been described by one judge as meaning in its ordinary sense 'to furnish or to serve'.[9] The breadth of the word has been emphasised on a number of occasions.[10] This is also inherent in the words of the legislation. VATA 1994 refers to 'anything ... done for

1 A business is defined in VATA 1994 as including any 'trade, profession or vocation' (s 94(1)). The comments made in relation to a trade in the context of corporation tax are equally valid in determining whether a trade is carried on for the purposes of VAT.
2 Ibid, s 2(1).
3 Ibid, s 30 and Sch 8.
4 Ibid, s 25(1).
5 Ibid, s 25(2).
6 Ibid, s 4(2).
7 *De Voil's Indirect Tax Service*, *op cit*, Division V3.101, 102, 104, 105, 106; Davies *Principles of Tax Law* (Sweet & Maxwell, 1996), pp 418–420; HM Customs and Excise Notice No 700 'The VAT Guide', para 2.4; HM Customs and Excise internal guidance manual, Vol 1, Part 3.
8 VATA 1994, s 5(2)(a).
9 *Williams v Pearce* (1916) 114 LT at 901, per Lord Reading CJ (in a Licensing Act case), adopted in *Carlton Lodge Club v Customs and Excise Commissioners* [1974] STC 507.
10 See *Customs and Excise Commissioners v Oliver* [1980] STC 73 at 74, Griffiths J said '"supply" is a word of the widest import'.

consideration'.[1] The fact that the legal framework within which a transaction takes place (ie under a contract) is void does not prevent a supply from occurring.[2]

Example 45

Hardware Technologies Ltd sells 1,000 computers to a retailer for a lump sum of £1 million.

Example 46

Global Internet Services Ltd provides an Internet access service to business subscribers. The annual subscription is £10,000, and the gross turnover is £5 million.

Example 47

Search Engine Services Ltd provides banner advertisements for businesses on its search engine web site. Gross turnover is £1 million.

8.5 WHAT IS CONSIDERATION?[3]

VAT is charged on consideration for the supply of goods or services.[4] It is inherent in the legislation that a direct link must exist between consideration and a supply.[5] If there is no link, then VAT cannot be charged on a supply. Everything therefore depends upon the contract under which the supply is provided. In addition the VAT charge applies only to consideration which is referrable to a particular supply. Consideration is not defined under either VATA 1994, or the Sixth VAT Directive. Some guidance on this matter is provided in the Sixth VAT Directive, which provides that the taxable amount, ie the consideration is: 'everything which constitutes the consideration which has been or is to be obtained by the supplier from the purchaser, the customer or a third party for such supplies including subsidies directly linked to the price of such supplies'.[6] This has been interpreted as meaning that consideration includes not only money or cash amounts, but goods or services received in exchange for a supply.[7] The fact that there is no definition of consideration means that it is to be given the widest possible meaning.[8]

---

1 VATA 1994, s 5(2)(a).

2 See eg *Customs and Excise Commissioners v Oliver* [1980] STC 73, [1980] 1 All ER 353 where a supply existed despite the fact that the contract relating to the sale of cars was void because the cars were stolen property.

3 See *De Voil's Indirect Tax Service*, *op cit*, Division V3.103. 1044; Davies *Principles of Tax Law* (Sweet & Maxwell, 1996), pp 421–423; HM Customs and Excise Notice No 700 'The VAT Guide', para 3.1(a); HM Customs and Excise internal guidance manual, Vol 1, Part 3.

4 VATA 1994, s 4(1); Sixth VAT Directive, Directive 77/338, Art 2(1).

5 See *Naturally Yours Cosmetics Ltd v Customs and Excise Commissioners* [1988] STC 879, per the Advocate General.

6 Sixth VAT Directive, Directive 77/338, Art 11(1)(a).

7 See eg *Naturally Yours Cosmetics Ltd v Customs and Excise Commissioners* [1988] STC 879 followed in *Empire Stores Ltd v Customs and Excise Commissioners* [1994] STC 623. In this case the European Court of Justice (ECJ) decided that the supply of services (arranging a party) and the payment of £1.50 constituted the consideration for a pot of cream, which otherwise retailed at £10.14. See the comments of the Advocate General.

8 Ibid.

Example 48

Harriet ('the subscriber') pays £10 each month plus £1.50 for each hour of service use to an Internet access provider. The Internet access agreement provides that in consideration for this payment each month the subscriber has a right to use the service which:

> 'consists of computing and information services and software, information and other content provided by [the Internet access provider], as well as access to services, software, information and other content provided by third parties.'

In the context of this licence agreement it is clear that all the services specifically mentioned are directly referable to the consideration of £10 per month, plus £1.50 for each hour the subscriber uses the service.

8.6 WHAT IS THE VALUE OF THE CONSIDERATION?

Normally anything done other than for consideration is not subject to a VAT charge, because it is not capable of being a supply.[1] Where, however, a person makes a disposal of goods which form part of the assets of his business free of charge, this is none the less treated as a supply of goods.[2] The disposal of goods free of charge will not be treated as a supply of goods if it is a gift costing less than £15, or it is a gift of samples.[3] In circumstances such as these, it will be necessary to ascertain the value of the consideration. For a VAT charge to be imposed it is necessary for the supply to be capable of being expressed in monetary terms.[4]

In assessing the value of consideration the Sixth VAT Directive makes no reference to objective criteria. The test is based on subjective criteria, because the VAT charge is imposed on the consideration actually received. To ascertain the value of the transaction it is therefore necessary to examine what is agreed upon between the parties.[5] Where an exchange takes place, the value of the supply is calculated by the value of the consideration provided by the other party. In other words, it is necessary to ascertain the value assigned to the supply by the parties. For example, if the consideration represents a supply of services for goods, the value of the consideration is the cost of the goods, because that represents what the recipient of the services was prepared to pay. In *Empire Stores Ltd v Customs and Excise Commissioners*,[6] the ECJ held that the consideration on an exchange must be ascertained in the following way:

---

1 VATA 1994, s 5(2); Sixth VAT Directive, Directive 77/338, Art 2(1).
2 VATA 1994, Sch 4, para 5(1).
3 Ibid, Sch 4, para 5(2).
4 See *Staatssecretaris van Financien v Cooperative Aardappelenbewaarplaats GA* [1981] ECR 445.
5 In *Naturally Yours Cosmetics Ltd v Customs and Excise Commissioners* [1988] STC 879 the ECJ examined the agreement between the supplier and an individual. Under the agreement, a pot of cream would be supplied below the wholesale price, on condition that the person arranged for a party to be held. In the event of no party being arranged, the pot of cream had either to be returned or paid for at the retail price. The ECJ held that in these circumstances the value of the consideration could be fixed as the difference between the wholesale price and the cost price, because this difference although not paid in monetary terms is paid for by the provision of a service, ie arranging the party.
6 [1994] STC 623, para 19 of the judgment.

> 'Where that value is not a sum of money agreed between the parties, it must, in order to be subjective, be the value which the recipient of the services constituting the consideration for the supply of goods attributes to the services which he is seeking to obtain and must correspond to the amount which he is prepared to spend for that purpose.'

Where the supply of goods is involved the value can only be the price which the supplier has paid for the article which it is supplying without any extra charge in exchange for the services.[1]

The *Empire Stores* case is a useful illustration of how VAT can be charged on the exchange of goods for services, or services for services, in the context of an Internet service. First consider the facts of this case before turning to an example of Internet business. In this case a retailer sold merchandise through a catalogue. In order to acquire new clientele it operated various schemes. Under one scheme, a person would provide personal information about themselves, including the implicit right to use the information to check creditworthiness. The customer list could then be sold by the catalogue retailer. The information provided therefore had economic value. Additionally, the retailer received the real advantage that if a person introduced themselves to the catalogue that the person would make purchases. Once the information was provided and accepted (ie after a credit check) a 'free' gift would be sent to the person providing the information.

The issue was whether VAT was chargeable, and if so what the amount was. In essence the retailer undertook to provide goods in exchange for information. The gift was intended as the quid pro quo for an advantage provided to the retailer by the person providing the information. In the Opinion of the Advocate General in *Empire Stores* there was a direct link between the provision of information and the supply of goods. A value could be placed on the supply of information because for the retailer it had an economic value. The value in this case had a subjective value, because the retailer was prepared to give for the information an article for which it had paid the cost price. On this basis, it was held that the retailer made a supply of goods for a consideration fixed at the cost price of the goods.

Example 49

A national catalogue operator provides an electronic version through the medium of the Internet to anyone who accesses the web site. The operator provides access free of charge to consumers. However, every person who accesses the site for the first time is required to register, and complete an extensive questionnaire. The data is then used by the operator and sold on to other retailers. In exchange for the provision of the data the catalogue operator provides 'free goods' from a range of goods to the consumer.

The issue from a VAT perspective is whether it is possible for a charge to arise. For the provision of information the operator supplies 'free goods'. This is based on the retail scheme similar to the *Empire Stores* case.

What is the value of the consideration? The value must be capable of being expressed monetarily. It is clear that the information provided by the public has economic value

1 [1994] STC 623, para 19 of the judgment.

because it enables the catalogue operator to generate revenue by onward sale of the information to retailers: on the basis of *Empire Stores* the value of the consideration is the cost of supplying the 'gift'.

8.7 WHAT IS A SUPPLY OF GOODS?[1]

A supply of goods is governed in UK domestic legislation by Sch 4 to VATA 1994. The meaning of a supply of goods has received judicial consideration.[2] It is important at this point to make a distinction between the physical product and the property that exists within the product. For example, a person who owns tangible property such as a device upon which a computer program is encoded, is entitled to sell, or lease the device etc. These rights of ownership are the property in the tangible property. Against this background it must be remembered that a VAT charge only arises where the property in the goods is:[3]

- transferred by sale;
- possession of goods is transferred under an agreement for the sale of the goods; or
- possession of goods is transferred under agreements which expressly contemplate that the property will also pass at some time in the future.

An agreement which transfers property in goods is a supply of goods. There does not necessarily have to be an instantaneous physical transfer of goods to the purchaser for a supply of goods to take place. All that is required is the transfer of the whole property in the goods. It is possible for a supply of goods to be achieved through the medium of electronic commerce.

Example 50

UK Merchandising Ltd carries on a trade in the sale of products which are a spin-off from television serials and films. The site is accessed by people throughout the world who place orders for novelty merchandise. Orders placed by UK individuals for the acquisition of merchandise will be subject to VAT on the basis that it is a sale of goods. This is because the order is essentially a basic transaction for the acquisition of

1 See *De Voil's Indirect Tax Service*, *op cit*, Division V3.112; Davies *Principles of Tax Law* (Sweet & Maxwell, 1996), pp 420–421; HM Customs and Excise internal guidance manual, Vol 1, Part 3, Chapter 1, Section 6, and Chapter 2A, Section 2.

2 In the ECJ decision, known as the *Theotrue* case the following explanation of what is a supply of goods is given [1983] VATTR 88 at 92:
'"Supply" for such purposes in relation to goods requires the transfer of goods from one taxable person to another, either immediately or at a future date, and implies the existence of the goods at such time of transfer. That, we consider, is inherent in the definition of "supply" given by Mr Justice Griffiths in the case of *Commissioners of Customs and Excise v JRB Oliver* in which he stated "Supply" is the passing of possession in goods pursuant to an agreement whereunder the supplier agrees to part with and the recipient agrees to take possession. By "possession" is meant in this context control over the goods, in the sense of having the immediate facility for their use. This may or may not involve the physical removal of the goods.'

3 VATA 1994, Sch 4, para 1(2). See also Sixth VAT Directive, Directive 77/338, Art 5(1), (4).

products, albeit facilitated by IT. However, not all transactions will be subject to VAT at the rate of 17.5 per cent. If the supply is classified as a zero-rated supply the consumer will pay no VAT since the rate for such a supply is nil. For instance, articles designed as clothing or footwear for young children which are not suitable for older persons are zero-rated.[1]

8.7.1 Software

Can standardised software transferred electronically be classified as a supply of goods? This is a particularly difficult issue in respect of software sold and transferred via the medium of the Internet. A good is not defined in VATA 1994 or the Sixth VAT Directive. However, it is defined in the Sale of Goods Act 1979 as including 'all personal chattels other than things in action and money'.[2] It is clear from this definition that there must be an element of tangible existence, such as a device like a CD-ROM upon which the software is recorded.[3] Software sold through the medium of the Internet, and installed directly onto the purchaser's computer hard disk will be regarded as a supply of services.[4] The Customs and Excise guidance manual provides that current practice is to recognise the supply and delivery of standardised computer software via a computer network as a supply of services.[5]

8.7.2 Goods forming part of the assets of a business

Where goods form part of the assets of a business, and these are transferred or disposed of under the direction of the person carrying on the business that action is deemed to be a supply of goods, irrespective of the fact that there is no consideration.[6]

8.7.3 Gifts and samples

Where a supply occurs in the context of a gift made in the course of business, or as a gift to any person of a sample, there is no supply of goods.[7]

Example 51

Computer Graphic Designs Ltd issues a CD-ROM containing its graphic package which retails for £85. The CD-ROM is attached free of charge on computer magazines. Access to the graphics package on the CD-ROM is limited to a 30-day trial period. After this time the computer program is locked and cannot be accessed. In

---

1 VATA 1994, Group 16.
2 Sale of Goods Act 1979, s 61.
3 See C. Reed *Computer Law* (Blackstone Press, 3rd edn, 1996), pp 55–58.
4 The VAT implication of supplying software through the medium of the Internet is examined in the chapter dealing with software.
5 Volume 1, Appendix G (Computer Networks): Reverse Charge.
6 VATA 1994, Sch 4, para 5(1).
7 VATA 1994, Sch 4, para 5(2)(a)(b). Other rules apply to multiple samples to the same person. See Sch 4, para 5(3). However, this phrase appears only to cover complimentary gifts intended generally to foster goodwill or publicise the taxable person's name, without there being any direct consideration; *Empire Stores v Customs and Excise Commissioners* [1994] STC 623, para 19 of the Opinion per the Advocate General.

these circumstances the graphics program is issued as a sample in the furtherance of business, as a promotion of the company's product. Any subsequent unlocking of the software, after payment of a sum would represent a supply of goods and consequentially subject to VAT.

8.8 WHAT IS A SUPPLY OF SERVICES?[1]

VATA 1994 provides that anything which is not a supply of goods, but is done for consideration is a supply of services.[2] The granting, assignment or surrender of any right if done for consideration is deemed to be a supply of services.[3] In some circumstances, a supply, although involving goods, will be classified as a supply of services. Schedule 4 to the 1994 Act provides that the transfer of any undivided share of property in goods, or the possession of goods is a supply of services.[4] The supply of software provided electronically is a supply of services.

8.9 WHO IS A TAXABLE PERSON?[5]

A taxable person is required to charge VAT and account for it to Customs and Excise.

8.9.1 VATA 1994

A taxable person is defined under VATA 1994 as a person who is, or is required to be, registered under the Act.[6] A person who makes taxable supplies is required to register for the purposes of VAT, where these supplies are in excess of £50,000 to the year ending for any month.[7] An obligation also exists to register where the person has reasonable grounds for believing that the value of supplies will exceed £50,000 within 30 days.[8] A person is not obliged to register where Customs and Excise are satisfied that the value of supplies will not exceed £48,000 in a period of one year.[9]

A person can cease to be registered under VATA 1994 only in specified circumstances. By Sch 1 to the Act, a person ceases to be liable to register where the Commissioners of Customs and Excise are satisfied that the person has ceased to make taxable supplies.[10] Where the conditions specified above obliging a person to

---

1 See *De Voil's Indirect Tax Service*, *op cit*, Division V3.113; Davies *Principles of Tax Law* (Sweet & Maxwell, 1996), pp 420–421; HM Customs and Excise internal guidance manual, Vol 1, Part 3, Chapter 1, Section 6 and Chapter 2A, Section 2.

2 VATA 1994, s 5(2)(b). See also Sixth VAT Directive, Directive 77/338, Art 6(1).

3 VATA 1994, s 5(2)(b). See also Sixth VAT Directive, Directive 77/338, Art 6(1).

4 VATA 1994, Schs 1–3.

5 See *De Voil's Indirect Tax Service*, *op cit*, Division V2.1; Davies *Principles of Tax Law* (Sweet & Maxwell, 1996), pp 423–428; HM Customs and Excise Notice No 700 'The VAT Guide', paras 2.1 and 2.5; HM Customs and Excise internal guidance manual, Vol 1, Part 5.

6 VATA 1994, s 3(1), Schs 1–3.

7 Ibid, Sch 1, para 1(1)(a). Liability must be notified to the Commissioners within 30 days of the end of the month in which the liability arises (para 5(1)).

8 Ibid, Sch 1, para 1(1)(b). The Commissioners must be notified within 30 days before the end of the period to which the liability arises (para 6(1)).

9 Ibid, Sch 1, para 1(3).

10 Ibid, Sch 1, para 3(a).

register are no longer satisfied, there is no obligation to remain registered.[1] A person is entitled to deregistration where Customs and Excise can be satisfied that the value of taxable supplies will not exceed £48,000 within one year.[2]

A person who is not obliged to register under VATA 1994 may none the less seek voluntary registration. This can occur where a person satisfies the Commissioners that he makes taxable supplies, or alternatively that the person is carrying on a business, and intends to make taxable supplies in the course of furtherance of business.[3] A person may want to register so that he can reclaim VAT incurred by him in making taxable supplies.

A person may also register where he makes a taxable supply outside the UK. For example, the export of goods may be a taxable supply. The rate of tax is sometimes nil, which would make it zero-rated. Registering would be advantageous because it enables the input VAT to be reclaimed.

An exemption from registration is available where the Commissioners are satisfied, and think it appropriate, that the person concerned makes or intends to make taxable supplies which are zero-rated.[4] An obligation exists to inform the Commissioners, within 30 days, of any material change in the nature of the supplies.[5] For example, an Internet trader who specialises in the sale of children's clothes could claim the exemption.

8.9.2 Sixth VAT Directive

By contrast to VATA 1994 which uses the concept of taxable person, the Sixth VAT Directive is based on non-financial turnover thresholds. By Art 4(1) of the Directive, a taxable person is defined as meaning 'any person who independently carries out in any place any economic activity ... whatever the purpose or results of that activity'. An economic activity is defined as 'all activities of producers, traders and persons supplying services ...'.[6] A person who carries on an economic activity under a contract of employment, does not carry on the activity independently.[7]

Any State, regional or local authority governed by public law is not, unless otherwise provided for, a taxable person in respect of activities carried on by them as public authorities. This prohibition applies even where the public authority collects fees, contributions or payments in respect of the services.[8] A public authority is however treated as a taxable person where it would lead to a significant distortion of competition.[9] Where the following activities are carried on by a public authority they are treated as taxable persons:[10]

1 VATA 1994, Sch 1, para 3(b).
2 Ibid, Sch 1, para 4(1). A person will not be deregistered because the supplies are suspended for a period of 30 days or more, or that the person will cease making taxable supplies (para 4(2)).
3 Ibid, Sch 1, para 9.
4 Ibid, Sch 1, para 14(1).
5 Ibid, Sch 1, para 14(2).
6 Sixth VAT Directive, Directive 77/338, Art 4(2).
7 Ibid, Art 4(4).
8 Ibid, Art 4(5).
9 Ibid.
10 See ibid, Annex D. For the purposes of this book only the activities relevant to IT and Internet transactions are listed.

- telecommunications;
- supply of new goods manufactured for sale;
- the running of trade fairs and exhibitions;
- the activities of commercial publicity bodies;
- the activities of travel agencies;
- transactions other than those specified in Article 13A(1)(q) of radio and television bodies.[1]

8.10 WHERE IS THE PLACE OF SUPPLY OF GOODS OR SERVICES?[2]

For the purposes of UK domestic legislation the place of supply is determined by reference to a number of specific rules. Table 14 summarises the place of supply rules for both goods and services. In the context of IT and e-commerce the place of supply rules are extremely important. This is because the cost of using technology is diminishing quickly. It is now relatively easy to send large portions of data across Continents through the use of submarine lines or via a satellite network. The advantage of locating a service supply outside of the UK to UK non-business customers, is that there is no VAT cost. In order to avoid a charge totally, it is imperative for a business to ensure that the supply is not only deemed to take place outside of the UK, but also that it is deemed not to be received in the UK.[3]

8.10.1 The territorial extent of the UK for VAT purposes

Where a supply takes place outside of the UK, a UK VAT charge cannot be imposed upon the supply. VATA 1994 defines the UK as including the territorial sea[4] of the UK.[5] Greater light is thrown on the matter by the Interpretation Act 1978 which provides that the UK comprises England, Scotland, Wales and Northern Ireland.[6] The Isle of Man is deemed to be part of the UK unless otherwise indicated.[7] By contrast the Channel Islands do not form part of the UK. At the time of publication VAT is not charged in the Channel Islands.

1 Sixth VAT Directive, Art 13A relates to the exemption of specific activities. The relevant paragraph in that Article exempts 'activities of public radio and television bodies other than those of a commercial nature'.

2 See *De Voil's Indirect Tax Service*, *op cit*, Division V3.124, and V3.181; HM Customs and Excise Notice No 700 'The VAT Guide', paras 2.4(b), 2.8(a), (b), and 4.1(c), and Notice No 741, Section 2; HM Customs and Excise internal guidance manual, Vol 1, Part 4, Section 2, Chapter 2B, Section 6.

3 This is necessary in order to avoid the reverse charge provisions. These are described below, and examined in the chapter dealing with the taxation of e-commerce.

4 See *De Voil's Indirect Tax Service*, *op cit*, Division V1.207 for an explanation of this phrase.

5 VATA 1994, s 96(11).

6 Interpretation Act 1978, ss 5 and 22(1) and Sch 1.

7 See Value Added Tax (Isle of Man) Order 1982, SI 1982/1067 and Value Added Tax (Isle of Man) (No 2) Order 1982, SI 1982/1068.

Table 14: Place of supply rules for goods and services – VATA 1994

Type of supply	*Place of supply*	*Reference (VATA 1994)*
Goods		
Goods not removed from the UK	Goods supplied in the UK	s 7(2)
Goods not removed to the UK	Goods not supplied in the UK	s 7(2)
Goods installed or assembled at a place in the UK to which they are removed	Goods supplied in the UK	s 7(3)(a)
Services		
Supply of services by a supplier who belongs in the UK	Service supplied in UK	s 7(10)(a)
Supply of services by a supplier who belongs in another country	Service supplied outside the UK	s 7(10)(b)

The place of supply rules for the purposes of the Sixth VAT Directive are summarised in Table 15.

Table 15: Place of supply the Sixth VAT Directive

Type of supply	*Place of supply*	*Reference (VAT Sixth Directive)*
Goods		
Goods dispatched, transported by the supplier, or by the person to whom they are supplied, or by a third person	Place where the goods are at the time of dispatch, or transport to the person to whom supplied begins	Art 8(1)(a)

Type of supply	*Place of supply*	*Reference (VAT Sixth Directive)*
Goods installed or assembled by or on behalf of the supplier	Place where goods are installed or assembled	Art 8(1)(a)
Goods not dispatched or transported	Place where the goods are when the supply takes place	Art 8(1)(b)
Services		
Supply of services	Place where supplier has: (a) established its business; or (b) fixed establishment from which the service is supplied or in the absence of (a), (b) where the supplier has its permanent address or where it usually resides	Art 9(1)
Cultural, artistic, sporting, scientific, educational, entertainment or similar activities, including the activities of the organisers of such activities, and the supply of ancillary services	Where services are physically carried out	Art 9(2)(c)
Intellectual property transfers and assignments of copyrights, patents, licences, trade marks and similar rights, or obligations to refrain from pursuing or exercising, in whole or in part these rights performed for customers outside the EU or taxable persons established in the EU but not in the same country as the supplier	Place where customer has established his business, or has a fixed establishment to which the service is supplied, or the place where the customer has his address or usually resides	Art 9(2)(e)

Type of supply	*Place of supply*	*Reference (VAT Sixth Directive)*
Advertising services performed for customers outside the EU or taxable persons established in the EU but not in the same country as the supplier	Place where customer has established his business, or has a fixed establishment to which the service is supplied, or the place where the customer has his address or usually resides	Art 9(2)(e)
Consultancy services performed for customers outside the EU or taxable persons established in the EU but not in the same country as the supplier	Place where customer has established his business, or has a fixed establishment to which the service is supplied, or the place where the customer has his address or usually resides	Art 9(2)(e)
Data processing services performed for customers outside the EU or taxable persons established in the EU but not in the same country as the supplier	Place where customer has established his business, or has a fixed establishment to which the service is supplied, or the place where the customer has his address or usually resides	Art 9(2)(e)
Supply of information performed for customers outside the EU or taxable persons established in the EU but not in the same country as the supplier	Place where customer has established his business, or has a fixed establishment to which the service is supplied, or the place where the customer has his address or usually resides	Art 9(2)(e)
Obligations to refrain from pursuing or exercising, in whole or in part, a business activity performed for customers outside the EU or taxable persons established in the EU but not in the same country as the supplier	Place where customer has established his business, or has a fixed establishment to which the service is supplied, or the place where the customer has his address or usually resides	Art 9(2)(e)

Type of supply	*Place of supply*	*Reference (VAT Sixth Directive)*
Banking, financial, insurance transactions including reinsurance performed for customers outside the EU or taxable persons established in the EU but not in the same country as the supplier	Place where customer has established his business, or has a fixed establishment to which the service is supplied, or the place where the customer has his address or usually resides	Art 9(2)(e)
Services of agents who act in the name and for the account of another, when they procure for their principal the services referred to in respect of IP, advertising, consultancy, data processing, supply of information, restrictive covenants and financial services performed for customers outside the EU or taxable persons established in the EU but not in the same country as the supplier	Place where customer has established his business, or has a fixed establishment to which the service is supplied, or the place where the customer has his address or usually resides	Art 9(2)(e)

Example 52

Dr Terras operates a legal practice in the Cayman Islands. He is happy to provide advice to both professional and lay clients in the UK via video-conferencing, and e-mail etc. A UK based firm of solicitors require clarification on trust law in the Cayman Islands. A video conference is held, and the fee payable to Dr Terras is the sterling equivalent of £30,000. Dr Terras is e-mailed by John and Rita who want to retire to the Cayman Islands. They seek his advice on the legal requirements to gain residence. The advice costs the sterling equivalent of £1,000.

Dr Terras, as supplier of the services belongs outside of the UK, and the EU. Dr Terras is under no obligation to charge and account for VAT to any EU tax authority. However, the UK based firm of solicitors will be required to account for UK VAT because they receive the service for business purposes.

8.11 DETERMINING WHERE A SUPPLIER BELONGS FOR THE PURPOSES OF A SUPPLY OF SERVICES

As Table 14 illustrates the key to determining place of supply of services is in locating where the supplier belongs. The test of 'belonging' is defined in VATA 1994 as being where:

(1) the supplier of the service has a business establishment or some other fixed establishment, and no other establishment elsewhere;[1] or
(2) where the supplier has no such establishment, the location of the supplier's usual place of residence;[2] or
(3) where neither (1) or (2) are met, the place of supply is where the establishment most directly concerned with the supply exists.[3]

A person who is a non-resident is treated as belonging in the UK in respect of a supply of services if he carries on business through a branch or agency in the UK.[4]

8.12 REVERSE CHARGE[5]

Where a service is received from abroad the place of supply is located outside of the UK, because under the rules for locating a supply, the supplier belongs in another country, VAT will not therefore be charged on the supply. Many supplies received in these circumstances will be by a trader. The business usually incurs the cost of this supply from abroad for its own business purposes, so that it can make supplies to its consumers. VAT will be imposed on these supplies, if they are taxable supplies. The business trader will be required to account for VAT on these supplies. This is designed to prevent distortion of trade otherwise businesses would acquire tax-free benefits by obtaining services from abroad.

VATA 1994 provides that where 'relevant services' are received by a person who belongs in the UK for the purposes of any business carried on by him, and those services are supplied by a supplier from abroad, then the recipient is treated as having supplied the services in the UK for the purposes of VAT.[6] The result of this is that the recipient is entitled to claim credit for input tax.[7]

Example 53

Supplies received from abroad costing £100. VAT on supply deemed to be made by recipient (£100 × 17.5 per cent) = £17.50. Recipient has incurred VAT of £40

1 VATA 1994, s 9(2)(a).

2 Ibid, s 9(2)(b). For the purposes of a company, this means the place where it is legally constituted (s 9(5)(b)).

3 Ibid, s 9(2)(c).

4 Ibid, s 9(5)(a).

5 See *De Voil's Indirect Tax Service*, *op cit*, Division V3.231; HM Customs and Excise internal guidance manual, Vol 1, Part 4, Chapter 2B, Section 16; and HM Customs and Excise Notice No 741/9/98, 'Place of supply of services'.

6 VATA 1994, s 8(1).

7 Ibid.

(including the supply from abroad) in making supplies in the course of its business. The company receives output tax of £540. Tax accounted for to Customs and Excise is £500.

8.13 RELEVANT SERVICES

The services in respect of which a reverse charge operates are set out in Sch 5 to VATA 1994, as follows:

> '1. Transfers and assignments of copyright, patents, licences, trademarks and similar rights.
> 2. Advertising Services.
> 3. Services of consultants, engineers, consultancy, bureaux, lawyers, accountants and other similar services, data processing and provision of information . . .
> 4. Acceptance of any obligation to refrain from pursuing or exercising, in whole or in part, any business activity or any such rights as are referred to in paragraph 1 above.
> 5. Banking, financial and insurance services (including reinsurance . . .)
> 6. . . .
> 7. . . .
> 7A. Telecommunications services, that is to say services relating to the transmission, emission or reception of signals, writing, images and sounds or information of any nature by wire, radio, optical or other electromagnetic systems, including the transfer or assignment of the right to use capacity for such transmission, emission or reception.[1]
> 8. The services rendered by one person to another in procuring for the other any of the services mentioned in paragraphs 1 to 7 above.
> 9. Any services not of a description in paragraphs 1 to 8 above when supplied to a recipient who is registered under this Act [ie VATA 1994].
> 10. Section 8(1) shall have effect in relation to any service –
> (a) which are of a description specified in paragraph 9 above; and
> (b) whose place of supply is determined by an order under section 7(1) to be in the United Kingdom,
> as if the recipient belonged in the United Kingdom for the purposes of section 8(1)(b).'

PART IV VALUE ADDED TAX

8.14 PLACE WHERE SUPPLY IS RECEIVED

The rules for determining where a supplier belongs have been described above. The location of where the recipient of a supply belongs is determined by rules specified in VATA 1994, s 9. Where a supply of services is made to an individual, which is received otherwise than for business purposes carried on by him, the individual is treated as belonging in whatever country he has as his usual place of residence.[2] Where the latter rule does not apply, a person is treated as belonging in a country if:

(a) he has a business establishment, or other fixed establishment, and no such other establishment elsewhere; or

---

1 Inserted into VATA 1994, Sch 5 by Value Added Tax (Reverse Charge) (Anti-avoidance) Order 1997, SI 1997/1523, art 3. The provision applies to services performed on or after 1 July 1997.

2 VATA 1994, s 9(3).

(b) failing this, the establishment at which the services are most directly used or to be used, is in that country.[1]

8.15 TIME OF SUPPLY

When a taxable supply takes place the obligation to charge VAT arises.[2] The time of supply is governed by specific rules in VATA 1994 which determine the liability to account for VAT. A summary of these rules is provided in Table 16.

Table 16: Time of supply

Method of supply	*Time of supply*	*VATA 1994*
Goods		
Goods are to be removed	Time of removal	s 6(2)(a)
Goods are not to be removed	Time when goods are made available to the person to whom they are supplied	s 6(2)(b)
Goods sent on approval or sale or return which are removed before it is known whether a supply will take place	When it becomes certain that the supply has taken place, or if sooner, 12 months after the removal	s 6(2)(c)
Services		
Supply of services *VAT Invoice*	When performed	s 6(3)
(1) Time of supply has not been established above, but a VAT invoice is issued	Time invoice issued	s 6(4)
(2) Supplier receives payment in respect of supply before time of supply established above	Time payment received	s 6(4)
(3) In the absence of rules (1) and (2) applying where an invoice is issued within 14 days after the time specified in respect of goods or services	Time invoice issued	s 6(5) An election can be made to displace this provision. A longer period may be imposed (s 6(6))

1 VATA 1994, s 9(4).

2 Ibid, s 4(1).

In relation to telecommunication services, such a service is performed on the expiration of the period to which a payment, a statement, or an invoice relates.[1] This rule applies where telecommunication services are supplied for a consideration, the whole or part of which is determined or payable periodically or from time to time, or in respect of which statements or invoices are issued periodically or from time to time.[2]

Example 54

Alpha Satellite Carrier Ltd issues invoices on a monthly basis to Data Processing Ltd, which uses the telecommunication services of the former company for the purposes of sending and receiving data. The invoice is issued at the end of each month, and relates to that 30-day period. The telecom service is deemed to be supplied at the end of the 30-day period immediately following issue of the invoice.

8.16 INPUT AND OUTPUT TAX

As described at the beginning of this chapter, a taxable person is required to account for VAT on all taxable supplies made by him in the course or furtherance of business.[3] A taxable supply is a supply which is not an exempt supply.[4] The person is entitled to credit the VAT incurred by him upon components, known as 'input tax', against the tax charged by him on supplies, known as 'output tax'.[5] Input tax is defined under VATA 1994 as VAT incurred on the supply of any goods or services used or to be used for the purpose of any business carried on by a taxable person.[6] By contrast output tax means VAT on supplies made by a taxable person.[7]

Example 55

Internet Services Ltd provides Internet access to its subscribers. In the appropriate accounting period for VAT purposes, it is paid subscriptions totalling £100,000. The VAT charge on this amount is £17,500. The company incurs VAT in the course of providing Internet access to its subscribers of £5,000. The amount payable to Customs and Excise is therefore £12,500 (£17,500 minus £5,000).

Where the input tax exceeds the amount of output tax (either because there is no amount of VAT, because it is zero-rated, or there is excessive input tax) the taxable person is entitled to a refund of the excess.[8]

---

1 Article 10(1) of the Value Added Tax (Reverse Charge) (Anti-avoidance) Order 1997, SI 1997/1523.
2 Ibid.
3 VATA 1994, s 25(1).
4 Ibid, s 4(2). The nature of exempt supplies is considered below.
5 Ibid, s 25(2).
6 Ibid, s 24(1). See also s 26.
7 Ibid, s 24(2).
8 VATA 1994, s 25(3).

8.17 ZERO-RATED SUPPLIES

Where a supply is classified as zero-rated for the purposes of VAT, it is a taxable supply, but the rate of VAT charged is set at zero, as opposed to the standard rate of 17.5 per cent (1998–99).[1] Zero-rated supplies are specified in Sch 8 to VATA 1994.[2] A summary of relevant zero-rated supplies for the purposes of e-commerce are as follows:

Group 1 – FOOD

[...]
1. Food of a kind used for human consumption.
2. Animal feeding stuffs.
3. Seeds or other means of propagation of plants comprised in (1) or (2) above.
4. Live animals of a kind generally used as, or yielding or producing, food for human consumption.

Excepted items:

1. Ice cream, ice cream lollies, frozen yogurt, and other similar frozen products.
2. Confectionery not including cakes or biscuits other than biscuits wholly or partly covered with chocolate or some other product similar in taste and appearance.
3. Beverages chargeable with any excise duty specifically charged on spirits, beer, wine or made-wine and preparations thereof.
4. Other beverages (including fruit juices and bottled waters) and syrups, concentrates, essences, powders, crystals or other products for the preparation of beverages.
5. Any of the following when packaged for human consumption without further preparation, namely, potato crisps, potato sticks, potato puffs, and similar products made from the potato, or from potato flour, or from potato starch, and savory food products obtained by the swelling of cereals or cereal products; and salted or roasted nuts other than nuts in shell.
6. Pet foods, canned, packaged or prepared; packaged foods (not being pet foods) for birds other than poultry or game; and biscuits and meal for cats and dogs.
7. Goods canned or prepared for use in making domestically of beer, wine.

Group 3 – BOOKS, ETC

[...]
1. Books, booklets, brochures, pamphlets and leaflets.
2. Newspapers, journals and periodicals.
3. Children's picture books and painting books.
4. Music (printed, duplicated or manuscript).
5. Maps, charts and topographical plans.
6. Covers, cases and other articles supplied with items 1 to 5 and not separately accounted for.

1 VATA 1994, s 30(1).
2 Ibid, s 30(2).

Group 4 – TALKING BOOKS FOR THE BLIND AND HANDICAPPED

[...]

Group 12 – DRUGS, MEDICINES, AIDS FOR THE HANDICAPPED ETC

[...]

1. [...]

1A. [...]

2. The supply to a handicapped person for domestic or personal use, or to a charity for making available to a handicapped persons by sale or otherwise, for domestic or their personal use of –

   [...]

   (b) Electrically or mechanically adjustable beds designed for invalids;

   [...]

   (e) hoists or lifters designed for use by invalids;

   [...]

   (g) equipment and appliances ... designed solely for use by a handicapped person;

[Item numbers 3, 4, 5, 6, 7, 8, 9, 10, 11, 12, 13, 14, 15, 16, 17, 18, 19, 20 – not directly relevant]

Group 15 – CHARITIES ETC

1. [...]
2. [...]
3. The export of any goods by a charity to a place outside member States of the European Union.
4. [...]
5. [...]
6. [...]
7. [...]
8. Supply to a charity, for the purposes of raising money for, or making known the objects or reasons for the objects of, the charity, of –

   (a) the broadcast on television or radio or screening in a cinema of an advertisement; or

   (b) the publication of an advertisement in any newspaper, journal, poster, programme, annual, leaflet, brochure, pamphlet, periodical or similar publication; or

   (c) any goods or services in connection with the preparation of an advertisement within (b) above.

   [...]

Group 16 – CLOTHING AND FOOTWEAR

[...]

1. Articles designed as clothing or footwear for young children and not suitable for older persons.
2. [...]
3. Protective helmets for wear by a person driving or riding a motor bicycle.

'Clothing' is defined as including hats and other headgear.[1] Various other rules apply which must be satisfied so that the exemption applies.

8.18 EXEMPT SUPPLIES

Where a supply is classified as exempt, no VAT is charged on the supply.[2] It will be recalled that VAT is only charged on a taxable supply, which does not include an exempt supply. There is accordingly no right to deduct VAT incurred on components acquired for the purposes of making exempt supplies. Exempt supplies are specified in Sch 9 to the Act.[3] A summary of relevant supplies classified as exempt for the purposes of an IT or Internet business are as follows:

Group 4 – BETTING, GAMING AND LOTTERIES

[...]
1. The provision of facilities for the placing of bets or the playing of any games of chance.
2. The granting of a right to take part in a lottery.'

Item 1 within Group 4 does not include, inter alia, the provision of a gaming machine.[4]

Group 5 – FINANCE

[...]

1. The issue, transfer or receipt of, or any dealing with money, any security for money or any note or order for the payment of money.
2. The making or any advance or the granting of any credit.
3. [...]
4. [...]
5. [...]
6. The issue, transfer or receipt of, or any dealing with, any security or secondary security being –
   (a) shares, stocks, bonds, notes
   [...]
7. [...]
8. The operation of any current, deposit or savings account.

[...]

Group 6 – EDUCATION

[...]

1. The provision by an eligible body of
   (a) education;
   (b) research supplied to an eligible body;
   (c) vocational training.

---

1 VATA 1994, Sch 8, Group 16, Note (1).
2 Ibid, s 4(2).
3 Ibid, s 31(1).
4 Ibid, Sch 9, Group 4, Note (1)(d).

2. The supply of private tuition, in a subject ordinarily taught in a school or university, by an individual teacher acting independently of an employer.
3. [...]
4. [...]
5. [...]
6. Provision of facilities by –
   (a) a youth club or an association of youth clubs to its members; or
   (b) an association of youth clubs to members of a youth club which is a member of that association.

A club is a youth club under VATA 1994 if, among other things it is established to promote the social, physical, educational or spiritual development of its members.

Group 9 – TRADE UNIONS AND PROFESSIONAL BODIES

[...]

1. The supply to its members of such services and, in connection with those services, of such goods as are both referable only to its aims and available without payment other than a membership subscription by any of the following non-profit-making organisations –
   (a) [...]
   (b) [...]
   (c) an association, the primary purpose of which is the advancement of a particular branch of knowledge, or the fostering of professional expertise, connected with the past or present professions or employment of its members.

Note:

(4) Paragraph (c) does not apply unless the association restricts its membership wholly or mainly to individuals whose present or previous professions or employments are directly connected with the purposes of the association.

Group 12 – FUND-RAISING EVENTS BY CHARITIES AND OTHER QUALIFYING BODIES

[...]

1. The supply of goods and services by a charity in connection with a fund-raising event organised for charitable purposes by a charity or jointly by more than one charity.
2. The supply of goods or services by a qualifying body in connection with a fundraising event organised exclusively for its own benefit.[1]

A 'fund-raising event' is defined as meaning a fête, ball, bazaar, gala show, performance or similar event which is separate from, and not forming any part of, a series or regular run of like or similar events.

1 VATA 1994, Sch 9, Group 12.

Table 17: Overview of VAT framework

Rule 1 *VAT charge*	*Rule 2* *Taxable person*	*Rule 3* *Taxable supply*	*Rule 4* *supply*
VAT must be charged on the supply of goods or services in the UK VATA 1994, s 1 VAT must be charged at the rate of 17.5% unless otherwise specified VATA 1994, s 2(1) The supply, in order to be subject to VAT must possess the following characteristics: 1. a taxable supply 2. by a taxable person 3. in the course or furtherance of any business 4. carried on by the person in 3. VATA 1994, s 4(1)	A person who is, or is required to be registered under VATA 1994 VATA 1994, s 3(1) A person is liable to be registered, in general terms, if taxable supplies are in excess of £50,000 VATA 1994, Sch 1 In appropriate circumstances a person who is not liable to be registered can voluntarily seek to become registered. To do this, the person must satisfy the Commissioners that: 1. he makes taxable supplies 2. is carrying on a business and intends to make such supplies in the course or furtherance of that business VATA 1994, Sch 1, para 9	This is a supply of goods or services made in the UK, other than an exempt supply. VATA 1994, s 4(2)	A supply is defined in the Act as including 'all forms of supply, but not anything done otherwise than for consideration' VATA 1994, s 5(2)(a)

Rule 5 *Classification as goods or services*	*Rule 6* *Time of supply*	*Rule 7* *Place of supply of services*	*Rule 8* *Reverse charge*
The Act provides that anything which is not a supply of goods, but is done for consideration is a supply of services VATA 1994, s 5(2)(b) The granting, assignment or surrender of any right, if done for consideration is a supply of services VATA 1994, s 5(2)(b)	Intellectual property, such as a patent is not a supply of goods. The only relevant rule is the time of supply for services A service is supplied at the time when the service is performed VATA 1994, s 6(3)	A supply of services is treated as taking place in the UK where: 1. the supplier belongs in the UK, and 2. not in the UK where the supplier belongs in another country VATA 1994, s 7(10) See also s 9	Where 'relevant services' are supplied by a person who belongs in a country other than the UK, and are received by a person who belongs in the UK for the purposes of any business carried on by him, that person, the recipient, shall be treated as though he had supplied the services in the UK in the course of furtherance of his business. The supply is treated as a taxable supply VATA 1994, s 8(1) A 'relevant service' includes 'Transfers and assignments of ... patents, licences' VATA 1994, Sch 5, para 1

Rule 9 ***Right to credit input tax against output tax***	***Rule 10*** ***Zero-rating***	***Rule 11*** ***Exempt supplies***	***Definitions***
A taxable person is required in respect of supplies made by him to account for and pay VAT in respect of those supplies VATA 1994, s 25(1) The person who is required to account for the VAT on supplies, is entitled to credit for 'so much of his input tax', which is then deducted 'from any output tax that is due from him' VATA 1994, s 25(1) Input tax is VAT which is attributable to supplies made in the course or furtherance of business which are (a) taxable supplies (b) supplies outside the UK which would be taxable supplies if made in the UK (c) such other supplies outside the UK, and such exempt supplies as the Treasury may by order specify VATA 1994, s 26(2)	Where a taxable person supplies goods or services, that would otherwise be charged to VAT on the supply but which are zero-rated no VAT is chargeable on the supply VATA 1994, s 30(1) However the supply is still treated as a taxable supply with the result that the supplier is entitled to credit for his input tax. The rate of VAT on these supplies is nil VATA 1994, s 30(1) Zero-rated supplies are classified in VATA 1994, Sch 8	Where a person makes an exempt supply no VAT is charged on the supply, and there is no right to claim input tax which is attributable to the making of that supply VATA 1994, s 31	'Business' includes any trade, profession or vocation VATA 1994, s 94(1) The Act provides that 'the disposition of a business as a going concern, or of its assets or liabilities (whether or not in connection with its reorganisation or winding up), is a supply made in the course or furtherance of that business' VATA 1994, s 94(6) 'Input tax' means: VAT on the supply to a taxable person of any goods or services used or to be used for the purpose of any business carried on or to be carried on by him VATA 1994, s 24(1) 'Output tax' means VAT on supplies which a taxable person makes VATA 1994, s 24(2)

Chapter 9

ACQUISITION OF GOODS: INTERNAL EUROPEAN UNION TRADE

9.1 INTRODUCTION

VATA 1994 governs the application of tax to the 'acquisition' of goods by businesses in the UK from other Member States of the EU. The tax charged in these circumstances is VAT at the standard rate of 17.5 per cent (1998–99).[1] Acquisitions which are classified as zero-rated goods are subject to a VAT rate of nil.[2] VAT is generally payable only on acquisitions made by businesses. The main exceptions to this rule are where:

(1) non-business users make 'relevant acquisitions', the broad effect of this is to make the non-business user liable to register for VAT purposes and consequently account for VAT on acquisitions; and
(2) where goods acquired are subject to a duty of excise.

The fact that a business recipient of goods is generally required to pay UK VAT on the acquisition of goods from another Member State of the EU does not mean that the UK non-business user escapes the payment of VAT. The non-business recipient of goods will probably pay VAT of the EU country from which the supply is made. This is typically as a result of what are known as the 'distance sale rules'.[3]

Broadly, supplies made to a UK business recipient by another business supplier located in another EU Member State are zero-rated as exports. This enables the supplier in the other EU Member State (ie country of origin) to claim back the VAT incurred by it in acquiring the goods up until the supply of the goods outside his home country. The recipient in the other EU Member State, such as the UK, will then come under a liability to account for VAT on the acquisition. The purpose of this chapter is to illustrate the main fabric of the VAT acquisition framework and to provide illustrations of how it might operate in the context of e-commerce.

1 VATA 1994, s 1.
2 Ibid, s 30(1).
3 See Chapter 12.

9.2 ACQUISITIONS: BUSINESS ACQUISITIONS BY UK TRADER

VAT is charged on the acquisition *in* the UK of goods from other Member States of the EU.[1] The duty to account for VAT in these circumstances is upon the person making the acquisition, and it must be accounted for at the time of the acquisition.[2] VAT is applied to the *value* of the acquisition at the *time* of the acquisition.[3] The VAT incurred as a result of the acquisition rules qualifies as input tax which can be set off against appropriate supplies upon which output tax is received.[4]

9.2.1 Rules

To simplify our understanding of how the VAT on acquisitions framework operates the basic rules of the system are summarised below.

Rule 1: Pre-conditions to a VAT charge on an acquisition
UK VAT is charged on an acquisition from another EU Member State where:[5]

(1) there is a taxable acquisition of goods;
(2) which takes place in the UK;
(3) is otherwise than in pursuance of a taxable supply;[6] and
(4) the person who makes the acquisition is a taxable person; or
(5) the goods are subject to a duty of excise.[7]

Rule 2: Taxable acquisition
VAT only applies to a taxable acquisition. A taxable acquisition occurs where:[8]

(1) it is not an exempt acquisition;[9] and
(2) the goods are acquired in the course or furtherance of
    (i) any business carried on by any person; or
    (ii) any activities carried on otherwise than by way of business by any body corporate or by any club, association, organisation, or other unincorporated body; or
(3) it is the person who carries on that business or, as the case may be, those activities which acquires the goods; and
(4) the supplier:

---

1 VATA 1994, s 1(1)(b).
2 Ibid, s 1(3).
3 Ibid, s 2(1)(b).
4 Ibid, s 24(1)(b). For the meaning and nature of the concepts of 'input' and 'output' tax, see Chapter 8.
5 Ibid, s 10(1).
6 VATA 1994 defines a taxable supply as 'a supply of goods . . . made in the United Kingdom other than an exempt supply' (s 4(2)).
7 Excise Duty is a tax on alcohol, petrol and tobacco.
8 VATA 1994, s 10.
9 VATA 1994 provides that the acquisition of goods from another EU Member State is an exempt acquisition if the goods are acquired in pursuance of an exempt supply (s 31(1)).

(i) is taxable in another Member State at the time of the transaction in pursuance of which the goods are acquired;[1] and
(ii) in participating in that transaction, acts in the course or furtherance of a business carried on by him.

Example 56

X Ltd a UK based business places an order for 20,000 widgets via an electronic commerce system with a French based company called SA. The French company is a taxable person for the purposes of French VAT law. The widgets are acquired by X Ltd for the purposes of a business carried on by it, which is registered for UK VAT purposes. In this situation X Ltd will be required to account for VAT at the standard rate of 17.5 per cent (1998–99) on the goods since the supply is an acquisition from another Member State of the EU. The UK VAT incurred by X Ltd qualifies as input VAT, which can be offset against output VAT obtained from the taxable supplies made by it.

Rule 3: Acquisition of goods from another Member State
This is the acquisition of goods from another Member State of the EU under a transaction in relation to which the following conditions are satisfied:[2]

(1) the transaction is a supply of goods (including anything treated for the purposes of VATA 1994 as a supply of goods); and
(2) the transaction involves the removal of goods from another Member State.

The fact that the removal of the goods from another Member State is under the direction of either the supplier or the person acquiring them is irrelevant.[3] Certain transactions are deemed as a matter of law not to amount to the acquisition of goods from another Member State.[4]

Rule 4: Time of acquisition
VATA 1994 requires VAT on an acquisition of goods from another Member State to be accounted for at the *time of acquisition*.[5] 'Unless otherwise provided for under VATA 1994 where goods are acquired from another Member State, the acquisition shall be treated as taking place on whichever is the earlier of the following:[6]

(a) the fifteenth day of the month following that in which the event occurs, which, in relation to that acquisition, is the first relevant event for the purposes of taxing the acquisition; and

PART IV
VALUE ADDED TAX

1 Broadly, VATA 1994 provides that references to a person being taxable in another Member State means a person who is a taxable person for the purposes of VAT in that Member State (s 92(2)(a)).
2 Ibid, s 11(1).
3 Ibid, s 11(2).
4 See Value Added Tax (Treatment of Transactions) (No 2) Order 1992, SI 1992/3132, and Value Added Tax (Special Provisions) Order 1995, SI 1995/1268. The former relates to the supply of gold to a central bank of a Member State, and the latter Order to VAT paid on supplies which is to be accounted for, and paid in another Member State in accordance with a profit margin scheme.
5 VATA 1994, s 12.
6 Ibid, s 12(1).

(b) the day of the issue, in respect of the transaction in pursuance of which the goods are acquired, of an invoice which is a tax invoice under the law of the EU Member State.'[1]

The 'event' for the purposes of taxing the acquisition is the first removal of the goods. Special rules apply for determining the time of acquisition of warehoused goods,[2] water, gas, power, ventilation and refrigeration.[3]

Example 57

X Ltd a UK based company orders the delivery of one hundred computer systems from a Spanish based company called Y SA. The order is placed by an e-commerce system. The goods are ordered on the 5 June, the date on which an invoice is raised, and removed from Spain in transit to the UK on 12 June. Because an invoice is raised on the 5 June that date is regarded under VATA 1994 as the time of acquisition for the purposes of UK VAT purposes.

Suspending the time of acquisition

There are two broad categories of scheme which exist under VATA 1994 that permit the suspension of the time of acquisition for VAT purposes. These are:

(1) goods subject to a warehousing regime; and
(2) goods subject to a fiscal warehousing regime.

The purpose of these schemes is to suspend the time of acquisition for the purposes of charging VAT. Effectively, when goods pass into a warehousing scheme the goods are deemed to be supplied outside of the UK until the goods leave the warehouse. The operation of these schemes may take place in the context of e-commerce. The nature of fiscal warehousing is examined below. Customs and Excise has published Notice No 702/8/96 which deals specifically with fiscal warehousing.

Effect of fiscal warehousing

VATA 1994 provides that the acquisition of goods which come within the fiscal warehouse scheme are deemed to take place outside of the UK while subject to the scheme.[4] Where the latter rule does not apply and the acquisition is treated as taking place in the UK, the acquisition is treated as taking place when the goods are removed from the fiscal warehousing scheme.[5] VAT must be paid at the time when the goods are removed from the fiscal warehouse.[6] The VAT is the liability of the person who removes the goods.

---

1 See Value Added Tax Regulations 1995, SI 1995/2518, reg 83.
2 See VATA 1994, ss 18 and 18B.
3 See Value Added Tax Regulations 1995, SI 1995/2518, reg 87.
4 VATA 1994, s 18B(3).
5 Ibid, s 18B(4).
6 Ibid, s 18D(2).

Conditions for application of effect of fiscal warehouse scheme
The effect of the fiscal warehouse scheme operates where:[1]

- there is an acquisition of goods from another Member State of the European Union;
- the goods acquired are eligible goods;
- either:
  - (a) the acquisition takes place while the goods are subject to a fiscal warehousing regime; or
  - (b) after the acquisition but before the supply, if any, of those goods which next occurs, the acquirer causes the goods to be placed in a fiscal warehousing regime; and
- the person making the acquisition, not later than the time of the acquisition, prepares and keeps a certificate that the goods are subject to a fiscal warehousing regime.

'Eligible goods' include those within Sch 5A to VATA 1994, and goods upon which import duties have been paid.[2] The goods within Sch 5A are mainly primary resources, such as tin, copper, nickel, cereals, oil seeds, tea, coffee (not roasted), raw sugar, wool, chemicals in bulk, mineral oils, potatoes and vegetable oils.

Rule 5: Place of acquisition
It will be recalled that under Rule 1, UK VAT is only applied to the acquisition of goods *in* the UK from another Member State of the EU. VATA 1994 provides the following rule for determining the place of acquisition.

(1) Goods are treated as acquired in the UK subject to any other provision:[3]
  - (a) if the goods are acquired under a transaction which involves their removal to the UK; and
  - (b) does not involve their removal from the UK; and
  - (c) shall otherwise be treated as acquired outside the UK.

(2) Goods are also treated as acquired in the UK where:[4]
  - (a) they are acquired by a person who for the purposes of their acquisition, makes use of a number assigned to him for the purposes of UK VAT;
  - (b) however (a) shall not require any goods to be treated as acquired in the UK where it is established, in accordance with regulations made by the Commissioners that VAT:
    - (i) has been paid in another Member State on the acquisition of those goods; and
    - (ii) that the VAT fell to be paid by virtue of provisions of the law of that Member State corresponding, to the provision referred to in (1) above made under UK law. In other words, VAT falls to be paid because goods are removed to that Member State.

PART IV
VALUE ADDED TAX

1 VATA 1994, s 18B(1).
2 Ibid, s 18B(6).
3 Ibid, s 13(2).
4 Ibid, s 13(3),(4).

(3) Warehoused Goods – the place of acquisition is altered in various circumstances where goods are transferred within a warehoused scheme permitted under VATA 1994. Relevant schemes are:
    (a) the warehousing regime;[1] and
    (b) fiscal warehousing.[2]

Example 58

X (UK) Ltd, orders via an e-commerce system 100,000 tyres from a German company called Y AG. The tyres are to be delivered in France. On making the order X (UK) Ltd makes use of its UK VAT registration number. In these circumstances there is an acquisition in the UK, unless X (UK) Ltd can show that it has paid VAT in France as the country to which the goods were sent.

Rule 6: Supplies by a UK trader to another trader within the EU

By regulations made under VATA 1994, s 30(8) the removal of goods from the UK which are acquired in another Member State of the EU are zero-rated. The Value Added Tax Regulations 1995 provide that where the Commissioners of Customs and Excise are satisfied that:

(1) a supply of goods by a taxable person involves their removal from the UK;
(2) the supply is to a person taxable in another EU State;
(3) the goods are removed to another EU State;
(4) the goods are not taxed by reference to the profit margin scheme provided for under VATA 1994, s 50A

then the supply, subject to such other conditions as the Commissioners may impose shall be zero-rated.[3] The net effect of this is that a UK taxable person will be able to obtain a full refund of input incurred in making the supply.

Example 59

X Ltd a UK based company, registered for VAT purposes incurs input tax of £50,000 on components which are subsequently supplied to Z Gmbh, based in Germany, which is subject to German VAT. Since the components are supplied to another Member State of the EU, and to a taxable person, the supply will be zero-rated. As a consequence X Ltd will be entitled to retain the input tax of £50,000.

9.3 NON-TAXABLE PERSONS AND ACQUISITIONS

Generally, a person who is not VAT registered, and who as a consequence is not a taxable person is not liable to pay UK VAT on the acquisition of goods from another Member State of the EU. However, there are two exceptions. These are where:

(1) a new means of transport is acquired; or

---

1 VATA 1994, s 18.
2 Ibid, s 18B.
3 Value Added Tax Regulations 1995, SI 1995/2518, reg 134.

(2) goods are acquired that are subject to excise duty.[1]

Another exception exists to the general rule which must be borne in mind. A non-taxable person will be required to pay UK VAT on acquisitions where 'relevant acquisitions' are made. VATA 1994 provides that, if at the end of a calendar month acquisitions exceed £50,000 (1999), that person is liable to register as a taxable person.[2] Customs and Excise must be notified within 30 days of the end of the month in which the threshold is met.[3] A person is also placed under an obligation to register where there are reasonable grounds for believing that he will make relevant acquisitions which shall exceed £50,000 (1999) within 30 days.[4] Such a person must notify Customs and Excise before the end of the 30 day period.[5]

Example 60

X Ltd a UK based company acquires on a regular basis electrical components from Z Gmbh, a company based in Germany. The placing of the order, delivery and payment is facilitated by an e-commerce system. X Ltd is currently not registered under VATA 1994 because it is not a taxable person. X Ltd places orders on a monthly basis. The last order placed was in mid August. The management are aware that it will make an acquisition of £50,000 worth of electrical components within 15 days from the end of August. X Ltd is under a responsibility in these circumstances to notify Customs and Excise for the purposes of registering as a taxable person.

1 See VATA 1994, s 10(1)(c).
2 VATA 1994, Sch 3, para 1(1).
3 Ibid, para 3(1)(a).
4 Ibid, para 1(2).
5 Ibid, para 3(1)(b).

Chapter 10

IMPORTS

10.1 INTRODUCTION

VATA 1994 governs the application of tax to the importation of goods from countries which do not form part of the EU. For example, goods imported from the USA under a transaction entered into via an e-commerce mechanism would be subject to import tax. The tax imposed is VAT, which is charged on the importation of such goods,[1] and is charged and payable as if it were a customs duty.[2] The rate of tax which currently applies to imported goods is the standard rate of 17.5 per cent (1998–99). However, there are exceptions, for example, some goods are exempt from duty, or the rate of tax is nil.[3]

From the 1 January 1993, the time of the creation of the Single European Market, goods which enter into the UK from countries outside the EU are treated as imports. Where goods enter into the UK from another Member State, these supplies to business recipients are treated as acquisitions.[4] VAT is charged upon both types of supply.[5] The VAT liability incurred on the import of goods is placed upon the importer. Where goods are acquired from another Member State the VAT liability is imposed upon the person acquiring the goods.[6]

10.2 ADMINISTRATION OF IMPORT VAT

Import VAT is collected by Customs and Excise. The legal authority for the collection and operation of import VAT is derived from various sources. The primary source of legislation is the Customs and Excise Management Act 1979 ('CEMA 1979') and VATA 1994. Under UK domestic legislation, VATA 1994 is the legal authority for the application of VAT to imports. VATA 1994 provides that the provisions of the CEMA 1979 including subordinate legislation and any EC legislation relating to Community customs duties are to apply to any goods imported from a place outside the Member States for the purposes of VAT.[7]

1 VATA 1994, s 1(1)(c).
2 Ibid, s 1(4).
3 See **10.6**.
4 See Chapter 9.
5 VATA 1994, s 1(1).
6 Ibid, s 1(3).
7 Ibid, s 16.

The scheme of import VAT is additionally governed by an array of secondary legislation known as Statutory Instruments. For example, various forms of relief from import VAT are provided for in the Value Added Tax (Imported Goods) Relief Order 1984.[1] Additional guidance can be obtained from the Customs and Excise manuals, and official notices of practice published by Customs and Excise. The most useful for the purposes of import VAT is Notice No 702 'VAT: Imports and Warehoused Goods'.

10.3 METHOD OF CHARGE AND COLLECTION

Import VAT is paid on the entry of goods into the UK from a country outside the EU. Broadly, goods are declared to Customs and Excise by completing Form C88. Goods subject to a warehousing scheme which operates to suspend the payment of import VAT are declared in a different document. Import VAT is either paid at the time of importation, or under duty deferment arrangements.

10.4 IMPORT VAT AND E-COMMERCE

E-commerce by its very nature facilitates international trade with the UK. The activities of overseas traders may result in the importation of goods into the UK either to domestic consumers or to business consumers who use the import for onward supply to UK consumers or specific export markets. The effect of import VAT is that it may be imposed upon overseas traders who will be required to account for it to Customs and Excise. The following example illustrates how e-commerce may result in import VAT issues arising.

Example 61

Alpha Ltd a UK company places an order via an electronic trading site for the purchase of 100 computers manufactured and sold by Beta Inc, a company based in the USA. Under the terms of the contract of sale, the purchaser agrees to pay all import duties and other taxes arising from the importation of goods. Additionally the effect of the contract of sale is to transfer ownership in the goods as soon as dispatched from the US distribution centre. In these circumstances Alpha Ltd is the importer for the purposes of VAT. Because Alpha Ltd is registered for VAT purposes, the import VAT can be reclaimed as input VAT, against the VAT received on supplies made by Alpha Ltd to UK consumers who purchase the imported computers.

10.5 ELEMENTS OF IMPORT VAT CHARGE

10.5.1 Goods imported from a place outside Member States of the EU

VATA 1994 provides various rules for determining when goods are imported from outside Member States. As a general rule, UK import VAT will apply to goods which

1 SI 1984/746.

arrive in the UK from outside the EU and are entered for home use, or to goods which have been placed in the UK under a customs arrangement, such as customs warehousing and are entered for removal to home use in the UK.[1]

10.5.2 Obligation to pay import duty

CEMA 1979 states that the obligation to pay import duty is upon the importer.[2] No imported goods can be removed or delivered on importation until the importer has paid any duty chargeable, ie VAT.[3] The duty must be paid at the time when the goods make entry into the UK.[4]

10.5.3 Time of payment

CEMA 1979 provides that the duty must be paid by the importer on 'making the entry'.[5]

10.5.4 Time of importation

The time of importation is critical, because this normally equates with when the import VAT is due on goods.[6] In other words, the time of importation is generally the time of 'making the entry' of goods. Unless goods are placed under either: (a) excise warehousing; or (b) a relevant customs arrangement, VAT is due at the time of importation. The time of importation under CEMA 1979[7] is summarised in Table 18.

Table 18: Time of importation

Method of entry	*Time of entry*
Sea	When ship comes within limits of port
Air	When aircraft lands in UK, or goods unloaded in UK (whichever is earlier)

Where goods from a country outside the EU are placed directly into a fiscal warehouse, the time of importation is suspended with the result that the payment of the import VAT is suspended.[8]

10.5.5 Importer: the meaning

CEMA 1979 defines 'importer' as:[9]

> 'in relation to any goods at any time between their importation and the time when they are delivered out of charge, includes any owner or other person for the time being possessed of or beneficially interested in the goods...'

PART IV
VALUE ADDED TAX

1 VATA 1994, s 15(1).
2 CEMA 1979, s 43(1).
3 Ibid, s 43(1).
4 Ibid.
5 Ibid, s 43(1).
6 See HM Customs and Excise Notice No 702, 'VAT: Imports and Warehoused Goods', para 4.1.
7 See s 5 of CEMA 1979.
8 The nature of fiscal warehousing was examined in Chapter 9.
9 CEMA 1979, s 1(1).

Any import duty is accordingly the liability of the importer. The importer may be the vendor or buyer. If title to the goods pass to a UK buyer prior to importation the liability to account for import duty will be upon the buyer. In these circumstances the foreign vendor will not be responsible for any import duty, and there will be no question of such a person being required to be VAT registered in the UK. It is to be noted from the definition that an importer does not actually need to be the owner of the goods.

10.6 RELIEF FROM IMPORT VAT

In some cases, no import VAT is payable on goods imported from a country not a Member State of the EU. The circumstances in which no import VAT is payable are as follows.

10.6.1 Zero-rated imports

Where goods classified in Sch 8 to VATA 1994 are imported into the UK from a place outside the EU, the import VAT charged is nil.[1] The nature of the Sch 8 classifications have been examined more fully elsewhere.[2] Table 19 summarises the goods groupings for which zero-rating is granted insofar as relevant to IT and e-commerce. It must be remembered that there are many exceptions to these classifications. While 'food' appears under Group 1 as zero-rated, it is subject to many excepted goods the supply of which are standard-rated and upon which import VAT would be payable.

Table 19: Summary of zero-rated goods

Zero-rated goods	*Excepted items from group (illustrative examples)*
food used for human consumption	ice cream, confectionery, beverages subject to excise duty
books, brochures, newspapers	plans, drawings for industrial, architectural, engineering, commercial purposes

10.6.2 Goods produced by the United Nations and other UN organisations

No import VAT is payable in respect of goods imported, irrespective of purpose which are produced by the United Nations or by other UN organisations.[3] The goods subject to relief are specified in Sch 1 to the Value Added Tax (Imported Goods) Relief Order 1984. The goods subject to relief include:

- holograms for laser projection;
- multi-media kits;

1 VATA 1994, s 30(3).
2 See Chapter 8.
3 Value Added Tax (Imported Goods) Relief Order 1984, SI 1984/746, art 4.

- materials for programmed instruction, including materials in kit form, with the corresponding printed materials;
- films of an educational, scientific, or cultural character;
- newsreels (with soundtrack).

10.6.3 Capital goods and equipment on transfer of activities from abroad

No import VAT is payable in respect of capital goods and equipment which are imported by a person into the UK for the purposes of a business which he has ceased to carry on abroad, but which he is to carry on in the UK.[1] It is a condition of relief that the business will be used to make exclusively taxable supplies, and that the imported capital goods and equipment were used in the business abroad at least 12 months before cessation of the business.

10.6.4 Goods used for promotion of a trade

The Value Added Tax (Imported Goods) Relief Order 1984 provides that certain goods distributed for the purposes of promotion of a trade are not subject to import VAT.[2] This is an important area of relief because many e-commerce traders will provide free goods, such as samples, as a way of soliciting trade. For example, an overseas trader could offer to send samples to all people providing their details via the trader's Internet business site.

The nature of the import relief given in the context of trade promotion is summarised in Table 20.

Table 20: Trade promotion

Item no	*Scope*
1	Articles of no intrinsic commercial value sent free of charge by suppliers of goods and services for the sole purpose of advertising
2	Samples of negligible value of a kind and in quantities capable of being used solely for soliciting orders for goods of the same kind
3	Printed advertising matter, including catalogues, price lists, directions for use or brochures, which relates to goods for sale or hire by a person established outside the UK, or to transport, commercial insurance or banking services offered by a person established in a third country, and which clearly displays the name of the person by whom the goods or services are offered
4	Goods to be distributed free of charge at an event, as small representative samples, for use or commercial consumption by the public

1 Value Added Tax (Imported Goods) Relief Order 1984, SI 1984/746, art 5, Sch 2, Group 1.
2 Ibid, Group 3.

Item no	Scope
5	Goods imported solely for the purpose of being demonstrated at an event
6	Goods imported solely for the purpose of being used in the demonstration of any machine or apparatus displayed at an event
7	...
8	Catalogues, prospectuses, price lists, advertising posters, calendars (whether or not illustrated), unframed photographs and other printed matter or articles advertising goods displayed at an event, supplied without charge for the purpose of distribution free of charge to the public at such an event

Items 4 to 8 relate to the distribution of goods for the purposes of an 'event'. The term 'event' is defined under the import relief regulations as meaning, among other things:

> '(a) any trade, industrial, agricultural or craft exhibition, fair or similar show or display, not being an exhibition, fair, show or display organised for private purposes in a shop or on business premises with a view to the sale of the goods displayed;'.[1]

10.6.5 Goods for testing

No import VAT is applied to goods imported 'for the purposes of examination, analysis or testing to determine their composition, quality or other technical characteristics, to provide information or for industrial or commercial research.'[2]

10.6.6 Printed material

Various forms of printed material imported from outside the EU are given relief from import VAT. The material relevant in the context of e-commerce/general Internet-based business activity that are given relief are documents sent for the purpose of free distribution to encourage persons to visit foreign countries, and particularly to attend cultural, tourist, trade or religious events.[3]

10.6.7 Material in connection with intellectual property rights

To obtain the protection of intellectual property laws under a national system such as the UK of technical knowledge, or commercial marketing symbols, documentary material must sometimes be submitted to the relevant Registry. Material imported for the purpose of being submitted to bodies competent to deal with protection of copyright and patent rights is not subject to import VAT.[4]

---

1 Value Added Tax (Imported Goods) Relief Order 1984, SI 1984/746, art 5, Sch 2, Group 3.
2 Ibid, Group 4.
3 Ibid, Group 7.
4 Ibid, Group 8, item 1.

10.6.8 Information carriers

No import VAT is payable in relation to recorded media, such as punched cards, sound recordings and microfilm which are sent free of charge for the purposes of transmission of information.[1]

10.6.9 Goods as gifts

No import VAT is payable in respect of goods sent on an occasional basis as gifts in token of friendship or goodwill between bodies, public authorities or groups carrying on an activity in the public interest. This relief does not include goods which are alcoholic beverages or tobacco products.[2]

10.6.10 Goods of limited value

No import VAT is payable in respect of 'any consignment of goods (other than alcoholic beverages, tobacco products, perfumes or toilet waters) not exceeding £18 in value.'[3]

10.6.11 Gifts between individuals

Gifts such as computer software between individuals not in excess of £36 in value (1998–99) imported from a country outside the EU, are not subject to import VAT.[4] The relief only applies to a consignment of goods of a non-commercial character. This is broadly a consignment of goods for no consideration, between individuals, intended solely for personal use by the recipient, or his family, and not for any commercial purpose.

Example 62

Cecil Rhodes sends a parcel containing a computer software program to John Rhodes his cousin who lives in the UK. The software program is a gift for John's son. In these circumstances no import VAT is payable unless the value of the computer software is in excess of £36 (1998–99).

10.6.12 Ring fencing schemes

A number of schemes exist which permit goods to 'enter' into the UK without any import VAT being incurred. These schemes exist to facilitate national trade. The schemes which suspend the obligation to pay VAT in one way or another are as follows:

(1) Goods subject to a customs or excise warehouse scheme.[5]
(2) Goods subject to a free zone.[6]

1 Value Added Tax (Imported Goods) Relief Order 1984, SI 1984/746, art 5, Sch 2, Group 8, item 4.
2 Ibid, item 7.
3 Ibid, item 8.
4 Value Added Tax (Small Non-Commercial Consignments) Relief Order 1986, SI 1986/939, art 3.
5 CEMA 1979, s 46. See generally EC Regulation No 2503/88 and Regulation 2561/90 (Customs Warehouses), and Excise Warehousing Regulations 1988, SI 1988/809.
6 See VATA 1994, s 17, and the Free Zone Regulations 1991, SI 1991/2727.

(3) Temporary importation of commercial vehicles and aircraft.[1]
(4) Goods temporarily imported for removal to another Member State of the EU.[2]

10.7 IMPORT VAT INCURRED ON IMPORTED GOODS FOR BUSINESS PURPOSES

Where a person incurs import VAT on goods, the extent to which the VAT can be reclaimed depends upon the person's status under VATA 1994. If a person is registered for VAT purposes, ie where turnover exceeds £50,000 in a year (1999), such a person is entitled to claim input tax incurred in making taxable supplies under his business activities.[3] That input tax is offset against output tax on those taxable supplies. Any excess of input tax is credited to the person concerned.[4] For the purposes of UK law VAT incurred on imports qualifies as input tax.[5]

Example 63

X Ltd a UK based company incurs import VAT on goods used to make taxable supplies in the UK. The goods are ordered by X Ltd through use of an e-commerce system. In the first quarter of 1998 the company incurs import VAT of £50,000, and makes taxable supplies to UK consumers worth £100,000. VAT at the standard rate of 17.5 per cent (1998–99) means that X Ltd receives output tax of £17,500 from UK consumers. X Ltd is entitled to set £50,000 of input tax against the £17,500 of output tax and to retain £32,500.

10.8 POSTAL IMPORTATION OF GOODS

Many goods purchased through the medium of the Internet, such as videos, computer software and audio tapes will be dispatched via the postal system. The UK has very strict rules on the posting of 'dutiable goods'. Under the Postal Packets (Customs and Excise) Regulations 1986,[6] all dutiable goods, ie goods chargeable with VAT[7] cannot be brought into the UK by post for delivery except:[8]

(1) in a parcel, letter packet, small packet or a datapost packet; or
(2) in a printed packet.

Where a packet or parcel is brought into the UK in this way it must comply with specified requirements under the Regulations.[9] For example, a parcel must have

---

1 See Temporary Importation (Commercial Vehicles and Aircraft) Regulations 1961, SI 1961/1523.
2 See Value Added Tax Regulations 1995, SI 1995/2518, reg 123.
3 VATA 1994, s 26(1),(2).
4 Ibid, s 25(2).
5 Ibid, s 24(1)(c).
6 SI 1986/260.
7 Ibid, reg 2(1).
8 Ibid, reg 6.
9 Ibid, reg 7.

affixed to it, or be accompanied by a customs declaration. The declaration must state the nature, quantity and value of the goods contained within the parcel.[1]

The Regulations permit an appropriate officer of the Post Office to demand payment of any duty on delivering a postal packet.[2] Any payment received is then transferred by the Post Office to Customs and Excise. When a demand for payment is not met, the Post Office with the agreement of Customs and Excise can dispose of the goods contained in the packet in any way it sees fit.[3]

PART IV VALUE ADDED TAX

1 Postal Packets (Customs and Excise) Regulations 1986, SI 1986/260, reg 7(2).
2 Ibid, reg 15(1).
3 Ibid, reg 15(2).

Chapter 11

EXPORT AND REMOVAL OF GOODS FROM THE UK

11.1 INTRODUCTION

The export of goods is broadly the physical transfer of goods from the UK to another country outside the Member States of the EU.[1] The main effect of exporting goods for VAT purposes is that it is normally zero-rated. Where goods are transferred to another Member State of the EU the terminology used is of a 'removal' or 'dispatch' instead of an 'export'. Generally, the transfer of goods to another Member State of the EU qualifies for zero-rating. The broad result of such treatment is that a UK trader registered for VAT purposes qualifies to retain all of its input tax incurred in making that taxable supply. Tax law relating to the export and removal of goods is principally contained in VATA 1994.

11.2 ZERO-RATING OF EXPORT GOODS

Where Customs and Excise are satisfied that goods supplied by a taxable person are exported to a place outside the Member States of the EU, or alternatively that the goods have been shipped as stores on a voyage or flight to an eventual destination outside the UK, or as merchandise for retail sale to people carried on such a voyage or flight, the supply is zero-rated.[2] The Value Added Tax Regulations 1995 provide that the following type of supply is zero-rated, subject to such conditions as Customs and Excise may impose:[3]

> '(a) goods intended for export to a place outside the Member States of the EU which have been supplied otherwise than to a taxable person, to:
> (i) a person not UK resident;
> (ii) a trader who has no business establishment in the UK from which taxable supplies are made; or
> (iii) an overseas authority; and
>
> (b) the goods are exported to a place outside the Member States of the EU.'

1 The Channel Islands are outside of the EU for VAT purposes.
2 VATA 1994, s 30(6).
3 SI 1995/2518, reg 129(1).

11.2.1 Electronically delivered software

Customs and Excise holds the view that software transmitted by telephone or by any other type of data network (ie Internet supplies) will not qualify for zero-rating as an export of goods.[1] This is because the supply of electronic data is regarded as a supply of services.

11.3 PROOF OF EXPORT

To obtain zero-rating a trader will need to satisfy Customs and Excise that goods have in fact been exported from the UK. The evidence necessary to satisfy Customs and Excise that an export has occurred is contained in Notice No 703. For example, in the context of air or sea freight, production of the air waybill or of the shipped bill of lading is appropriate evidence to support a claim for zero-rating.

Example 64

X Ltd a UK based Internet trader, who is registered for VAT purposes sells goods via the Internet. Barbara who is a citizen of the USA places an order via the Internet site of X Ltd from her home state of California. The cost of the goods is £150 which she pays for by credit card. X Ltd dispatches the goods via air freight.

X Ltd will be able to satisfy Customs and Excise that the goods have been exported because it will be in possession of the air waybill. Because the supply is zero-rated it will be able to reclaim the input tax on the supply to Barbara.

11.4 ZERO-RATING OF GOODS REMOVED FROM THE UK TO THE EU

Where goods are removed from the UK, and acquired in another Member State of the EU by a person who is liable to pay VAT on the acquisition in that other Member State, which corresponds to the obligation of a person in the UK to pay acquisition VAT,[2] the supply will be zero-rated.[3] Other conditions may also be imposed before the supply can be zero-rated. Before the supply will be zero-rated, Customs and Excise must have evidence of the removal of the goods from the UK.[4]

Example 65

Y Ltd a UK based Internet trader, who is registered for VAT purposes sells goods via the Internet. Vania who is a citizen of Italy, places an order via the Internet site of Y Ltd from her home city of Naples. Vania carries on business in Italy and the goods are acquired for the purposes of her business. The cost of the goods is £450, which she

1 HM Customs and Excise Notice No 703, section 6.6.
2 See VATA 1994, s 10.
3 Ibid, s 30(8).
4 Ibid.

pays for by credit card. Y Ltd dispatches the goods via air freight. Vania is liable to pay acquisition VAT in Italy. Accordingly, the supply can be zero-rated for UK purposes. For this reason Y Ltd will be entitled to reclaim the input tax incurred upon this supply.

11.5 OTHER MATTERS

The law on exports and VAT is very detailed. This chapter has touched on the basic framework. There are many categories of goods which are zero-rated on export. For example, the export of motor vehicles.[1] Some forms of zero-rating will not apply to e-commerce. For instance, the retail export scheme only applies where the customer makes a purchase in person, and the customer is an 'overseas visitor'.[2]

1 See the Value Added Tax Regulations 1995, SI 1995/2518, regs 132 and 133.

2 See ibid, reg 131.

Chapter 12

VAT AND OVERSEAS TRADERS

12.1 INTRODUCTION

The purpose of this chapter is to pull together the areas of VAT which are directly relevant to the commercial activities of an offshore e-commerce trader. Although an offshore trader may have no physical trading presence within a jurisdiction, such as the UK, or even Europe for the purposes of a direct tax charge, such as corporation tax, it may none the less be subject to VAT laws. The ingredients of the VAT tax charge can be satisfied without the existence of any physical office within the UK.

12.2 PLACE OF SUPPLY OF GOODS

Before a supply can be taxable, it must take place within the UK. The rules relating to place of supply are contained in VATA 1994, and are summarised in Table 21.

Table 21: Place of supply – VATA 1994

Type of supply (Goods)	*Place of supply*	*Reference (VATA 1994)*
Goods not removed from the UK	Goods supplied in the UK	s 7(2)
Goods not removed to the UK	Goods not supplied in the UK	s 7(2)
Goods removed to the UK: 1. under the direction of the supplier 2. the goods are acquired in the UK by a non-taxable person, from another Member State 3. supplier is liable to be registered under VATA 1994, Sch 2, or would be so liable if not registered or liable to be registered under Sch 1 of VATA 1994 4. Sch 4, para 5(1) or 6 to VATA 1994 do not apply	Goods supplied in the UK	s 7(4)
Goods imported from outside the Member States, and the person who supplies them is the person who gives the direction for them to be imported.	Goods supplied in the UK	s 7(6)

PART IV
VALUE ADDED TAX

As Table 21 illustrates, some overseas suppliers are potentially liable to account for VAT to Customs and Excise, because the place of supply is deemed to be within the UK. The following paragraphs explore the liability of offshore traders in more detail.

12.3 IMPORTED GOODS FROM OUTSIDE THE EU

Where goods are imported into the UK under the directions of an overseas supplier the place of supply is the UK. Specifically VATA 1994 provides that where the supply of goods involves them being imported from a place outside the Member States of the EU, and the person who supplies them is the person by whom, or under whose directions, they are so imported the place of supply is the UK.[1] The wording of the place of supply rules should be noted carefully. Place of supply is only in the UK in respect of goods removed from a country outside the Member States of the EU where *the supplier* and *not the customer* directs the importation of the goods.

Example 66

Britannia Ltd places an order via the Internet for the supply of £50,000 worth of goods from a trader, US Inc based in the USA. US Inc arranges for the importation of the goods into the UK. In these circumstances the place of supply of the goods is the UK because the supplier, ie (US Inc) is the person who arranges, ie directs their importation.

12.4 GOODS IMPORTED BY A UK AGENT

Customs and Excise practice provides that where goods are imported for onward supply into the UK, and the value of any other supplies in the UK does not exceed UK registration thresholds, a non-UK trader can appoint an agent, who is VAT registered and resident in the UK, for the purposes of importing on his behalf and supplying the non-UK trader's goods to UK consumers.[2] However, for the arrangement to work the agent must issue tax invoices for the supplies. Additionally, the services of the agent for the non-UK trader will be subject to VAT at the standard rate (17.5 per cent, 1998–99).

The agent is treated as the principal importer and will be required to enter goods into the UK as the importer, and pay any relevant VAT. However, the agent will be able to reclaim any such VAT as input tax, and set it off against the VAT received on the further supply of the goods to the UK consumer.

1 VATA 1994, s 7(6).

2 HM Customs and Excise Notice No 702 'VAT: Imports and Warehoused Goods'.

12.5 VAT REGISTRATION: SUPPLIES BY TRADERS FROM OTHER EU MEMBER STATES

Broadly, a trader in another Member State of the EU is required to register for UK VAT purposes where turnover meets a specified threshold. The requirement to register arises where a person makes 'relevant supplies' which exceed in a year £70,000 in value.[1] A 'relevant supply' is defined as being a supply which:[2]

- involves the removal of goods to the UK by or under the directions of the person making the supply (ie the trader in another EU Member State);
- *does not* involve the installation or assembly of the goods at a place in the UK;
- is a transaction under which goods are acquired in the UK from another Member State of the EU by a person who is not a taxable person (ie a person who is not UK VAT registered);
- is made after 1 January 1993 and in the course or furtherance of a business carried on by the supplier; and
- is neither an exempt supply nor a supply of goods subject to a duty of excise, nor a new means of transport, nor the supply of assets forming part of a business.

12.6 DISTANCE SALES OF GOODS FROM EU MEMBER STATES TO THE UK

The term 'Distance sales' within the EU describes the situation where a supply of goods is made by a taxable person to a consumer who is not a taxable person for the purposes of VAT. In other words, a non-taxable person is an individual or company who is not required to account for VAT.

Where a taxable person in another Member State of the EU makes a supply of goods to a non-taxable person in the UK the supply is treated as taking place in the UK under the distance sales rules where:[3]

- the supply of goods involves their removal to the UK by or under the directions of the person who supplies them (ie an EU trader);
- the supply is a transaction under which the goods are acquired in the UK from another Member State of the EU by a person who is not a taxable person;
- the supplier (ie the EU trader) is liable to be registered under Sch 2 to VATA 1994 (value of supplies exceed £70,000), or would be so liable to be registered if he were not already registered under Sch 1; and
- the supply is not a supply of goods consisting in a new means of transport.

Broadly, traders in other Member States of the EU will be required to register for VAT purposes where supplies exceed £70,000. Once this threshold is met the place of supply of goods becomes the UK as a result of the rules outlined above. Until this threshold is met the non-UK, but EU trader will continue to charge VAT on the supply according to the rate prevailing in their own country (ie country of origin). EU traders

1 VATA 1994, Sch 2, para 1(1).
2 Ibid, Sch 2, para 10.
3 Ibid, s 7(4).

must pay close attention to the volume of supplies to other EU Member States. If relevant thresholds are met, this will result in VAT having to be accounted for in another EU Member State (ie country of destination) as a result of distance selling rules.

Example 67

Z SA operates an Internet trading site and sells goods via this medium. Isabelle, based in the UK places an order via the Internet site for the supply of goods. Z SA has a gross turnover of £100,000 in respect of Internet derived trade from the UK. In these circumstances the Spanish trader would be liable to be registered as a taxable person, supplies of this nature would be deemed to take place in the UK with the result that UK VAT must be accounted for by Z SA to Customs and Excise.

12.7 REPRESENTATIVE OFFICE

An overseas trader is unlikely to have any physical representation in the country to which it makes supplies via the medium of e-commerce. However, it is clear that a person who makes supplies to the UK is required once a specific threshold is met to register for VAT purposes. Customs and Excise has the power to order, or an EU trader can request, the appointment of a person within the UK as that EU trader's VAT representative for UK purposes.[1] Broadly, once appointed the representative becomes responsible for his principal's VAT responsibilities in the UK. Effectively the representative must ensure the principal discharges his VAT liabilities and compliance obligations under VATA 1994. Where a UK representative fails in discharging these obligations, he will be held jointly and severally liable with the principal.

12.8 DISTANCE SALES FROM THE UK TO ANOTHER EU MEMBER STATE

Where a UK trader makes supplies of goods to another Member State of the EU, to a non-taxable person VATA 1994 provides that the place of supply will not be the UK in the following circumstances:[2]

- the supply of goods involves the removal of the goods, by or under the directions of the person who supplies them (ie by the UK trader) to another Member State of the EU; and
- the person who makes the supply is taxable in another Member State of the EU (ie the UK trader is subject to VAT in the country the goods are supplied to by the trader, the country of destination) under rules comparable to those where a trader in another Member State of the EU makes distance sales to a non-taxable person in the UK (ie under Sch 2).

1 VATA 1994, s 48.
2 Ibid, s 7(5).

Where the place of supply is outside of the UK, the place of supply will effectively be the country within the EU to which the goods are dispatched. In other words, the UK trader will be required to account for VAT under the rules of that other country and not those of the UK. If the UK trader is not responsible for the removal of the goods from the UK, or is not taxable in the other Member State of the EU, this will mean that the place of supply will be in the UK.[1] Effectively until a UK trader meets the EU threshold for registration in another country, UK VAT will continue to be charged.

Each Member State of the EU has the option of applying a distance selling threshold of either: (a) 35,000 ECU; or (b) 100,000 ECU (about £71,000). The UK applies the 100,000 ECU threshold. Some countries, such as Belgium and Ireland, have indicated that they will apply the 35,000 ECU threshold.

Example 68

UK Goods Ltd makes a supply of goods to Zorro who is a non-taxable person in Spain for VAT purposes. The value of the goods is £500 and UK Goods Ltd is responsible for the delivery of the goods to Spain. Supplies to Spain do not exceed more than £20,000 each year. UK Goods Ltd is not liable to pay Spanish VAT. UK Goods Ltd is not required to account for Spanish VAT, because it does not make supplies which render it liable for VAT purposes. However, the supply may be subject to UK VAT. This is because UK Goods Ltd is a taxable person and the place of supply will be deemed to be the UK.[2]

12.9 COMPLIANCE

The application of VAT to e-commerce raises a number of potential compliance problems. An overseas trader must establish systems which enable the trader to identify accurately and to the satisfaction of tax authorities precisely what type of supplies are made. As Table 22 illustrates, a UK overseas trader must monitor the recipient of goods. An EU recipient who is a non-taxable person must pay UK VAT, but a taxable person who receives goods is not required to pay UK VAT, but must instead account for acquisition VAT under his own country's VAT system. Other problems exist. Within the EU the UK supplier must monitor the monetary value of supplies it makes to other EU countries. If it exceeds specific monetary thresholds the UK supplier must account for VAT under the system of that EU Member State.

1 VATA 1994, s 7(7).
2 Ibid.

Table 22: Compliance and VAT

Event	*Tax*
Supply to UK from outside EU	Import VAT
Supply from EU to UK non-taxable person	EU Member State VAT, but supplies in excess of £70,000 subject to UK VAT
Supply from UK to EU country non-taxable person	UK VAT, but in excess of relevant threshold subject to EU VAT
Supply from UK to EU country taxable person	UK zero-rated, and taxable as acquisition in EU Member State
Supply from EU to UK taxable person	UK acquisition and zero-rated in EU Member State

Chapter 13

CUSTOMS DUTY[1]

13.1 INTRODUCTION

Customs duty is levied upon goods, which must be declared[2] at the point of entry into the EU.[3] The goods are physically present; by whatever means, whether electronic or not, that has been used to obtain them from wherever.[4] The customs officer must categorise them by reference to the Common Customs Tariff.[5] This is effected by reference to the 99 chapters of the combined nomenclature ('CN'), which attempts to describe every category of goods that may be traded.[6] Customs duties attach the goods *in rem* and are *ad valorem*, subject to any preference, quota, relief or suspension.

Community customs duty is defined by Pt II, Sch 1 to the European Communities Act 1972 as '... such duty of customs as may from time to time be fixed for ... goods by directly applicable Community provisions as the duty charge will on the importation into member states'. Thus, the substantive charge is directly applied from EU legislation, in particular the Customs Code[7] which establishes the basic rules and principles which must be used in conjunction with a Commission regulation, which lays down provisions for its implementation – that is say, detailed rules and procedures.[8] The collection of customs duty is administered by the Commissioners of Customs and Excise[9] and, generally speaking, their decisions may be subject to appeal

1 This chapter was written by Robin Mathew QC.

2 Community Customs Code Regulation (EEC) 2454/93 (OJ 1993 L253/1), Arts 198 *et seq*. As to computerised declarations, see Arts 222 to 224 as amended by Council Regulation (EEC) 3665/93 (OJ 1993 L335/1).

3 Community Customs Code Regulation (EEC) 2913/92 (OJ 1992 L302/1) Arts 37 and 38: 'goods' means products which can be valued in money and are capable of forming the subject of commercial transaction: see Art 23 of the EC Treaty; and Case 7/68 *Commission of the European Communities v Italy* [1968] ECR 423.

4 See generally the Press Release 'Electronic Commerce: UK Policy on Taxation Issues' *Simon's Taxation Intelligence* (Butterworths, 1998), p 1436 – in particular paras 31–34 on customs duties, which are less than informative.

5 Common Customs Tariff Regulation (EEC) 2658/87 (OJ 1987 L256/1), Art 4(1) on the tariff and statistical nomenclature (see below) and the common customs tariff as amended: see also Regulation (EEC) 2913/92 (OJ 1992 L302/1), Art 20(3).

6 Each chapter is by reference to the material of which the goods are made. The chapters have headings and subheadings. The degree of processing to goods sets the order of each chapter. There are explanatory chapter notes, heading notes and subheading notes which are legally binding. The CN is in tabular form.

7 Regulation (EEC) 2913/92 (OJ 1992 L302/1).

8 Community Customs Code, Regulation (EEC) 2454/93 (OJ 1993 L258/1) as amended by Regulation (EC) 3665/93 (OJ 1993 L335/1).

9 Customs and Excise Management Act 1979, s 6.

(after statutory review)[1] to the VAT and Duties Tribunal and possibly to the ECJ on matters of categorisation or interpretation, pursuant to Art 234 of the EC Treaty. Penalties, methods of enforcement and such procedures are matters for local (ie domestic) enactment for as long as they are compatible with the substantive principles of Community law.[2] In the UK, these are primarily found in the Customs and Excise Management Act 1979, as amended.[3]

The challenge posed by the creation of the customs union of the EU, is to ensure uniform and consistent application of the rules.[4] There is a complete prohibition on customs duties on imports between Member States of the EU. Article 25 of the EC Treaty banned collateral charges having the equivalent effect to customs duty. Thus, the customs law of the EU is administered by domestic authorities, who have the duty of consistent administrative practice and ensuring that anomaly, weakness or inefficiency do not distort trade patterns.

13.2 THE CHARGE TO DUTY

Three factors have to be considered upon the imposition of customs duty.

(1) The goods must be accurately classified in terms of the CN.
(2) The origin of the goods must be satisfactorily established as many Community measures may apply on the basis of their origin.
(3) The goods must be valued (obviously, for *ad valorem* duty).

It must also be remembered that the tariff classification governs the application of not only customs duty, but also other trade measures such as quantitative restrictions on imports or quota, anti-dumping duties, preferential tariff rating, export refunds and suspension of custom duties[5] (including the application of inward and outward processing relief).

Once goods from third countries, countries outside of the EU, have satisfactorily been imported into the EU,[6] they are then said to be in 'free circulation' in any particular Member State. Such goods may be transferred from one Member State of the EU to another without hindrance. Of course, free circular means that the goods are not in, or have been satisfactorily taken from, a bonded warehouse.

It should be noted that if the goods come from a country with which the EU has an arrangement for the provision of preferential duty[7] treatment (for goods of that

---

1 Finance Act 1994, ss 15 and 16; and Value Added Tax Tribunal Rules 1986, SI 1986/590, as amended; and see **13.3**, note 5, below.

2 Case 181/84 *R v Intervention Board for Agricultural Produce ex parte ED&F Man (Sugar) Ltd* [1985] ECR 2889. See also, Case 52/77 *Leonce Cayrol v Giovanni Rivoiri & Figli* [1977] ECR 2261.

3 See Pt XI of the 1979 Act.

4 For instance, Case 353/93 *Neckerman Versand AG v Hauptzollamt Frankfurt am Main Öst* [1994] ECR 1–4027 at para 5; and Case 114/80 *Dr Ritter GmbH & Co* [1981] ECR 895.

5 Regulation (EEC) 2658/87 (OJ 1987 L256/1) and see 'Taric' below.

6 Regulation (EEC) 2913/92 (OJ 1992 L302/1) Art 37 having been satisfactorily presented to the customs officer: Arts 42–45; ibid, and Arts 59–78, ibid, and Arts 198–253 of Regulation (EEC) 2454/93 (OJ 1993 L253/1).

7 See Art 20(3)(d) of Regulation (EEC) 2913/92 (OJ 1992 L302/1). Legal certainty being the objective: Case 388/90 *Hamlin Electronics v Hauptzollamt Darmstradt* [1992] ECR I–2333.

description in the CN) then such a preference would not be given until goods comply with the CN categorisation and satisfactory evidence of origin has been supplied.[1] Special rules apply where goods have been produced in more than one country.[2]

13.3 COMMON PROBLEMS

Common difficulties for importers are among the following:

(1) Whether the tariff classification by reference to the description in the CN is correct.[3]
(2) Whether the goods exactly comply with the description in a Binding Tariff Information[4] which has been issued by a competent customs authority.
(3) Whether the origin of goods is truly the origin upon the certificate (with the consequence, for example, that the goods are entitled to the benefit of the generalised system of preferences).[5]
(4) Whether identical or similar goods are receiving different treatment by different customs authorities within the EU.[6]
(5) Whether goods fall foul of quota[7] or anti-dumping restrictions. Such a question usually involves substantiating the origin of the goods and consideration of the integrity of documentation.[8]
(6) Whether the 'transaction value'[9] of goods should include or should not include other collateral terms and conditions relating to the sale or use of the goods.
(7) Whether customs duty which was undercharged or not collected may be recovered or the amount of any penalties, and forfeiture[10] of goods.

13.4 CLASSIFICATION OF GOODS

The basis of the CN is the Harmonised System ('HS') administered by the World Customs Organisation (formerly known as the Customs Co-operation Council). The

1 Article 47 of Regulation (EEC) 2454/93 (OJ 1993 L253/1) for contents required of a Certificate of Origin. For Community produced goods see, ibid, Art 48.
2 Ibid, Arts 69–74.
3 See notes to Example 69 given at **13.5** below.
4 Article 6 of Regulation (EEC) 2454/93 (OJ 1992 L302/1); and Art 243 of Regulation (EEC) 2913/92 (OJ 1993 L302/1). Customs Reviews and Appeals (Tariff and Origin) Regulations 1997, SI 1997/534.
5 Article 66 *et seq* of Regulation (EEC) 2454/93 (OJ 1992 L302/1) as amended by Regulation (EC) 12/97 (OJ 1997 L911).
6 See **13.1** (p 192), note 3, above.
7 Community procedue for administering quantitative quotas Regulation (EC) 520/94 (OJ 1994 L66/1). As to implementing measures, see Regulation (EC) 738/94 (OJ 1994 L87/47) as amended by Regulation (EC) 1150/95 (OJ 1995 L116/3).
8 See Art 47 of Regulation (EEC) 2454/93 (OJ 1993 L253/1), and also Art 20(3)(d) of Regulation (EEC) 2913/92 (OJ 1992 L302/1).
9 See **13.7** *et seq*, below.
10 Schedule 3 to the Customs and Excise Management Act 1979; and see **13.10** *et seq* below.

HS has been established since 1 January 1988 and is the worldwide system of goods classification. The common customs tariff (including the statistical nomenclature) sets out not only the basic rules and procedures for classification, but by an Annex contains the CN which applies only in the EU. The CN is an eight digit code of which the first six digits are based on the HS and the remainder are described under 'Taric', see **13.6**. The CN is updated by an annual Commission Regulation.

There are a number of aids and rules to interpretation. These are:

(1) the case-law of the ECJ;
(2) the general rules for the interpretation of the CN;[1]
(3) the Explanatory Notes of the HS;[2]
(4) the Explanatory Notes of the CN;[3] and
(5) a formal, binding clarification by the Nomenclature Committee which is issued as a Commission Regulation[4] (the Nomenclature Committee being composed of delegates of Member States under the chairmanship of the Commission: Art 7 of Regulation (EEC) 2658/87 of 23 July 1987).

The HS Explanatory Notes are not legally binding as a source of interpretation but are authoritative according to the ECJ. The CN Explanatory Notes may be referential to the HS Explanatory Notes, but do not take the place of them and are regarded as complementary and to be used in conjunction with them.

13.5 ELECTRONIC GOODS

Both the HS and the CN have been outpaced by scientific advance in terms of the description, which they give, of computers and allied electronic equipment (usually described as automatic data processing machines).[5] The Explanatory Notes of the HS and CN have proved of little assistance. Categorisation has often concerned the purpose to which the goods have been put, rather than their objective and verifiable characteristics which is the fundamental test laid down by the ECJ for appraisal of goods by an EU customs authority.[6]

---

1 Section 1A of Pt I of Annex I to Regulation (EEC) 2658/87 (OJ 1987 L256/1) as amended by Regulation (EC) 2086/97 (OJ 1997 L317/1). The chapter and heading notes of the CN must be heeded: Case 38/75 *Douaneagent de NV Nederlandse Sporswegen v Inspecteur de Invoerrechten* [1975] ECR 1439, para 22.

2 Case 183/85 *Hauptzollamt Itzehoe v HS Reperning GmbH* [1986] ECR 1873 established that they are of a 'consultative nature only' (ie valid aids to interpretation if of no legal force): see also Case 35/93 *Develop Dr Eisbein GmbH & Co v Hauptzollamt Struttgart West* [1993] ECR 1–2655.

3 They are an important factor in interpretation but do not modify the headings: Case 149/73 *Otto Witt KG v Hauptzollamt Hamburg-Ericus* [1973] ECR 1587.

4 They do not have retrospective effect: Case 40/84 *Casteels PVBA v The Commission* [1985] ECR 667.

5 See Note 5(A) to Chapter 84 set out at **13.5** below.

6 See, for instance: Case 114/80 *Dr Ritter GmbH & Co v Oberfinanzdirektion Hamburg* [1981] ECR 895: Case C353/93 *Neckerman Vensand AG v Hauptzollamt Frankfurt am alfaia-Ost* [1994] ECR 1–4027; and some VAT and Duties Tribunal cases such as *International Computers Limited v Customs and Excise* (1995) Value Added Tax and Duties Reports 459; and *Videotron Corporation Ltd v Customs and Excise* (C00016 – 24 June 1996, unreported) and as an early but accurate and wise consideration of Chapter 85 of the CCT see *Tratec UK Ltd v Customs and Excise* (1995) Value Added Tax and Duties Reports 72.

Example 69

Startronics Ltd imports advanced electronic machines from the manufacturer in the US. By letter, Startronics Ltd requested a Binding Tariff Information (BTI) in respect of these machines. Unexpectedly, the machines are categorised differently than earlier models and at a higher *ad valorem* customs duty rate. Startronics Ltd appeals to the VAT and Duties Tribunal, after a statutory review by Customs and Excise has upheld the original decision. The issue is whether the machines are powerful, advanced, independent automatic data processors within heading CN 8471 (in particular, CN heading 8471 41 00) or an apparatus used to facilitate the transmission of data within a computer network within heading CN 8517 (in particular CN 8517 50 90). The pertinent CN headings are set out below. At the appeal, the chairman of the Tribunal is assisted by a lay assessor or expert in electronic machinery. Expert evidence is led by the Crown and the importer. Both experts are cross-examined. The CN headings are interpreted according to ECJ decisions (for instance, that the use to which goods are put is irrelevant unless that use is mentioned in the CN heading[1] and that the test is on objective and verifiable assessment of the goods). Reference is also made to the general interpretative rules and the Explanatory Notes of both the CN and the HS. The Tribunal gives a written decision on facts and law. If Startronics Ltd loses then it may take an appeal into the High Court on a point of law[2] (a perverse finding of material fact may equate to a point of law). In any event Customs and Excise may refer the result to the Nomenclature Committee.[3]

CN heading 8471 provides (in part):

> '8471 00 00 00/80 Automatic data processing machines and units thereof; magnetic or optical readers, machines, for transcribing data onto data media in coded form and machines for processing such data not elsewhere specified or included:
>
> 8471 41 00 00/10 Other digital automatic data-processing machines:'

CN heading 8517 provides (in part):

> '8517 00 00 00/80 Electrical apparatus for line telephony or line telephony, including line telephone sets with cordless handsets and telecommunication apparatus for carrier—current line systems or for digital line systems; videophones:
>
> 8517 50 00 00/80 Other apparatus for carrier-current line systems or for digital line systems:
>
> 8517 50 90 00/80 Other'

For the purposes of Chapter 84, the following heading and subheading notes are pertinent. The most significant only are reproduced.

> **'NOTES**
>
> 5(A) For the purposes of heading no 8471, the expression "automatic data processing machines" means:
>
> (a) digital machines, capable of

1 See Note 5(A) *et seq* to Chapter 84 set out below.
2 Tribunals and Enquiries Act 1992, s 11(1).
3 Established by Art 2 of Regulation (EEC) 2658/87 (OJ 1987 L256/1).

PART IV
VALUE ADDED TAX

(1) storing the processing program or programs and at least the data immediately necessary for the execution of the program;
(2) being freely programmed in accordance with the requirements of the user;
(3) performing arithmetical computations specified by the user; and
(4) executing, without human intervention, a processing program which requires them to modify their execution, by logical decision during the processing run;

(b) analogue machines capable of simulating mathematical models and comprising at least: analogue elements, control elements and programming elements;
(c) hybrid machines consisting of either a digital machine with analogue elements or an analogue machine with digital elements.

(B) Automatic data-processing machines may be in the form of systems consisting of a variable number of separate units. Subject to paragraph (E) below, a unit is to be regarded as being a part of a complete system if it meets all of the following conditions:

(a) it is of a kind solely or principally used in an automatic data processing system;
(b) it is connectable to the central processing unit either directly or through one or more other units; and
(c) it is able to accept or deliver data in a form (codes or signals) which can be used by the system.

(C) Separately presented units of an automatic data processing machine are to be classified in heading no 8471.

(D) Printers, keyboards, X-Y co-ordinate input devices and disk storage units which satisfy the conditions of paragraphs (B)(b) and (B)(c) above, are in all cases to be classified as units of heading No 8471.

(E) Machines performing a specific function other than data processing and incorporating or working in conjunction with an automatic data processing machine are to be classified in the headings appropriate to their respective functions or, failing that, in residential headings.

...

A machine which is used for more than one purpose is, for the purposes of classification, to be treated as if its principal purpose were its sole purpose.

...

Subheading notes

1. For the purpose of subheading 8471 49, the term "systems" means automatic data processing machines whose units satisfy the conditions laid down in note 5(B) to Chapter 84 and which comprise at least a central processing unit, one input unit (for example, a keyboard or a scanner), and one output unit (for example, a visual display unit or a printer).'

The language used in the CN code with regard to electronics goods can also be particularly difficult. As mentioned above, this is exacerbated by the rapid changes in technology and the development of new products. The basic description is that a computer is a sophisticated electronic device which automatically processes data in accordance with instructions (or established programs). Computer systems may be described as being of three different types according to the method used to process data: digital, analog or hybrid. As has been seen, the classification terms are considered in the heading 'automatic data processing machines and units thereof', CN heading 8471. The conditions for inclusion of each type of automatic data processing machine are found in the HS notes and in Chapter 84. The relevant notes set out that a digital data processing system (under CN heading 8471) must be capable of fulfilling simultaneously a number of conditions. These are:

(1) storing the processing program (or the data immediately necessary for execution of the program);
(2) being freely programmed in accordance with instructions of the user;
(3) performing arithmetical computations as instructed; and
(4) executing a processing program (without human intervention, which requires it to modify its execution by logical decision during the processing run).

A digital data processing machine usually consists of a number of individual interconnected units which form a system. And the HS notes define this as being:

(1) a central processing unit;
(2) an input unit; and
(3) an output unit.

Each individual unit of the system has its own heading in the tariff and consequently cannot be classified under a single tariff heading (with the exception of laptop computers with different specifications).

13.6 TARIC

Mention should be made of the Taric which is the name given to the integrated tariff of the EU.[1] The Taric is based on the CN and lists the usual customs duty rates which apply to imports from third countries as well as preferences, suspensions and anti-dumping measures or quota restrictions that may apply to goods of a particular description. The first eight digits are the CN code whilst the ninth digit is reserved for Member State national statistical subdivision and the tenth and eleventh are Taric digits which codify specific Community measures applicable to the goods.

13.7 VALUATION

Once the categorisation exercise is complete then the issue of valuation for custom duty purposes arises.[2] This legislation is based on the General Agreement on Tariffs and Trade ('GATT') customs valuation code, which, of course, applies worldwide.

Subject to certain special valuation rules for carrier media in data processing machines,[3] the primary rule for determining the customs value of imported goods is

---

1 Article 2 of Regulation (EEC) 2658/87 (OJ 1987 L256/1); and Commission of the EC 'Integrated Tariff of the EC' (OJ 1998 L115/1).

2 Article 29 of Regulation (EEC) 2913/92 (OJ 1992 L302/1), and see Case 65/85 *Hauptzollamt Hamburg-Ericus v Van Houten International GmbH* [1986] ECR 447.

3 See **13.8** below, and Art 167 of Regulation (EEC) 2454/93 (OJ 1993 L253/1).

the 'transaction value'. This is the price actually paid or payable for the goods when sold for export into the EU, with certain adjustments. Each element in the definition of 'transaction value' has to be examined:

- 'price actual paid or payable' is the total payment made or to be made by the buyer to, or for the benefit of, the seller for the imported goods. If the buyer pays a third party then that is indirect payment. Activities such as marketing which are undertaken by the buyer at his own cost are not relevant even if agreed with the seller.[1]
- 'sold'. There must be actual sale – that is to say, purchase for consideration.
- 'for export to the customs territory' means the goods must be sold for export to the territory of the EU and the presentation to the customs officer (for determination of the correct CN heading or categorisation) indicates they have been sold for export and the last sale, in any series of sales, is the pertinent sale for valuation purposes and it is that price which may be paid or payable which constitutes the transaction value. If a prior sale is the true sale in terms of export to the EU, then that is the sale which must be taken as the 'transaction value'.[2]

The adjustments to 'transaction value' are to reflect the terms of the transaction between the buyer and the seller and these are to be included in the price if they are not incurred by the buyer.[3]

(1) Commissions (excluding a buying commission), brokerage and the cost of containers and packing (whether of labour or materials).
(2) Obligations undertaken by a buyer to the seller in connection with the manufacture and sale of the goods (for instance, the provision of materials or components).
(3) Payment of licence of royalty fees from patents, know-how, designs etc, which are pertinent to the goods and payable by the buyer. There must be a legal obligation to pay, of course.
(4) The value of the proceeds of any subsequent re-sale or use of the goods directly or indirectly which accrues to the seller.
(5) The costs of transport, insurance to the place of introduction into the territory of the EU (pertinent place being the land frontier when goods are imported by air).

Costs incurred by a buyer once the goods have been imported are not included in the customs value (the same applies to other such charges).

Where the customs value cannot be determined under the rules described so far, there are four methods (method (3) and method (4) may be reversed if the importer so requests) of secondary valuation.

(1) The transaction value of identical goods sold for export to the EU and exported at or about the same time as the goods being valued.

---

1 Case 299/90 *Hauptzollamt Karlsruhe v Geber Hepp GmbH & Co KG* [1991] ECR 1–4801. Costs relating to the acquiring export quotas are not part of the transaction value: Case 7/83 *Ospig Textilgesellschaftg KG W Ahlers v Hauptzollamt Bremen – Ust* [1984] ECR 609.

2 Article 31 of Regulation (EEC) 2913/92 (OJ 1992 L302/1).

3 Ibid, the exact rules are set out in Arts 29 *et seq*: see also Annex 23 of Regulation (EEC) 2454/93 (OJ 1993 L253/1).

(2) The transaction value of similar goods sold for export to the EU and exported at or about the same time as the goods being valued.
(3) The value based on the unit price at which the imported goods for identical or similar imported goods are sold within the EU in the greatest aggregate quantity to persons not related to the sellers.
(4) The computed value consisting of the sum of the costs of material used in the manufacture (including containers and packaging), profits and usual general expenses for producers in the exporting country concerning goods of the same kind for export to the EU and the cost of transport, insurance, loading and handling associated with the transport.[1]

There may be no identifiable 'transaction value' because of the restrictions on free disposal of the goods by the buyer (and so their value being materially affected). When the buyer and seller are related, then the importer will have to demonstrate that his relationship did not influence the price and that the 'transaction value' must be accepted as the customs value. This is usually done by approximation to the transaction value of unrelated sales concerning identical or similar goods.[2]

If none of the criteria mentioned to find the 'transaction value' can be applied then the customs authority is entitled to determine the value according to any 'reasonable means' on the basis of data available in the EU statistical base, but it must be in a manner consistent with the GATT customs valuation code and the EU Customs Code.

13.8 SPECIAL VALUATION RULES FOR DATA PROCESSING EQUIPMENT

By Art 34 of the Customs Code, certain carrier media for use in data processing equipment are excepted from the provisions of Art 29 to 34 of the Customs Code.[3] Article 167 of the implementing regulation[4] reads as follows:

> '1. Notwithstanding Articles 29 to 33 of the Code, in determining the customs value of imported carrier media bearing data or instructions for use in data processing equipment, only the cost or value of the carrier medium itself shall be taken into account. The customs value of imported carrier media bearing data or instructions shall not, therefore, include the cost or value of the data or instructions, provided that such cost or value is distinguished from the cost or value of the carrier medium in question.
>
> 2. For the purposes of this Article –
>
> (a) the expression "carrier medium" shall not be taken to include integrated circuits, semiconductors and similar devices or articles incorporating such circuits or devices;
> (b) the expression "data or instructions" shall not be taken to include sound, cinematographic or video recordings.'

1 Article 30(2)(a), (b), (c), (d) of Regulation (EEC) 2913/92 (OJ 1992 L302/1).
2 Ibid, Art 31.
3 See the 'transaction value' described at **13.7**, above.
4 Regulation (EEC) 2454/93 (OJ 1993 L253/1).

Thus, in determining the customs value of imported carrier media or computer hardware bearing data or instructions for use in data processing equipment, only the cost or value of the carrier medium itself is taken into account. The phrase 'carrier medium' is not to be taken to include integrated circuits or similar equipment which incorporates such circuits or devices[1] (that is to say, silicon chips and printed circuits). The customs value does not include, on such goods, the cost or value of the data or instructions on imported equipment provided the cost or value can be distinguished.

There appears to be no ECJ case-law on this provision at the time of writing.

13.9 INWARD AND OUTWARD PROCESSING RELIEF

Two special customs regimes which may be significant in the manufacture and development of electronic machines are inward processing relief[2] and outward processing relief.[3] These cumbersome titles describe a beneficial regime for those who make temporary imports of goods, into the EU, for the processing (for instance, adaptation, further manufacture or, say repair) and, conversely, arrangements to enable EU traders who have goods processed by having a product manufactured outside the EU and to export the goods for that processing. The former regime provides that the goods are exempted from payment, on import, provided that they are exported once the processing has been completed. Outward processing means that the customs duty on importation of the finished product (known as the compensating product) is reduced to an amount corresponding to the duty, which would have been payable on the importation of those goods if they had been directly imported. Both reliefs involve some complex form filling, and conditions, and are given by the customs authorities of the relevant EU Member State. The policy considerations are the interests of traders within the EU undertaking such processing work. Inward processing relief is aimed at promoting exports from the EU. These provisions, of course, are not applicable to intra-EU trade. Outward processing relief applies to all EU goods other than those whose export gives rise to repayment or remission of import duties or which prior to export were released for free circulation with total relief from import duties (because of their end use, but only so long as conditions granted such relief continue to apply or whose export gives rise to the grant of export refunds or in respect of which a financial advantage arises other than refunds under the Common Agricultural Policy ('CAP')).

13.9.1 Inward processing

The application of this procedure is authorised by the domestic customs authorities of the Member State of the EU where the inward processing takes place. There are three conditions:[4]

---

1 See Art 167(2)(a) of Regulation (EEC) 2454/93 (OJ 1993 L253/1).

2 Article 114 of Regulation (EEC) 2913/92 (OJ 1992 L302/1).

3 Ibid, Art 145, and for an example: Case 49/82 *Commission of European Communities v The Netherlands* [1983] ECR 1195.

4 Article 117 of Regulation (EEC) 2913/92 (OJ 1992 L302/1).

(1) The applicant must be established in the EU.
(2) The goods imported must be identified in the compensating product. There is some relaxation in the strict application of this rule (ie where it is impracticable to distinguish between the origin of components).
(3) The economic interests of EU traders or producers are not adversely affected.

The economic conditions are qualified according to the nature of the work (ie repairs, adjustments and presentation, etc are of little economic importance). Another condition would be that there are no comparable goods produced in the EU or there are too few or that comparable EU goods cannot be supplied within an appropriate time. If the EU goods are too expensive or of inadequate quality or specification then that is significant. Finally, the applicant must obtain at least 80 per cent of his requirements for components from EU traders. These conditions are not strict and may be mitigated in certain circumstances.[1] There are other special rules (for instance, the equivalent compensation, prior exportation and triangular traffic rules) which do not merit detailed consideration in this outline. But they may apply to all kinds of imported components or to a situation where opportunities exist for the export of compensating products where, for instance, there are quota restrictions.

13.9.2 Outward processing[2]

As mentioned above, the regime is a converse of inward processing. It entitles EU traders to export components temporally for processing outside the EU and subsequently to import the compensating product (with total or partial relief from import duty).

It is a restricted regime and not open to all EU manufactured components. It is not available where the export gives rise to repayment or remission of import duties; where prior to export the goods have been released for free circulation in the EU with total relief from import duty because of the end use or EU goods, the export of which gives rise to refunds or other financial advantages under the CAP.[3]

Three complicated cumulative requirements must be met for outward processing relief.[4] They are set out here in brief outline only.

(1) The applicant, for authorisation, must be established in the EU. Usually this is the processor. The essential interests of EU traders must not be prejudiced. The processing operation must consist of incorporating the EU goods into third country goods which are subsequently imported into the EU.
(2) Compensating products have resulted from the processing of the EU goods exported. Distinctive marking may demonstrate this. Under the standard exchange system there may be outward processing for the purposes of repair in a third country. The replacement products must be equivalent to the compensating products replaced.
(3) The application must not result in serious harm to Community processing industry interests. A reasonably liberal regime is in place.

1 Regulation (EEC) 2913/92, Arts 118 *et seq.*
2 Ibid, Arts 145 *et seq.*
3 Ibid, Art 146.
4 Ibid, Art 148.

It is outside the scope of this book to give a detailed analysis of these. There is a transit procedure to facilitate the transport of goods within the EU, and in particular to simplify the formalities which have to be undergone when the goods cross EU internal frontiers. The conditions must satisfy Arts 23 and 24 of the EC Treaty. There are elaborate arrangements which attempt to result in simplified and special procedures involving guarantees, etc. There are special rules for customs warehousing as well as free zones in warehouses. There are arrangements for processing under customs control as well as numerous specific reliefs from import or export duties where the goods are put into free circulation or are exported.

13.10 ADMINISTRATION AND PRACTICE

Enforcement of EU customs rules is, of course, the duty placed on the Commissioners of Customs and Excise.[1] The Customs and Excise Management Act 1979 has been significantly amended in recent years to provide the legislative framework for the administration and collection of these duties. But the implementation Regulation (2454/93, OJ 1993 L253/1) is precise about all other procedural or administrative matters from the size of forms to the remission of duties. So the scope of UK enactments is now very limited. The EU legislation is directly enforceable, although any amount of duty owing is a debt due to the Crown. The sanction (by s 43(1) of the 1979 Act) is that imported goods may not be delivered or removed upon importation until the importer has paid the relevant duty. The definition of 'importer' in s 1(1) of the 1979 Act is remarkably imprecise and includes (between importation and delivery out of charge): '... any owner or other person for the time being possessed of or beneficially interested in the goods'.

Specialist agents in the import/export trade may not strictly fall within this definition. The wording of sales contracts sometimes can be significant, therefore, in terms of responsibility for customs duty.[2]

13.11 POST CLEARANCE RECOVERY AND THE POWER TO WAIVE COLLECTION OF DUTY

There are special provisions where too little customs duty is collected but the importer acted in good faith when the declaration was made albeit on the wrong basis (say, as to categorisation of the goods in terms of the CN). The basic rule it that the domestic customs authority must proceed to collect the duty. There are two exceptions, in broad terms:

(1) post-clearance recovery cannot be made in respect of goods more than three years previously;[3]

---

1 Section 6 of the Customs and Excise Management Act 1979.

2 See Regulation (EEC) 2913/92 (OJ 1992 L302.1), Arts 859 *et seq.*

3 Article 221(3) of Regulation (EEC) 2913/92 (OJ 1992 L302/1).

(2) post-clearance recovery is waived where the duty rate, at import, was shown to be wrong by a later court decision or it was wrong due to customs error '... which could not have been reasonably detected or there is a special exemption'.[1]

Generally, these reliefs have been restrictively applied.[2] As to erroneous advice by the customs authority, the Court of Appeal in *Customs and Excise Commissioners v Invicta Poultry and another*,[3] held the issue was whether the error could reasonably have been detected, not whether it was reasonable for traders to accept the customs advice. A reference to the Official Journal on each occasion was required to verify goods classification by the importer, if the relief was justifiably to be invoked. That, of course, is less than fair or realistic.

However, the nature of the error, the experience of the importer and the degree of care taken by the importer are relevant. Good practice requires co-operation in provision of the paperwork and the correct information. Waiver of customs duty over 2,000 ECU is in the power of the Commission only.[4]

13.12 SUSPENSION OF DUTY

Finally, duty suspension is an exceptional measure for reduced or nil-rate duty on particular goods[5] or categories of goods. This is applied on the basis of 'economic impact' where there is inadequate production within the EU. Under Art 28 of the EC Treaty, the decision to suspend duty is that of the Council on recommendation by the Commission.[6] Applications in the UK are made to the Customs and Excise after advice from officials.

1 Regulation (EEC) 2913/92, Art 220(2)(a)(b)(c).

2 Case 348/89 *Mecanrante-Metalúrgica da Lagoa Ltd v Oporto* [1991] ECR 1–3277.

3 [1998] TLR 353: see also Case C-153/204/94 *R v Customs and Excise ex parte Faroe Seafood Co Ltd* [1996] ECR 1–2465

4 Article 869(b) of Regulation (EEC) 2454/93 (OJ 1993 L253/1), as presently drafted.

5 Article 84, *et seq*, of Regulation (EEC) 2913/92 (OJ 1992 L302/1).

6 See Case 227/84 *Texas Instruments v Hampzollant München-Mitte* [1985] ECR 3639.

Part V

SPECIAL TOPICS

Chapter 14

E-COMMERCE

14.1 INTRODUCTION

Increasingly, businesses are examining the opportunities of supplying goods and services via the Internet. The music industry sells a considerable volume of audio goods in this way. It is estimated that the value of on-line music sales will reach US $1.6 billion by the year 2002, which will account for about 7.5 per cent of the global market.[1] Businesses are seriously examining and implementing solutions for the provision of high end consumer products via the Internet. These products include travel bookings for airlines, and banking.

Another reason for the increasing interest in this area is because of the challenges it poses for tax administrations and taxpayers. At a conference held by the OECD in Turku, Finland (November 1997), concerns were voiced as to the ability to identify taxpayers, and the potential for widespread tax avoidance. The growth in, and improvement of, the technology making up the Internet will facilitate easier access to offshore business centres which offer anonymity.[2] With continuing improvements in technology an Internet trader need have no physical presence within the jurisdictions in which it trades. This poses fundamental problems for tax authorities where tax charges are based upon a physical presence such as residence, or the carrying on of a trade through a branch or agency. At this point in time, no specific scheme of UK taxation exists in respect of Internet commerce. As a result, transactions must be slotted into the general framework of tax law.

14.2 STRUCTURE

The UK Office of Telecommunications ('Oftel') defines the Internet in its glossary to a number of consultative documents on the telecommunications industry as: 'A global network of networks, mainly narrowband, accessed by users with a computer and a modem via a service provider.'

The nature of the Internet was examined in Chapter 1. The Internet is in simple terms the application of IT in a way which enables two or more persons through the medium of computers to distribute information between each other. The Internet can be used for the purposes of buying and selling products or services.

1 'Business: Surf music' (August 1997) *The Economist*, p 57.

2 OECD conference papers on 'Electronic Commerce: The Challenge To Tax Authorities And Taxpayers', Turku, Finland (November 1997), para 39.

Before continuing further, it is of use to note that the US Internet Tax Freedom Act defines e-commerce as meaning 'any transaction conducted over the Internet or through Internet access, comprising the sale, lease, licence, offer, or delivery of property, goods, services, or information, whether or not for consideration, and includes the provision of Internet access'.[1]

14.3 OBJECTIVES

The object of this chapter is to focus on specific areas relating to taxation of activities arising from use of the Internet. This question has two aspects to it. On the one hand, how are businesses which supply goods or services through the medium of the Internet to be taxed under UK law? A business can make these supplies either from outside or inside the UK. What are the tax charges which will apply to such businesses? A business can supply goods via the medium of the Internet by entering into a contract whilst on-line with a customer. The business will then arrange for delivery of the goods. What are the tax implications of these delivery arrangements? Alternatively, services can be supplied on-line, such as the supply of computer software, access to an information database, or possibly the provision of gambling services.

(1) In what circumstances can computer hardware such as servers which operate an Internet business site constitute a tax point for a country's tax authority?
(2) What are the tax implications of delivery arrangements for goods purchased via the Internet?
(3) In what circumstances will electronic traders be subject to UK tax law?
(4) Who is obliged to account for taxes arising from Internet commerce?
(5) What taxes apply to Internet commerce?

14.4 CHARACTERISTICS OF INTERNET TRADING SITES

Once accessed, a shopping site usually allows the consumer to view a range of available products. These products can then be selected by the consumer. Once the consumer has finished selecting the products of his choice, he then proceeds to the electronic check-out. The products are purchased by the consumer completing electronic forms which require billing and delivery information, such as name, address, and e-mail to be completed. The trading site is also used to make a payment. This is achieved by the consumer supplying credit card details on-line, such as the card number, issuer and expiry date. In this way, a contract is entered into via the Internet between the consumer and the trader. Depending upon the nature of the product purchased the trader will initiate an appropriate method of delivery. If it is possible to send the product via the Internet, such as computer software this will be installed directly upon the buyer's computer. If the product is of a physical nature, such as an audio cassette, food or wine the trader will send delivery instructions to either its own warehouse or an independent distributor with whom it has prior arrangements for making its deliveries.

1 HR 4105, s 155(4).

14.5 TAXATION OF CORPORATE INTERNET TRADERS: SUMMARY

The specific rules relating to the taxation of resident and non-resident people were examined in Chapter 5. What follows is a short summary of these rules, and an examination of them in the context of e-commerce. Where a corporate Internet trader is resident in the UK, it is subject to tax on profits wherever arising.[1] A company is treated as resident if it satisfies one of the following conditions:[2]

- it is incorporated in the UK[3]; or
- the central management and control of the company is located in the UK. [4]

Problems in the application of the central management and control test will be particularly acute where a business can be actively controlled from other continents by the use of instantaneous methods of communication such as e-mail or video-conferencing.

This problem is recognised in the Inland Revenue Statement of Practice which describes it in the following terms:

> 'The case law test examined in this Statement is not always easy to apply. The courts have recognised that there may be difficulties where it is not possible to identify one country as the seat of central management and control. The principles to apply in those circumstances have not been fully developed in case law. In addition, the last relevant case was decided almost 30 years ago, and there have been many developments in communications since then, which in particular may enable a company to be controlled from a place far distant from where the day-to-day management is carried on.'[5]

Under the common law test, it is possible for a company to have more than one place of residence.[6] A company may be regarded as resident in Country X because it is incorporated in that State, but it may also be regarded as a resident of the UK because its real place of business, ie its central management and control is based in the UK. The Inland Revenue holds the view that the residence of a company can be established

1 ICTA 1988, s 8(1).

2 A company which is regarded as resident in the UK for the purposes of the Tax Acts is excluded from residence where under a double taxation agreement the company is regarded as resident outside the UK and not resident in the UK, Finance Act 1994 ('FA 1994'), s 249.

3 FA 1994, s 66 (with effect from 15 March 1988).

4 *De Beers Consolidated Mines Ltd v Howe* (1906) 5 TC 198 at 213, per Lord Loreburn LC. In that case, Lord Loreburn LC said 'a company resides, for the purposes of income tax, where its real business is carried on ... I regard that as the true rule; and the real business is carried on where the central management and control actually abides'. In *Unit Construction Co Ltd v Bullock (Inspector of Taxes)* [1959] 3 All ER 831 at 836 HL, Lord Radcliffe said that this principle was firmly enshrined into the tax law. See also *American Thread Co v Joyce* (1916) 6 TC 163 at 165; *New Zealand Shipping Co Ltd v Thew* (1907) 8 TC 208; and *Bradbury v English Sewing Cotton Co* (1933) 8 TC 481. The test was re-formulated in *American Thread Co v Joyce* (1916) 6 TC 163 at 165 in the following terms: '... the real test ... and that which has been accepted as a test, is where what we should call the head office in popular language is, and where the business of the company is really directed and carried on in that sense.'

5 Inland Revenue Statement of Practice, SP 1/90, para 19 (9 January 1990).

6 See *Swedish Central Ry Co Ltd v Thompson* (1925) 9 TC 342 at 352; per Rowlatt; and *Unit Construction Co Ltd v Bullock (Inspector of Taxes)* [1959] All ER 831 HL at 833, per Viscount Simonds.

in the UK if a dominant person within a company, such as a managing director, exercises powers bestowed upon him in the UK, or if an influential shareholder exercises voting rights in the UK.[1]

14.6 TAX CHARGES APPLICABLE TO A CORPORATE RESIDENT

The sources which will be generally relevant to an Internet business are those within Cases I and V of Schedule D.[2] Case I is used to compute receipts derived from a trade.[3] Tax is assessed on 'profits' under this Case.[4] Case V is used to compute receipts derived from foreign possessions.[5] Receipts sourced to this Case are also assessed to tax on 'profits'.[6] These are the two main ways in which receipts from Internet business will be assessed for the purposes of a charge to tax in the UK.

14.7 TRADE WITHIN THE UNITED KINGDOM

A non-resident Internet trader can be brought within the charge to UK corporation tax where it is carrying on a trade through a branch or agency or it may be subject to income tax on the basis that it carries on a trade within the UK.[7] Where a DTA is in place between the UK and the non-resident's country, it is not sufficient to merely show that a trade is exercised within the UK. This is because, if we assume that the DTA is based on the principles of the OECD Model Tax Convention, the UK will only be entitled to tax the business profits of a non-resident where profits are derived from a permanent establishment. This is the nature of the relief conferred by a DTA on a non-resident. The taxation of a non-resident is made more difficult than the domestic UK legislation would otherwise require.[8] The Inland Revenue touches upon this in the internal guidance manual, *Double Taxation Relief*.[9] It is clear that many types of

---

1 Inland Revenue Statement of Practice, SP1/90, para 13.
2 ICTA 1988, s 18.
3 Ibid.
4 Ibid, s 70(1).
5 Ibid, s 18.
6 Ibid, s 70(2).
7 Ibid, s 18.
8 Appendix 2 lists the countries with which the UK has entered into a DTA. Appendix 3 lists those countries with which the UK has no DTA.
9 Inland Revenue guidance manual *Double Taxation Relief*, Part 3 (Income arising in the UK to Non-Residents), at para 1704 the following passage provides:
'If the non-resident is a resident of a country with which the United Kingdom has a double taxation agreement then we have to consider the provisions of the agreement as well as domestic law before we can decide whether there is liability. Our domestic law cannot generally override an agreement. However an agreement cannot impose a charge to tax where one does not already exist at all under our domestic law. Therefore an agreement may exempt where our domestic law would charge and an agreement may contemplate liability which our domestic law cannot enforce. Our domestic law, in deciding whether a non-resident trader should be taxed, simply asks the question – is the trade being exercised in the United Kingdom? However the business profits Article in the

Internet trade will not be susceptible to UK taxation where a DTA exists, which based on the OECD principles limits the application of tax to situations where there is a permanent establishment located in the UK. With Internet trade, there is usually no form of presence capable of amounting to a permanent establishment.

The following cases illustrate the requirements for a trade to be recognised as being exercised within the UK. In *Grainger & Son v William Lane Gough*,[1] Lord Herschell said it is a question of fact whether or not a person is exercising a trade within the UK.[2] What are the elements which constitute a trade within the UK? Lord Herschell said '... there is a broad distinction between trading *with* a country and carrying on a trade *within* a country'.[3] His lordship commented that the export of goods to the UK does not in itself amount to a trade within the UK, and that soliciting orders does not amount to a trade, whether by agent, circulars or advertisements.[4] In *Werle & Co v Colquhoun*[5] Fry LJ said that the following circumstances may be material in considering whether or not a trade is carried on in the UK. The following list is a generalisation of the circumstances put forward by Fry LJ:

- Where is payment made by the purchasers, eg to an agent in the UK?
- Where are the receipts given in the UK?
- Where are the goods delivered? Who is the carrying agent selected by the purchaser in the UK or the seller in the foreign country?
- Did the non-resident corporations agents issue advertisements or circulars in the UK for the purpose of causing contracts to be entered into in the UK?

In the course of giving judgment, Esher MR, said:[6]

> '... in each case, when you come to consider is there a trade carried on in England, it is a question of fact. It is a question of fact which is divided into two. Is there a trade carried on and, if so, is that trade carried on in England? It is a question of fact in each case.'

Esher MR, went on to say that 'a trade may be carried on in England without having an establishment at all'.[7] This view was concurred with by Lopes LJ.[8]

PART V SPECIAL TOPICS

OECD model agreement ... provides that country A can tax the profits of an enterprise of a resident of country B, an agreement partner, only if it has a permanent establishment ... in country A. In considering whether the business profits of an enterprise of a country A with which there is an agreement are taxable in the United Kingdom, it is necessary to decide (a) whether a trade is being carried on in the United Kingdom, (b) if it is, whether it is carried on through a permanent establishment in the United Kingdom. For companies it is also necessary, for the purpose of a charge to Corporation Tax, to determine whether the trade is carried on through a branch or agency. Most non-residents, whether companies or not, who trade in the United Kingdom do so through a branch or agency. In many cases a branch or agency will be a permanent establishment and vice versa. A non-resident may however trade in the United Kingdom through a branch or agency that is not a permanent establishment, or may have a permanent establishment here of which the activities do not amount to trading in the United Kingdom.'

1 [1896] AC 325
2 Ibid, at 335.
3 Ibid.
4 Ibid, at 336.
5 (1888) 20 QBD 753, 1 TC 402.
6 *Werle & Co v Colquhoun* (1888) 20 QBD 753, 1 TC 402 at 408.
7 Ibid, 1 TC 402 at 411.
8 Ibid, 1 TC 402 at 415.

His lordship said that it is not essential that profits be received in the UK, or that there be an establishment in the UK. The essential factor is whether the contracts are made in the UK. If so then the trade is carried on in the UK. This is because the making of contracts is the very substance and essence of a trade.[1]

Fry LJ said that 'the question whether a trade is carried on is not a matter of law, or one in respect of which you can lay down any one distinguishing incident, but is a compound fact made up of a variety of things.[2]

In *Maclaine v Eccott*[3] the following summary of the law was given by Viscount Cave LC,[4] with the concurrence of Viscount Haldane, Lord Atkinson, Lord Shaw of Dunfermline and Lord Sumner:

> 'The question whether a trade is exercised in the United Kingdom is a question of fact, and it is undesirable to attempt to lay down any exhaustive test of what constitutes such an exercise of trade; but I think it must now be taken as established that in the case of a merchant's business, the primary object of which is to sell goods at a profit, the trade is (speaking generally) exercised or carried on (I do not myself see much difference between the two expressions) at the place where the contracts are made. No doubt reference has sometimes been made to the place where payment is made for the goods sold or to the place where the goods are delivered, and it may be that in certain circumstances these are material considerations; but the most important, and indeed the crucial, question is, where are the contracts of sale made? Statements to this effect by Lord Justice Brett and Lord Justice Cotton in *Erichsen v Last* ((1881) 8 QBD 414) were quoted with approval in this House in the case of *Grainger v Gough* ([1896] AC 325); and the same principle was the basis of the decisions in *Werle v Colquhoun* (1888) 20 QBD 753), *Lovell and Christmas v Commissioners of Taxes* ([1908] AC 46), *Greenwood v Smidth* ([1922] 1 AC 417), and *Wilcock v Pinto* ([1925] 1 KB 30).'

However, it must be emphasised that the place where the contract is formed is not conclusive. In *Firestone Tyre Co Ltd v Lewellin*,[5] Lord Radcliffe made the following observations:

> '[. . .] the place of sale will not be the determining factor if there are other circumstances present that outweigh its importance, or unless there are no other circumstances that can. Since the courts have not attempted to lay down what those other circumstances are or may be, singly or in combination, and it would be, I believe, neither right nor possible to try to do so, I think it true to say that, within wide limits which determine what is a permissible conclusion, the question whether a trade is exercised within the UK remains, as it began, a question of fact for the Special Commissioners.'[6]

Lord Radcliffe quoted with approval the observations of Atkin LJ in *FL Smidth & Co v Greenwood* where he said:[7]

> 'The contracts in this case were made abroad. But I am not prepared to hold that this test is decisive. I can imagine cases where the contract of resale is made abroad, and yet the

1 *Werle & Co v Colquhoun* (1888) 1 TC 411 at 411–412.
2 Ibid, 1 TC 413.
3 (1926) 10 TC 481, 131 LT 601.
4 Ibid, 10 TC 481 at 574–575.
5 [1957] 1 All ER 561, HL.
6 Ibid, at 568.
7 (1922) 8 TC 193 at 203.

> manufacture of the goods, some negotiation of the terms, and complete execution of the contract take place here under such circumstances that the trade was in truth exercised here. I think that the question is, where do the operations take palce from which the profits in substance arise?'

The central principle to be extracted from this line of case-law is that the location of the contract is not determinative. It is necessary to look at the nature of the transaction between the parties. For instance, the location of the place of manufacture or appropriation of stock, the place of delivery, receipt of payment are all relevant considerations. Although in some cases of e-commerce the contract will be formed abroad, there will be situations where other factors will tend to show that the centre of operations is in the UK from which profits arise. In these circumstances the e-commerce trader will be trading in the UK.

14.8 INTERNET CONTRACTS

The formation of contracts via the Internet is an area which is not the subject of specific legislation. The formation of a contract will be a matter for the common law. The application of common law principles to Internet activity is beyond the scope of this book. Further guidance can be obtained elsewhere.[1] Generally, it appears that, where communications are made over the World Wide Web, it is instantaneous. On this basis the rules relating to contracts made over the telephone or fax are likely to apply. Where a consumer responds to an offer from an Internet trading site, a contract will be formed when the notification of acceptance is received by the offeror. The country where the Internet contract is formed is the country where the notification of acceptance is received by the offeror.[2]

Example 70

Z Inc carries on business as an Internet trader in audio cassettes. The e-commerce machinery and the trader are based in New York. The web site is accessed by a consumer in the UK. Merchandise is selected, billing information is completed and the consumer transmits an offer to purchase the selection to the traders computer via the Internet site. The computer based in the USA automatically sends notification of acceptance, and that the audio tapes will be delivered within three weeks. In these circumstances a contract is formed in the UK. The extent to which the profits from such an activity can be taxed depends upon whether a permanent establishment exists in the UK.

The observations about DTAs must be borne in mind. Where a DTA does not exist, a non-resident Internet trader may be subject to income tax where as in the above example the contract is formed in the UK and it is the place where the profits in substance arise. In the absence of a DTA there is no additional requirement for a permanent establishment to exist and accordingly the Inland Revenue's power of taxation will not be restricted.

---

1 C. Gringras *The Laws of the Internet* (Butterworths, 1997), Chapter 2.

2 *Entores v Miles Far East Corporation* (1955) 2 QB 327; *Brinkibon Ltd v Stahag Stahl GmbH* [1983] 2 AC 34.

The parties to a contract can stipulate the mode of contract formation. With the appropriate structure in place, it would be possible to ensure that a contract is not made in the UK.

14.9 THE NATURE OF FOREIGN POSSESSIONS[1]

If a trade is exercised wholly outside the UK by a corporate resident, receipts will be chargeable under Case V as income from foreign possessions. The precise nature of the receipts brought within this Case is 'income arising from possessions out of the United Kingdom not being income consisting of emoluments of any office or employment'.[2] The tax legislation does not define the word 'possessions'. In *Colquhoun (Surveyor of Taxes) v Brooks*,[3] Lord Herschell delivered the following opinion on the nature of the word 'possessions' within the context of this charging provision:

> 'When, therefore, the term "possessions" is employed it seems to indicate an intention to cover by it something more than "property". And it is difficult to see why, unless the intention were to embrace something more, the latter word was not used. "Possessions" is a wide expression; it is not a word with any technical meaning; the Act supplies no interpretation of it. And I cannot see why it may not fitly be interpreted as relating to all that is possessed in Her Majesty's dominions out of the United Kingdom, or in foreign countries. And if so, I do not think any violence would be done to the language if it were held to include the interest which a person in this country possesses in a business carried on elsewhere.'

The opinion of Lord Herschell was concurred with by Lord Halsbury and Lord Fitzgerald. Lord Macnaghten said in the course of delivering his opinion that 'The word "possessions" is not a technical word. It seems to me that it is the widest and most comprehensive word that could be used.' Where a trade is carried on outside of the UK, it is clear that the receipts derived from such a trade will be taxable under Case V. This is the implication of the charge which encompasses 'income arising from possessions out of the United Kingdom'.

Example 71

Z Ltd is a UK resident which has located an automated computer server in the Bahamas. This server operates an Internet business which sells computer software. Payment is made by the use of a credit card, and all payment receipts are credited by the computer server to an account held in the Cayman Islands. The computer software is delivered to the consumer by installing it directly upon the consumer's computer. The profits derived from this trade are the sterling equivalent of £300,000 for 1998–99. Z Ltd receives other profits generated in the UK of £1.5million. The Inland Revenue assess the profits of £300,000 to corporation tax under Case V of Schedule D. Total corporation tax payable is £558,000 (31 per cent of £1.8 million). The real problem for the Inland Revenue will be in detecting offshore transactions such as these. Failure to disclose such arrangements would of course be unlawful.

---

1 See Shipwright and Keeling *Revenue Law* (Blackstone Press, 1997), Chapter 35.

2 ICTA 1988, s 18 (3).

3 [1886–90] All ER Rep 1063, 2 TC 490.

Diagram 5

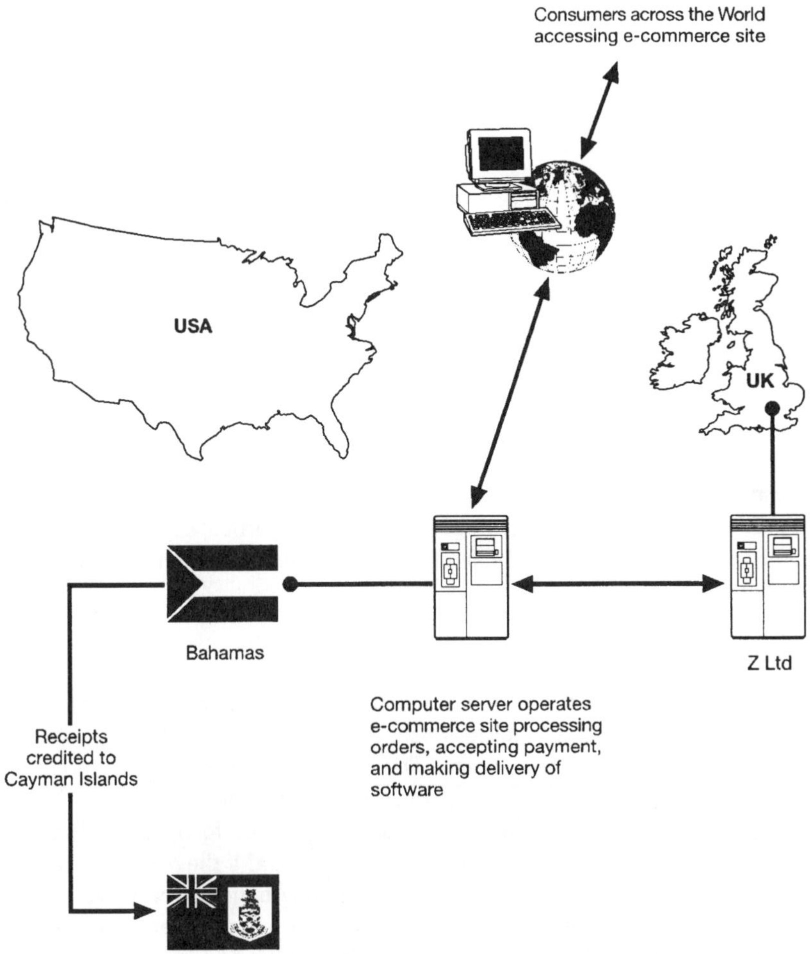

If part of a business is carried on outside of the UK, and also partly within the UK, any receipts would be taxed under Case I of Schedule D. This is because tax is only charged under Case V in respect of 'possessions out of the United Kingdom'. Receipts arising under Case V are taxed in accordance with the same principles as those applicable to receipts derived from a trade under Case I.[1] It is important to appreciate that receipts arising in respect of foreign possessions will be taxed in the hands of a company whether or not those receipts are received in or transmitted to the UK.[2] A UK company will therefore receive no tax advantage in delaying the repatriation of profits derived from an Internet business located outside these shores.

1 ICTA 1988, s 70(2).
2 Ibid, s 70(1).

14.10 'BRANCH OR AGENCY' OF A NON-RESIDENT

A non-resident company is subject to corporation tax if it carries on a trade through a branch or agency within the UK.[1] The level of profits subject to corporation tax are limited to those derived from the branch or agency, and also those profits derived from property used by the branch or agency.[2] The tax legislation defines a 'branch or agency' as 'any factorship, agency, receivership, branch or management'.[3]

The term 'branch' is a reference to a physical presence, such as the existence of offices rather than to a legal relationship.[4] Either the concept of branch or agency can be used as a force of attraction in respect of subjecting Internet business to UK corporation tax. It cannot be overlooked that a second condition must be satisfied to bring a non-resident within the charge to corporation tax, which is that a trade must be carried on within the UK through the branch or agency.[5] In this respect, a distinction must be drawn between trading with the UK and exercising a trade within it.[6]

Although a non-resident company may have no 'branch or agency' which operates to attract corporation tax, it may none the less be possible to impose income tax where the company receives annual profits or gains from a trade exercised within the UK, or from property in the UK.[7] This charge to tax may be particularly important, as the example below illustrates, to the Inland Revenue as a means of capturing e-commerce across the Internet.

Example 72

USA Shopping Mall Inc operate an Internet site on a computer server located in the UK of their clothing merchandise which can be accessed solely by wholesale distributors authorised by the company. The wholesalers purchase the merchandise by accessing the web site, through which orders are placed, and payment can be made via use of a credit card. A UK wholesaler places an order for merchandise worth $150,000. Is USA Shopping Mall Inc assessable to UK tax? If the profits in substance arise in the UK it is likely that this will amount to trading in the UK. However, if a DTA exists UK tax can only be imposed if derived from a permanent establishment. Whether profits are taxable will depend upon whether it is a branch or agency for the purposes of corporation tax, for the purposes of an income tax charge whether the activity amounts to trading in the UK.

1 ICTA 1988, s 11(1).
2 Ibid, s 11(2).
3 Ibid, s 834(1).
4 In *Hughes (HM Inspector of Taxes) v Bank of New Zealand* [1938] 1 All ER 778 the Bank was subject to tax in the UK because it derived profits from offices opened in London.
5 See earlier discussion of the circumstances when a trade is exercised in the UK.
6 See *Grainger v Gough* [1896] AC 325 at 335, per Lord Herschell.
7 ICTA 1988, s 18(1). See also C. Whitehouse *Revenue Law: Principles and Practice* (Butterworths, 1996), p 559.

14.11 BRANCH

In the context of ICTA 1988 a 'branch' is defined as 'any factorship, agency, receivership, branch or management'.[1] This definition of branch can be amplified by reference to the *Shorter Oxford English Dictionary*,[2] which defines it as: 'A subordinate establishment of a library, bank, or other business, serving a particular area.'

This concept is clearly based upon a physical presence of a business organisation within the UK. Typically, this would be where a non-resident opens offices which it furnishes, and employs staff to carry on its business within a particular area. The definition clearly requires an establishment. It is inherent within this language that there is a degree of fixation or permanence. The *Shorter Oxford English Dictionary* defines an establishment as: 'An institution or business; the premises or personnel of this'. It is also worth referring to the meaning of establish, which is defined as 'Set up on a permanent or secure basis; bring into being, found, (a government, institution, business, etc.)'.

These definitions do not depend upon any legal entity being in existence within the UK. What must exist is a physical thing which is used to carry on not a business, but a trade within the UK.[3] Against this background is it possible for physical hardware, by which an Internet business activity is carried on, to constitute a branch? In the tax chapter of *The Laws of the Internet*[4] the author entertains the possibility that a computer server can constitute a branch. The author states:

> '... the situation can be imagined where the server carries out a certain amount of processing: it could, for example, be the server which authorises credit card transactions. It could be that the web server will be treated as a branch of the company.'[5]

It is doubtful that a computer server would constitute a branch of a non-resident. This is because a principal badge of a branch is that it carries on an economic activity on behalf of the non-resident. A computer server is often a passive piece of machinery within the jurisdiction. The non-resident will send commands to the computer server via other pieces of machinery located within the home jurisdiction. The computer server will generally perform the function of a mere conduit for passing information back to the non-resident. Generally, a piece of equipment within the home jurisdiction will be used to process orders, trigger payment, issue despatch orders for delivery of goods or services. Additionally, the place of delivery of the goods or services may be triggered from another location entirely different from that of the purchaser and seller by another piece of machinery. The situations will be comparatively rare where a non-resident seller structures his e-commerce business so that a computer server performs all the activities necessary for a branch to exist within a jurisdiction for tax purposes.

---

1 ICTA 1988, s 834(1).
2 Oxford University Press, 1993.
3 ICTA 1988, s 11 (1).
4 C. Gringras, *op cit*.
5 Ibid, p 308.

Under UK law, only the profits attributable to the branch can be taxed. As the OECD conference in Turku highlighted, what happens where an Internet trader operates several computer servers in multiple jurisdictions? In these circumstances, how will it be possible to determine the level of profits attributable to particular computer server located in the UK? It must be remembered that under most DTAs, a permanent establishment must exist for a tax authority to impose a charge. Under OECD principles this requires a 'fixed place of business'.[1] How will it be possible to identify that a server within the UK is being used as a branch for a trade?

14.12 AGENCY

ICTA 1988 defines agency in the same terms as a branch, which is as 'any factorship, agency, receivership, branch or management'.[2] However, unlike a branch, an agency is based on the concept of a legal relationship[3], and not a physical presence, although it is inherent within the concept of agency that an agent is in existence within the UK. An agency can only exist where there is an entity in existence with legal personality, such as a corporation. It is clear that, in this context, computer hardware used for the purposes of carrying on an Internet business cannot form the basis of an agency. No tax can be attracted to an Internet business in these circumstances.

However, a person who is a non-resident and who sells goods or services through the medium of the Internet, may need to enter into arrangements for the transfer of those goods or services to the consumer in the jurisdiction concerned. This may be achieved by the appointment of an agent or distributor. Such an appointment may operate to attract a tax charge on the non-resident provided a trade is being carried on through the agent. However, regard must in this context be had to any DTAs, which are between the UK and the country in which the seller is a resident.

There are clear rules within the OECD Model Convention that some agents cannot be a permanent establishment for the purposes of allowing the UK Inland Revenue to raise a tax assessment. Because much of the UK's DTA network is based upon the principles of the OECD framework, it is appropriate to have regard to the provisions within it dealing with agency.[4] Where no DTA exists, all that is required for a corporation tax charge in these circumstances is a simple agency through which a non-resident carries on a trade.[5]

---

1 The OECD Turku conference notes state '... difficulties would arise where a number of mirror web sites on different servers located in different countries would be used so that a customer could be directed to any site for any function depending on electronic traffic.' (para 97).

2 ICTA 1988, s 11 (1).

3 *Bowstead on Agency* (Sweet & Maxwell, 1985), p 1, defines as an agency as 'the fiduciary relationship which exists between two persons, one of whom expressly or impliedly consents that the other should act on his behalf, and the other of whom similarly consents so to act or so acts. The one on whose behalf the act or acts are to be done is called the principal. The one who is to act is called the agent. Any person other than the principal and the agent may be referred to as a third party.'

4 See **14.15**.

5 Appendix 2 details the countries with which the UK has no DTA.

Example 73

Z Inc is an Internet trader specialising in the operation of gambling sites. It locates an automated computer server in the USA which carries on gambling operations. The profits from this activity are $2 million. Z Inc has a branch in the UK, which has located a computer server in the UK and Russia. Profits from each of these servers is the sterling equivalent of £200,000 and £1 million respectively. In these circumstances the UK Inland Revenue is entitled to assess corporation tax on the branch of Z Inc, in respect of the receipts arising in the UK, and possibly the receipts from the Russian computer server.[1] It is not entitled to assess the profits derived by Z Inc in the USA.

14.13 DOUBLE TAXATION AGREEMENTS

In considering how UK tax will be applied to e-commerce carried on by a non-resident, it is appropriate to refer to the principles of the double taxation convention settled by the OECD. Since the publication of the OECD Model Convention most of the UK's DTAs are based upon the concepts of the Model. The purpose of a DTA is to relieve tax on the profits of a non-resident who carries on a business activity within a country such as the UK. A DTA limits the extent to which UK tax can be applied. The scope of that relief will depend upon the precise terms of the relevant DTA. To date the UK is signatory to approximately 100 DTAs. The countries with whom the UK has a double taxation agreement are summarised in Appendix 2. If a DTA does not exist, it will be easier to tax an Internet trade carried on by a non-resident. This is because the tax charge will not be limited by the requirement for a permanent establishment to exist. All that must exist in the absence of a DTA for the application of corporation tax is a branch through which a trade is carried on in the UK, or for an income tax charge a trade which is carried on in the UK.

Where a DTA exists, it is necessary to consider the operation of the agreement because it may relieve tax where there would otherwise be a charge under the normal principles of domestic tax law. However, DTAs cannot operate to impose a wider tax charge than that which exists in domestic legislation.[2] This is an important point in the context of e-commerce.

DTAs contain important limits upon the right of a State to tax a non-resident. For example, Art 7(1) of the Model Convention dealing with business profits permits a non-resident only to be taxed by the country of source on profits arising from a permanent establishment.

This type of Article will limit the right of the UK to tax a non-resident where there is not a permanent establishment. For example, the right to impose tax where a non-resident is exercising a trade in the UK will be extinguished by a DTA unless a permanent establishment does exist. The OECD conference held in Turku, Finland,

1 See ICTA 1988, s 11(2); see also Bramwell *Taxation of Companies and Company Reconstructions* (Sweet & Maxwell, 1999), paras 15–18.

2 Baker *Double Taxation Conventions and International Tax Law* (Sweet & Maxwell, 1994), pp 7–10.

recognised that a computer server was in fact capable of constituting a permanent establishment.[1]

Example 74

X Inc, is an Internet trader which has a computer server located in the UK. In the 1998–99 tax year profits of £200,000 are derived from a trade of selling computer software to people in the UK who access the UK computer server. Orders and payment are processed by a US computer server. Delivery is initiated by the US server, but the actual transfer is from the UK server. X Inc asks for your advice as to whether the Inland Revenue can impose corporation tax on these profits on the basis that the UK server constitutes a branch or agency. If not the company also wishes to know whether it would be assessable to income tax on the basis that it is exercising a trade in the UK. An illustration of the method of business is shown in diagram 6 below.

Diagram 6

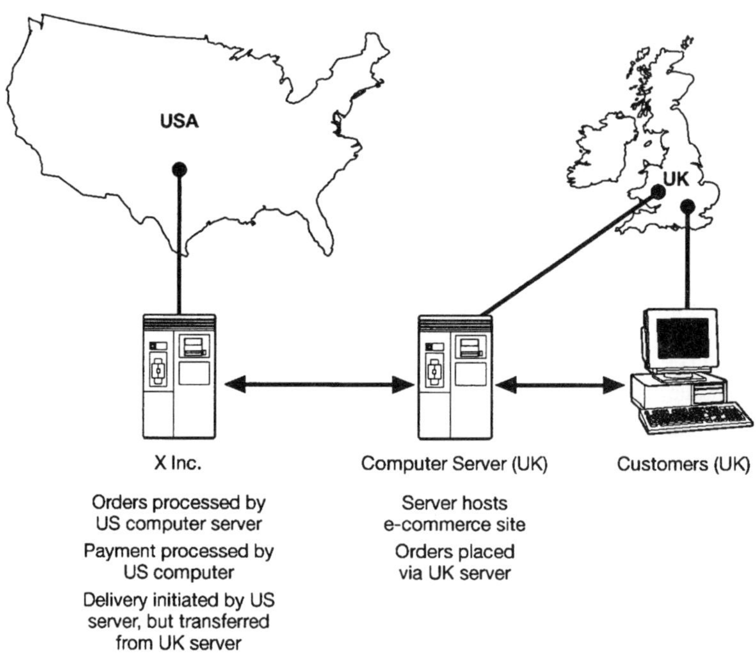

The answer to this question of tax liability depends upon whether the computer server (ie automated machinery) can constitute a branch or agency for the purposes of corporation tax. If a DTA is in place between the USA and the UK, reference must be made to the rights the UK has to tax a resident of the USA. Under the UK/USA Double Taxation Agreement Order 1980, SI 1980/568, art 7(1), the right to tax a US resident is limited to profits which are solely attributable to a permanent establishment.

1 OECD 'Electronic Commerce: The Challenges to Tax Authorities And Taxpayers' (1997), paras 93–102.

However, the treaty cannot extend UK tax charges which are limited to taxing the profits of a non-resident derived from a branch or agency. In this example, there is nothing to constitute a UK branch or agency. If corporation tax cannot be imposed on this basis, could income tax be charged on the basis that the Internet trade is exercised in the UK? The DTA only permits taxation of a non-resident's profits where they are derived from a permanent establishment. Can it be said that a trade is exercised through a permanent establishment where there is only a computer server located in the UK? The answer to this will turn upon whether the operations are such that profits in substance arise in the UK. Clearly, in this example the economic function of the servers is minimal. There can be no income tax charge.

14.14 USE OF DTAs AND INTERACTION WITH DOMESTIC TAX LAW

The definition of a permanent establishment is cast in wide terms. Article 5 of the OECD Model Tax Convention provides:

> '1. For the purposes of this Convention, the term "permanent establishment" means a fixed place of business through which the business of an enterprise is wholly or partly carried on.'

The Model Convention goes on to define the type of thing which is included within the concept of permanent establishment. Article 5(2) provides:

> '2. The term "permanent establishment" includes especially:
>
> a) a place of management;
> b) a branch;
> c) an office;
> d) a factory;
> e) a workshop, and a mine, an oil or gas well, a quarry or any other place of extraction of natural resources.'

It will be recalled that the word 'branch' is used for making a non-resident subject to corporation tax. In the OECD Article the term 'branch' is an illustration of what is a permanent establishment, while the corporation tax charge under UK law is limited to a branch. In other words, something can constitute a permanent establishment but not be a branch. It must be remembered that there is no specific reference to automated machinery within the UK DTA network. Consideration must accordingly be given to general principles.

The OECD Model Tax Convention is supplemented by Commentaries that explain among the many concepts within the Model Convention that of permanent establishment. The Model Convention envisages that a Contracting State is only entitled to tax the profits of a non-resident that are attributable to a permanent establishment. For example, Art 7(1) of the UK–Italy DTA[1] which is based upon the Model Convention provides:

> 'The profits of an enterprise of a Contracting State shall be taxable only in that State unless the enterprise carried on business in the other Contracting State through a permanent

1 Double Taxation Relief (Taxation on Income) (Italy) Order 1990, SI 1990/2590.

> establishment situated therein. If the enterprise carries on business as aforesaid, the profits of the enterprise may be taxed in the other State but only so much of them as is attributable to that permanent establishment.'

Clearly the DTA envisages the possibility of taxing anything which comes within the concept of permanent establishment through which a business is carried on. Assistance in the interpretation of permanent establishment can be obtained from the Commentaries to the Model Convention.[1] The use to which these Commentaries can be put is therefore of significance.

14.15 AGENCY AND THE OECD MODEL TAX CONVENTION

As previously discussed, the concept of agency is important in bringing a non-resident into the charge to corporation tax. Where a DTA exists, based upon the principles of the OECD Model Convention, no agency can be used as a tax charge unless it is a permanent establishment within the meaning of the Model Convention. Where an agency is not a permanent establishment, only the non-resident's country is entitled to tax it. The rules relating to the taxation of agents is important in the context of Internet commerce, because arrangements will be in place within jurisdictions for the delivery of goods via the Internet.

Article 5(5) of the OECD Model Tax Convention (1992) provides that a person who acts on behalf of an enterprise and

> 'habitually exercises, in a Contracting State an authority to conclude contracts in the name of the enterprise, that enterprise shall be deemed to have a permanent establishment in that State in respect of any activities which that person undertakes for the enterprise, unless the activities of such person are limited to those mentioned in paragraph 4 [reproduced below] which, if exercised through a fixed place of business, would not make this a fixed place of business a permanent establishment under the provisions of that paragraph.'

14.16 EXCLUSIONS FROM DEFINITION OF PERMANENT ESTABLISHMENT

Article 5(4) of the OECD Model Tax Convention is in the following terms:

> '... the term "permanent establishment" shall be deemed not to include:
>
> (a) the use of facilities solely for the purposes of storage, display or delivery of goods or merchandise belonging to the enterprise;
> (b) the maintenance of a stock of goods or merchandise belonging to the enterprise solely for the purpose of storage, display or delivery;
> (c) the maintenance of a stock of goods or merchandise belonging to the enterprise solely for the purpose of processing by another enterprise;
> (d) the maintenance of a fixed place of business solely for the purpose of purchasing goods or merchandise or of collecting information, for the enterprise;
> (e) the maintenance of a fixed place of business solely for the purpose of carrying on, for the enterprise, any other activity of a preparatory or auxiliary character;

---

1 See **14.17**.

(f) the maintenance of a fixed place of business solely for any combination of activities mentioned in sub-paragraphs a) to e), provided that the overall activity of the fixed place of business resulting from this combination is of a preparatory or auxiliary character.'

It is clear that where these principles are included in a DTA, a non-resident Internet trader who enters into a contract with a UK consumer, who dispatches delivery orders to a person in the UK (who holds stock for the foreign company) that the UK holder of merchandise will not constitute a permanent establishment.

Do these principles apply where a server is used within a particular jurisdiction for the delivery of computer software? Can it be said that such servers are facilities for the delivery of goods? Traditional concepts of taxation such as these are based in an era when transactions only occurred in respect of tangible and not electronic items. It is unlikely that this point will apply to electronic software, because Customs and Excise and the Inland Revenue treat off-the-shelf or standardised software downloaded from a computer network as the provision of services.

Example 75

X Inc carries on an Internet trade from the USA, with consumers who are based in the UK. The US company has all its automated machinery located in the USA through which payments are made. Delivery of ordered merchandise is achieved by sending delivery instructions to a UK company, which holds stock on behalf of the US Internet trader. The nature of the trade is shown in Diagram 7 below.

Diagram 7

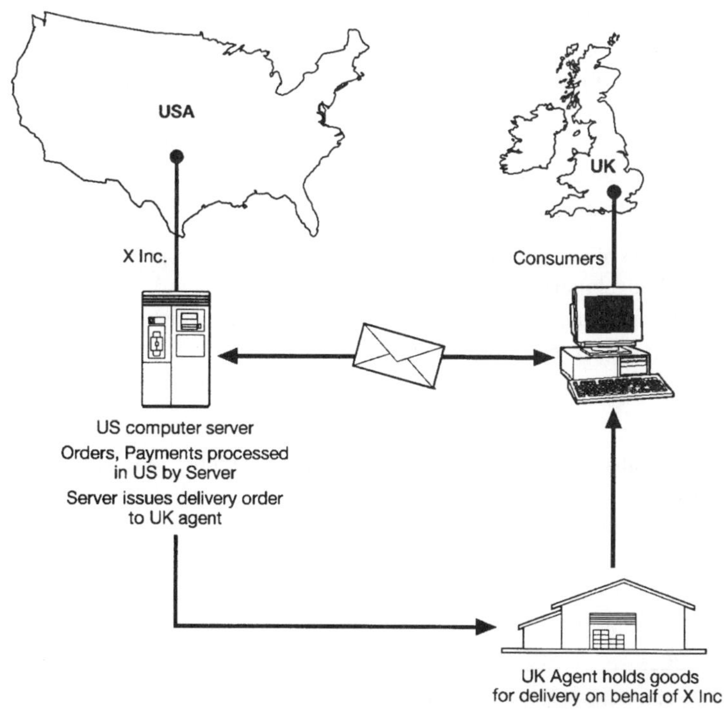

In this example, the US company has no presence in the UK which is capable of forming the basis of a tax charge. There is no branch or agency for the purposes of corporation tax, and the UK company which delivers merchandise for the US company is not, assuming OECD principles are contained in the DTA, capable of being an agency sufficient to constitute a permanent establishment. It is only where a permanent establishment exists that the UK tax authority will be entitled to impose a charge (this is the nature of the tax relief given to non-residents through a DTA).

It is also necessary to bear in mind the wording of Art 5, para (6), which provides that an enterprise shall not be treated as having a permanent establishment solely for the reason that it carries on business in a country through a broker, general commission agent or any other agent of an independent status. For this rule to apply the person must be acting in the ordinary course of business. The Commentaries make it clear that a person will come within the scope of this part of the Article, if the person is independent of the enterprise both legally and economically and he acts in the ordinary course of business when acting on behalf of the enterprise (Commentary to Art 5, para 37).

14.17 COMMENTARIES RELEVANT TO INTERNET BUSINESS

Considerable weight must be attached to the Commentaries of the OECD. They are used as an aid by the courts, and the Commentaries have also influenced the practice of the Inland Revenue in the UK. The concept of permanent establishment and particularly the terms 'branch or agency' will be of critical importance in determining the extent to which corporation tax or income tax can be imposed upon a non-resident Internet trader. The Commentaries make a number of important observations which can assist in determining the extent to which Internet business will be captured by UK tax legislation. The term 'permanent establishment' is identified by the key characteristic of a 'distinct situs', a 'fixed place of business'. The Commentaries draw the following inferences from the definition of permanent establishment which must be satisfied for it to exist:[1]

- the existence of a 'place of business', ie a facility such as premises, or in certain instances, machinery or equipment;
- this place of business must be 'fixed', ie it must be established at a distinct place with a certain degree of permanence;
- the carrying on of the business of the enterprise through this fixed place of business.

This usually means that persons who, in one way or another, are dependent on the enterprise (personnel) conduct the business of the enterprise in the State in which the fixed place is situated.

1 OECD Commentaries (1992) to Art 5. See para 2.

It is worth pausing to highlight the inference drawn in the Commentaries that 'machinery or equipment' is capable of forming the subject matter of a place of business. This must, therefore, extend to computer hardware from which an Internet business is operated by computer software. It does not follow that because automated machinery is capable of constituting a permanent establishment that corporation tax can be imposed on a non-resident, because of its use of automated machinery. This will occur only where it constitutes a branch or agency. It is clear that the concepts of branch or agency are narrower in meaning than the overall concept of permanent establishment. Where a DTA is in place, a permanent establishment is relevant to a charge to UK income/corporation tax because this must exist in addition to a trade being exercised in the UK. The following observations from the Commentaries are of relevance in determining the extent to which an Internet business comes within the concept of permanent establishment.

- the fact that an establishment fulfils a 'productive character' to a whole organisation, it does not necessarily follow that it is a permanent establishment to which profits can be attributed (Commentary to Art 5, para 3);
- 'place of business' includes any facilities or installations used for carrying on the business (Commentary to Art 5, para 4);
- a place of business can exist whether premises, facilities or installations are owned or rented by the enterprise concerned (Commentary to Art 5, para 4);
- a place of business may be situated in the business facilities of another enterprise (Commentary to Art 5, para 4);
- a place of business must be a fixed one (Commentary to Art 5, para 5);
- equipment constituting a place of business does not have to be fixed on the soil on which it stands (Commentary to Art 5, para 5);
- the place of business must have a degree of permanency;
- a permanent establishment does not exist where the place of business has a purely temporary nature (Commentary to Art 5, para 6);
- an enterprise must carry on a business activity through the place of business either wholly or partially. The activity is not required to be permanent;
- there can be an interruption to the operation of the business activity, but the activity must be carried out on a regular basis (Commentary to Art 5, para 7);
- a permanent establishment may exist if the business of an enterprise is carried on mainly through automatic equipment, and the activities of personnel of an enterprise are restricted to setting up, operating, controlling and maintaining such equipment (Commentary to Art 5, para 10);
- the Commentaries give as an example the illustration of gaming or vending machines which are set up by an enterprise in a Contracting State. A permanent establishment may exist if the enterprise which sets up the machines also operates and maintains the machines for its own account (Commentary to Art 5, para 10).

Against this background, it appears that the existence of a computer server in the UK, which operates an Internet trade in every sense of the word would be sufficient to allow the UK to tax a non-resident. However, an Internet trader with no physical presence in the UK, can use a DTA to protect itself from an income tax charge by ensuring that nothing is situated in the UK capable of constituting a permanent establishment.

14.18 WITHHOLDING TAXES – COPYRIGHT AND COMPUTER SOFTWARE

The only specific requirement to deduct tax at the basic rate of income tax at source is on payments made to a non-resident owner of copyright.[1] Payments made for the right to use computer software on computer hardware are regarded as utilisation rights. Payments of this nature are not regarded as being the subject of withholding tax. Payments for the right to reproduce computer software are regarded as being subject to withholding tax. The rights acquired in this context are referred to as 'partial rights' under the OECD proposed commentary amendments to Art 12. The acquisition of standardised software via the Internet involves the acquisition of a licence which is classified as a utilisation right. In this context, there is no obligation upon the UK consumer to impose withholding tax upon the payment for the software.

14.19 VALUE ADDED TAX

As a sales tax VAT is capable of being applied in many areas of Internet and associated commerce. Consider the following situations.

(1) Communication services, whether satellite or earth-based to an Internet access provider.
(2) A licence permitting the use of a search engine database by a mirror-site.
(3) Sale of computer software through the medium of an Internet transaction.
(4) Financial services accessed by subscribers via the Internet.

Each of the situations listed above has the potential to fall within the VAT legislation. The purpose of this section is to examine the application of VAT to Internet commerce. This means things supplied via the medium of the Internet (for example, computer software on-line), and things supplied in pursuance of an Internet contract.

14.19.1 Ingredients of the VAT charge: a summary[2]

The key to the application of the tax charge is s 4 of VATA 1994. By this section, a VAT charge will apply in the following circumstances:

- a supply of goods or services;
- the place of supply of which is in the UK;
- which is a taxable supply;
- made by a taxable person;
- in the course or furtherance of business[3] carried on by the supplier; and
- the supply is not an exempt supply.

---

1 ICTA 1988, s 536.

2 See Chapter 8 for further explanation.

3 A business is defined in VATA 1994 as including any 'trade, profession or vocation' (s 94(1)). The comments made in relation to a trade in the context of corporation tax are equally valid in determining whether a trade is carried on for the purposes of VAT.

Where VAT applies to a supply, there are two types of rate. A VAT charge of 17.5 per cent applies on standard rated supplies,[1] while no charge applies to zero-rated supplies.[2] The taxable person who charges VAT on supplies made by him, known as output tax, is required to account for that amount to Customs and Excise.[3] In accounting for this amount, the taxable person is entitled to subtract the amount of VAT incurred by him in making those supplies, known as input tax.[4] The right of set-off exists only where a taxable person makes taxable supplies. Where a person makes exempt supplies there is no right of set-off.[5]

14.19.2 The place of supply of goods or services[6]

Place of supply is determined by reference to a number of specific rules. In the context of Internet business, the place of supply rules are extremely important. One of the difficulties with Internet trade is identifying the place of supply, especially where computer servers effectively operate the business.

The place of supply is an important point for both suppliers and the consumers of those supplies. The advantage of locating a supply outside of the UK, is that there is no UK VAT payable by the non-business user. The result of this is that the supplier can sell goods or provide services on a cheaper and more competitive basis if it can arrange for the supply to fall outside of VAT.[7] Many services can be provided via the Internet from outside of the UK. The advances in technology make it a commercial reality to provide services such as gambling, and banking etc via the Internet.

The rules for determining the place of supply of goods or services have been designed to ensure that there is equal treatment in the application of VAT between Member States of the EU. The rules that have been adopted are those which achieve the avoidance of double taxation between Member States, non-taxation of supplies and those that prevent economic distortion. The place of supply rules in respect of goods and services, insofar as relevant to Internet trade, are summarised in the following Tables.

---

1 VATA 1994, s 2(1).
2 Ibid, s 30 and Sch 8.
3 Ibid, s 25(1).
4 Ibid, s 25(2).
5 Ibid, s 4(2).
6 See *De Voil's Indirect Tax Service* (Butterworths), Division V3.124, V3.181, V3.182 and V3.183; HM Customs and Excise Notice No 700, paras 2.4(b), 2.8(a), (b), and 4.1(c), and Notice No 741, Section 2; HM Customs and Excise internal guidance manual, Vol 1, Part 4, Section 2, Chapter 2B, Section 6.
7 Up until 1 July 1997 this advantage was being used by telecommunication and Internet access providers. This loop-hole of avoidance in relation to business users has now been closed. Such services are now subject to the reverse charge. See Value Added Tax (Reverse Charge) (Anti-avoidance) Order 1997, SI 1997/1523, art 3.

Table 23: Place of supply of goods

Type of supply (Goods)	*Place of supply*	*Reference (VATA 1994)*
Goods not removed from the UK	Goods supplied in the UK	s 7(2)
Goods not removed to the UK	Goods not supplied in the UK	s 7(2)
Goods removed to the UK 1. under the direction of the supplier 2. the goods are acquired in the UK by a non-taxable person from another member state 3. supplier is liable to be registered under VATA 1994, Sch 2, or would be so liable if not registered or liable to be registered under VATA 1994, Sch 1 4. VATA 1994, Sch 4, para 5(1) do not apply.	Goods supplied in the UK	s 7(4)
Goods imported from outside the Member State, and the person who supplies them is the person who gives the direction for them to be imported	Supplied in UK	s 7(6)

Table 24: Place of supply of services

Type of supply (Services)	*Place of supply*	*Reference (VATA 1994)*
Supply of services by a supplier who belongs in the UK	Service supplied in UK	s 7(10)(a)
Supply of services by a supplier who belongs in another country	Service supplied outside the UK	s 7(10)(b)
Supply of services within VATA 1994, Sch 5, and the recipient of the supply: 1. belongs in a country, other than the Isle of Man, which is not a Member State, or 2. is a person who belongs in a Member State other than the one in which the supplier belongs, and (i) receives the supply for the purposes of a business, and (ii) is not treated as having himself supplied the services on the basis that there is a reverse charge (VATA 1994, s 8)	Supplied where recipient belongs	Value Added Tax (Place of Supply of Services) Order 1992, SI 1992/3121, reg 16[1]

The services specified in Sch 5 to VATA 1994 are also those which are subject to the reverse charge where received in the UK.[2] Where the services classified within Sch 5

1 SI 1997/1523, reg 3.

2 See **14.19.5**.

are supplied to a person outside of the UK to a non-EU country, no UK VAT is charged in these circumstances. This is because the place of supply is deemed to take place outside of the UK. Although no UK VAT will be chargeable on a supply in these circumstances, a business recipient in the EU of the supplies will be required to account for VAT in their own country on the supply, if part of the EU.[1] This is the effect of Art 21 of the Sixth VAT Directive (the reverse charge provision).[2] Schedule 5 services insofar as they are relevant to e-commerce are: advertising services, data processing and provision of information, banking, financial and insurance services (including reinsurance), and telecommunications services. A non-business recipient within the EU will be subject to UK VAT on service supplies.

Example 76

Z Ltd operates an Internet trading site based in the UK. It provides an on-line Internet service to subscribers of worldwide stock market prices. The subscription is £10,000 per year for corporate users. Y based in the Cayman Islands subscribes to the service. Because this service relates to the provision of information within Sch 5 of the VATA 1994, it will be deemed to be supplied where the recipient belongs.[3] In this case the recipient is in the Cayman Islands. No UK VAT will be payable.

14.19.3 Key concepts in the place of supply of services[4]

In determining the place of supply of services under VATA 1994, the key concept is in locating where the supplier belongs. The test of 'belonging' is defined in VATA 1994 as being where:[5]

(1) the supplier of the service has a business establishment or some other fixed establishment, and no such establishment elsewhere;[6]
(2) where the supplier has no such establishment, the location of the supplier's usual place of residence;[7]
(3) where neither (1) or (2) are met, the place of supply is where the establishment most directly concerned with the supply exists.[8]

A person who is a non-resident is treated as belonging in the UK in respect of a supply of services if he carries on business through a branch or agency in the UK, on the basis that he has a business establishment within the UK.[9] The concept of branch or agency has previously been discussed in the context of direct taxation. It is clear from VATA

1 See HM Customs and Excise interval guidance manuals, Part 4 (Place of Supply), Chapter 2B, Section 14A, paras 14.2 and 14.3.
2 Directive 77/338. The nature of the reverse charge is examined later in this chapter. However, broadly it means that VAT must be accounted for by the recipient.
3 Value Added Tax (Place of Supply of Services) Order 1992, SI 1992/3121, art 16.
4 See *De Voils Indirect Tax Service*, *op cit*, Part V3.183; HM Customs and Excise Notice 700 'The VAT Guide', at section 2.8.
5 See HM Customs and Excise interval guidance manuals, Part 4, Chapter 2B, Section 5.
6 VATA 1994, s 9(2)(a).
7 Ibid, s 9(2)(b). For the purposes of a company, this means the place where it is legally constituted (s 9(5)(b)).
8 Ibid, s 9(2)(c).
9 Ibid, s 9(5)(a).

1994 that the concepts of branch or agency are equated to the status of a business establishment. In the context of Internet trade, services can be supplied from outside the EU and as a result no VAT will be payable by the EU non-business recipient. An Internet trader can achieve this objective by locating either its place of business or a fixed establishment outside of the EU. Such arrangements will work only where a supply is not deemed to be received in the UK under the reverse charge provisions. When this occurs, VAT must be accounted for by the business recipient. However, the VAT cost incurred by a business user can be recovered. If supplies are made directly to non-business consumers, the reverse charge will not apply because the service is not received for business purposes. The important point is that no VAT is payable by non-business consumers in these circumstances.

14.19.4 Establishments

The concept of branch or agency does not mark the outer limits of what can amount to an establishment for the purposes of a charge to VAT. The equation of branch or agency is limited to a business establishment. A fixed establishment is also relevant to where a supply is made. It is clear for the purposes of UK VAT legislation that a fixed establishment is capable of bearing a different meaning than business establishment. The concept of business establishment (referred to under VATA 1994) and place where the supplier has established his business (referred to under the Sixth VAT Directive) effectively means the registered place of business of the enterprise supplying the services (this is the interpretation placed on the phrase in the Sixth VAT Directive by the Advocate General in *Berkholtz*).[1] The important question for the purposes of place of supply of services is whether an automated computer server can amount to a fixed establishment. If so, it will be possible in appropriate circumstances to locate services outside of the UK and to supply them to UK consumers free of VAT. This will create incentives to locate services outside of the VAT charge.

Example 77

Z Ltd incorporated in the UK operates a worldwide Internet trade by the use of automated computer servers. One such server is located in the Cayman Islands. The business relates to the supply of computer software through the medium of the Internet. In other words, computer software is installed directly onto the buyer's computer. The question arises as to whether VAT must be charged on the supply of this service to UK buyers (non-business consumers). The application of VAT will depend upon the location of the supplier. Is the place of supply to be determined by reference to the place of business of Z Ltd (based in the UK), or the computer server in the Cayman Islands? The computer server can only constitute a reference point if it is a fixed establishment. The application of VAT legislation in this area is explored in the following sections. Much will depend upon the economic functions performed by the server.

The concept of fixed establishment

The concept of fixed establishment is interpreted by Customs and Excise as 'an establishment (including the business establishment) from which business activities

1 *Gunter Berkholz v Finanzamt Hamburg* [1985] ECR 2251.

are carried out and which has both the human and technical resources necessary for making or receiving the supplies of services in question'.[1]

The concept of fixed establishment has received consideration at the highest levels within the European Community. In the case of *Gunter Berkholz v Finanzamt Hamburg*,[2] gaming machines were installed on ferries operating between Denmark and West Germany. The tax authority in Germany sought to apply VAT on the gaming machines. The owner of the gaming machines employed individuals to maintain the machines and collect money from them. This was done on board the vessels. In 1980 the operation of these machines earned the owner 346,701.20 DEM. Turnover tax was assessed on the whole amount. Two questions arose. The first was as to whether the gaming machines were fixed establishments for the purposes of determining the place of supply of services. The second issue was how to determine the place of supply where the principal place of business of the supplier and any fixed establishment do not coincide.

As to the first question the Advocate General in his Opinion said that the term 'fixed'

> 'is synonymous with "permanent" and is the opposite of "uncertain" or "occasional". But this is not sufficient. A business, particularly if it supplies services extending over a period of time, requires a minimum kind of organisation. However, there is no organisation, ie an orderly system of human and material resources, which does not involve division of labour. Therefore the person supplying the services must have material resources or employees to help him in operating and administering the services.'

The Advocate General went on to say:

> 'With this, the court making the references has the interpretation which it was seeking: the fixed establishment within the meaning of Article 9(1) can perfectly well be an installation (such as a gaming machine), but subject to the proviso that it is installed permanently in a certain place and requires the use of human resources for its management.'

As to the second question, the Advocate General said that in the absence of specific rules in the legislation he would propose adopting the general principle whereby VAT is levied at the place of consumption. In this case, it would be the place of the fixed establishment, ie the gaming machines.

When this case went before the panel of the ECJ it was recognised that Art 9 of the Sixth VAT Directive refers to a number of different concepts which can be used to pinpoint the place of supply of services. The ECJ said that the main reference for determining the place of supply is the supplier's place of business. However, the existence of another establishment which is connected with a particular service is only relevant where 'that establishment has a sufficient minimum strength in the form of the permanent presence of the human and technical resources necessary for supplying

1 HM Customs and Excise internal guidance manuals, Part 4 (Place of Supply), Chapter 2B, Section 5.6.

2 [1985] 3 CMLR 667, ECJ.

specific services'.[1] Applying this principle to the installation of gaming machines on a ferry, the ECJ said:

> 'It does not appear that the installation on board a sea-going vessel of gaming machines which receive intermittent maintenance can constitute such an establishment, particularly in a case where the permanent place of business of the person operating the machines constitutes an appropriate point of connection for the purposes of taxation.'

The ECJ said that in reading Art 9 of the Sixth VAT Directive the preferred point for determining the place of supply of services was the supplier's place of business, except where this point would 'not lead to a rational solution from the tax viewpoint or results in a conflict with another Member State'. The ECJ also used the phrase that a fixed establishment may be used as the point for determining the place of supply where it would be 'impractical to connect the services with the place where the supplier has established his business'.

In the decision of *Customs and Excise Commissioners v DFDS A/S* the Advocate General (A La Pergola) summarised the approach, as stated in *Berkholtz* between the place of business and a fixed establishment in the following way:

> 'With regard to the connection between the two points of reference, the court went on to make it clear that an order of precedence must be observed. Specifically, it is only if "the reference to the place where the supplier has established his business does not lead to a rational result for tax purposes or creates a conflict with another member State" that account must be taken of another establishment from which the services are supplied (see *Berkholz* (at 2263, para 17)). In short, the place where the supplier has established his business must be seen as the "primary point of reference" (see *Berkholtz* (at 2263, para 17)).'[2]

How are we to decide which place of supply is to be preferred?

(1) In the decision of *Customs and Excise Commissioners v DFDS A/S* the Advocate General (A La Pergola) said that the place of taxation must coincide with that at which the service is supplied to the consumer. The Advocate General said 'the VAT system must be applied in a manner as far possible in harmony with the actual economic situation'[3]

(2) The place of supply as between the place of business or a fixed establishment should be that which leads to a rational result for the purposes of taxation. In *Customs and Excise Commissioners v DFDS A/S* the ECJ accepted the UK's view that for a rational result to be achieved it is necessary to take account of the actual place where the service is supplied. In that case, it was where travel tours were marketed (para 22 of the ECJ decision). Where a business establishment and fixed establishment exist it is likely that the latter will be chosen as the place

---

1 In *Faaborg-Gelting Linien A/S v Finanzamt Flensburg* [1996] STC 774 the ECJ, referring to *Berkholz* described the choice between the different concepts of place of business and fixed establishment in the following way: '... services cannot be deemed to be supplied at an establishment other than the place where the supplier has established his business unless that establishment is of a certain minimum size and both the human and technical resources necessary for the provision of particular services are permanently present' (para 17).

2 *Customs and Excise Commissioners v DFDS A/S* [1997] STC 384; see also the ECJ judgment at para 19 and 20.

3 Ibid, para 32.

of supply because as the ECJ observed in *Customs and Excise Commissioners v DFDS A/S* the

> 'Systematic reliance on the place where the supplier has established his business could in fact lead to distortions of competition, in that it might encourage undertakings trading in one member state to establish their business, in order to avoid taxation, in another member state which has availed itself of the possibility of maintaining the VAT exemption for the services in question.'[1]

This statement was made against the context of VAT and travel services. However, the same is true in respect of Internet business. A strict adherence to the place of business might encourage services to be located outside Europe creating fixed establishments which facilitate trade within Europe.

From the case-law a number of inferences can be drawn as to the impact of VAT on Internet business transactions.

(1) Installed hardware such as a computer server can theoretically constitute a fixed establishment.
(2) Computer hardware will only constitute a fixed establishment where the necessary human and technical resources for supplying the services accompany the establishment.
(3) Computer hardware which constitutes a fixed establishment will only be used for determining the place of supply of services where it is more practical than choosing the supplier's place of business.

The concept of fixed establishment is relevant to the following areas for the purposes of an Internet trade:

- determining where a supplier of services belongs (VATA 1994, s 9(2));
- determining where a supply of services is received (VATA 1994, s 9(4)).

Multiple establishments

It is possible for a supplier to have more than one establishment and this may cause potential difficulties in identifying the place of supply of services. Although the VAT legislation contains no rules on multiple establishments, Customs and Excise adopts the following approach:[2]

> 'When a supplier has establishments in different countries, the place of belonging under UK law is determined by reference to the establishment most directly concerned with the supply.'

> 'The "most directly concerned" test is not expressly provided for in EC law, but we regard it as consistent with the purpose of the relevant EC provisions (Article 9 of the Sixth VAT Directive) and we would contend that Article 9 provides the necessary EC vires for this test.'

1 *Customs and Excise Commissioners v DFDS A/S* [1997] STC 384, para 23.
2 HM Customs and Excise internal guidance manual, Vol 1, Part 4 (Place of Supply), Chapter 2B, Section 5.8. See also HM Customs and Excise Notice No 741 'VAT: Place of Supply of Services' para 2.2.

In *Berkholz* the ECJ said that a fixed establishment should be used for the purposes of determining the place of supply where it is practical to do so: for example, where there would otherwise be a conflict between Member States.

14.19.5 Reverse charge[1]

In addition to the place of supply rules under VATA 1994, s 7, and Art 9 of the Sixth VAT Directive, a service will be deemed to be received in the UK under the reverse charge provisions. Typically when a service is received from abroad the place of supply is located outside of the UK, because under the rules, the supplier belongs in another country. VAT will not therefore be charged on the supply. However, in relation to 'relevant services' under VATA 1994 these are deemed to be supplied in the UK. This is designed to prevent distortion of trade. Without a reverse charge businesses would acquire tax free benefits by obtaining services from abroad. This would enable foreign suppliers to gain a competitive advantage at the expense of suppliers operating within the EU.[2] The requirement to impose the reverse charge is provided for under Art 21(1)(b) of the Sixth VAT Directive.

The law
VATA 1994 provides that where 'relevant services' are received by a person who belongs in the UK for the purposes of any business carried on by him, and those services are supplied by a supplier from abroad, then the recipient is treated as having supplied the services in the UK for the purposes of VAT.[3] The result of this is that the recipient is required to account for output tax on the supply.[4] The recipient is entitled to claim that output tax back as input tax under the general rules. Under no circumstances is VAT accounted for to the foreign supplier.

Example 78

Internet Software Services Ltd acquires the right to produce Internet browser software developed in the USA. In the 1998–99 tax year the US owner of the copyright in the software grants an exclusive licence to the UK company for the right to produce the software. The licence payment is a lump sum of £40,000.

Under the reverse charge provisions (Sch 5, para 1 to VATA 1994), the licence will be treated as a supply received within the UK. The result of this is that VAT must be charged on the supply at the standard rate. The company will then be entitled to deduct the VAT liability as input tax.

If the reverse charge did not operate it would clearly be beneficial to acquire such licences from abroad, to the prejudice of domestic supplies of the same nature which will be subject to VAT.

1 See *De Voil's Indirect Tax Service*, (Butterworths) Division V3.193, V3.231; HM Customs and Excise internal guidance manual, Vol 1, Part 4 (Place of Supply), Chapter 2B, Section 16; and HM Customs and Excise Notice No 741, *op cit*.
2 For this reason telecommunication and IAP services are now subject to the reverse charge.
3 VATA 1994, s 8(1).
4 Ibid.

Limitations on the reverse charge

It is to be noted that the reverse charge does not apply where a supply specified in Sch 5 (relevant services) is supplied within the UK, or where a person receives the supply for non-business purposes. In these circumstances the place of supply will be determined under the default rules. Because of these rules, it is possible for Internet traders located outside the UK to conduct business effectively with non-business customers without any VAT being incurred by the UK consumer.

Relevant services

The services in respect of which a reverse charge operates are set out in Sch 5 to VATA 1994. Similar provisions are contained in Art 9(2)(e) of the Sixth VAT Directive which is the Schedule for the purposes of the reverse charge imposed by Art 21 of the Directive. The services subject to the reverse charge are not defined either at the domestic or European level. However, significant guidance is given by Customs and Excise as to the type of services which come within the classifications.[1] Although the guidance does not have force of law, it is certainly of use in determining current practice by the UK tax authorities. The list below is limited to those services directly relevant to Internet commerce.

Schedule 5 services

1. . . .

2. Advertising Services

Example of services:

Within: supplies of advertising services in the media, eg television time

3. . . . data processing and provision of information . . .

Example of services:

Within:

- There is no definition of data processing but Customs and Excise has adopted the definition contained in the Data Protection Act 1984,[2] which provides: 'Processing', in relation to data, means amending, augmenting, deleting, or re-arranging the data or extracting the information constituting the data and, in the case of personal data, means performing any of those operations by reference to the data subject.
- The guidance states that 'Data processing involves the performing of mathematical and logical operations on data according to programmed instructions in order to obtain required information'.[3]
- Appendix G of the Customs and Excise manual gives illustrations of the type of services received through a computer network which do not amount to data processing, for example, provision of access to the Internet.
- Information in respect of stock market prices.

1 HM Customs and Excise internal guidance manual, Vol 1, Part 4 (Place of Supply), Chapter 2B, Section 14B, paras 14.10 *et seq*.

2 HM Customs and Excise internal guidance manual, Part 1, para 1(7).

3 HM Customs and Excise internal guidance manual, Vol 1, Part 4 (Place of Supply), Chapter 2B, Section 14B, para 14.12.

- Information via ' "on-line" information services where the subscriber receives the information and not simply the right to access the system or network.'

4. . . .
5. banking, financial and insurance services (including reinsurance)
6. . . .
7. . . .

> '7A. Telecommunication services, that is to say services relating to the transmission, emission or reception of signals, writing, images and sounds or information of any nature by wire, radio, optical or other electromagnetic systems, including the transfer or assignment of the right to use capacity for such transmission, emission or reception.'

8. to 10 . . .

VATA 1994 provides that the reverse charge will not apply to services which are described in Sch 9 to the Act.[1] This Schedule defines services that are exempt from a VAT charge. The main services which will fall outside of the reverse charge provisions are as follows:

- Insurance (Group 2).
- Finance (Group 5).

Where a person receives these type of services for business purposes, no reverse charge will be applied. However, there will be no advantage in receiving these services from abroad simply because supplies of this nature will be exempt from VAT wherever the supplier is based. Of the services specified in Sch 5, it is clear numbers 2, 3 and 5 can all be offered through the medium of the Internet.

Telecommunication services
The reader might consider that there is a VAT advantage to be obtained by non-business users in acquiring telecommunication services from outside the UK. Such an advantage was available until 17 March 1998. Where telecommunication services are supplied on or after 18 March 1998 the place of supply rules have been modified.[2] The Value Added Tax (Place of Supply of Services) Order 1992[3] provides that where a supply of services consists of telecommuncation services,[4] and those services would be treated as supplied in a place outside the Member States of the EU, then the service 'shall be treated as supplied in the UK to the extent that the effective use and enjoyment of the services takes place in the UK.'[5] As a result, a foreign overseas telecommunications provider must account for UK VAT on the supplies, if the relevant registration thresholds are breached.

Example 79

Z Inc supplies telecommunication services to non-business users in the UK. The value of the supplies amounts to the sterling equivalent of £1 million. In the absence of the

1 VATA 1994, s 8(2).
2 Value Added Tax (Place of Supply of Services) (Amendment) Order 1998, SI 1998/763.
3 SI 1992/3121.
4 As defined in Sch 5, para 7A, to VATA 1994. It is important to note that the 'content' of a transmission is not included.
5 Value Added Tax (Place of Supply of Services) Order 1992, SI 1992/3121, art 18.

Value Added Tax (Place of Supply of Services) Order 1992 applying, the supply would be outside of the UK. However, the impact of the 1992 Order is that since the registration threshold for VAT is breached, and the 'effective use and enjoyment' of the telecommuncaiton services is in the UK, the foreign provider must account for UK VAT.

14.19.6 Place where supply received

The rules for determining where a supplier belongs have been described above. Where the recipient belongs of a supply is determined by rules specified in VATA 1994. Where a supply of services is made to an individual, which is received otherwise than for business purposes carried on by him, the individual is treated as belonging in whatever country he has his usual place of residence.[1] Where the latter rule does not apply, a person shall be treated as belonging in a country if he has a business establishment, or other fixed establishment, and no such other establishment elsewhere, or the person's usual place of residence is in that country, or failing this, the establishment at which the services are most directly used or to be used, is in that country.[2] The meaning of business establishment and fixed establishment have already been considered in the context of where a supplier belongs for the purposes of determining place of supply of services.

14.19.7 Internet access providers

Many Internet access providers usually confer more than the right to use a computer network in exchange for a subscription. The packages offered vary in nature but the core elements usually consist of the following:

- provision of e-mail addresses;
- provision of access to the World Wide Web;
- use of computer memory space for the purposes of operating an Internet web site page;
- chatline facilities;
- weather and news information pages;
- games;
- home banking;
- access to electronic shopping sites.

In relation to determining place of supply for such Internet packages, Customs and Excise issued a 'Business Brief'.[3] This publication essentially provides the following core advice in relation to Internet packages:

- packages offered for a single inclusive price represent a single supply for tax purposes;
- separate services are separate supplies and must be accounted for under each relevant VAT rule;

---

1 VATA 1994, s 9(3).
2 Ibid, s 9(4).
3 10 October 1997.

- a supply with a variety of elements will come within a number of the sub-paragraphs of Sch 5.[1] These elements should be separately identified;
- packages supplied within the UK are subject to VAT;
- packages supplied to non-business users within other Member States of the EU should be charged with UK VAT;
- packages supplied to business users within other Member States of the EU should not be charged with UK VAT if received for business purposes. In this regard adequate evidence should be retained.

14.19.8 Zero-rated supplies

Where a supply is classified as zero-rated for the purposes of VAT, it is a taxable supply, but the rate of VAT is set at zero, as opposed to the standard rate of 17.5 per cent.[2] Zero-rated supplies are specified in Sch 8 to the Act.[3] A distinction needs to be drawn between:

(1) supplies which are consumed directly through the medium of the Internet, such as access to an electronic database, or the purchase and electronic transfer of software to a computer; and
(2) supplies which are acquired through use of the Internet, such as a contract that is entered into for the supply of food, books, or tangible computer software.

The distinction is very important because very few supplies through the Internet are zero-rated.

Zero-rating is important to businesses because it enables them to acquire important cash flow advantages: for example, if a business incurs input tax of £100,000 on components used to make a supply by itself, which is zero-rated, the business will be entitled to a refund of the input tax on the cost components acquired in making that supply.

Relevant zero-rated supplies within (1) above for the purposes of Internet business potentially fall into one category which is 'Books'.[4] The question which arises here is the extent to which the supply of this type of media across the Internet constitutes a zero-rated supply. The category is defined as:

'Group 3 – BOOKS

1. Books, booklets, brochures, pamphlets and leaflets.
2. Newspapers, journals and periodicals.
3. Children's picture books and painting books.
4. Music (printed, duplicated or manuscript).
5. Maps, charts and topographical plans.
6. Covers, cases and other articles supplied with items 1 to 5 and not separately accounted for.'

---

1 VATA 1994.
2 Ibid, s 30 (1).
3 Ibid, s 30 (2).
4 See *De Voil's Indirect Tax Service*, *op cit*, Part V4, at V4.273.

Where the material referred to in Group 3 is supplied through the medium of the Internet it is doubtful that such supplies will qualify for zero-rating. This is because the classification is focused entirely upon physical media. In other words, zero-rating is permitted only in respect of text or images which are recorded on a paper format. This interpretation is applied by Customs and Excise. In their notice headed 'Printed and similar matter'[1] the passage referring to 'Books and booklets' states:[2]

> 'These normally consist of text or illustrations, bound in a stiffer cover than their pages. They may be printed in any language or character (including braille or shorthand), photocopied, typed or hand-written, so long as they are bound in book or booklet form.'

There is no scope within the guidance which permits zero-rating in respect of text transferred through the medium of the Internet. The definition applied by Customs and Excise in their guidance broadly corresponds in spirit with the definition of a book in the *Shorter Oxford English Dictionary*.[3]

However, if the Internet is used to enter into a contract for the supply of books, this would be a supply of goods, and hence a supply of books which would qualify for zero-rating. Group 3 provides that zero-rating extends to newspapers, journals and periodicals. Some proprietors of these media provide electronic versions via the Internet. These media qualify only where they are supplied in a physical format. The guidance describes a newspaper as 'several large sheets of printed matter folded rather than bound together',[4] while journals and periodicals are described as '... magazines issued in a series at regular intervals, but more frequently than once a year, either in newspaper format or as paper-bound publications'.[5]

The exclusion of zero-rating to supplies made otherwise than through physical media is confirmed in the Customs and Excise guidance. The relevant passage provides:[6]

> 'Any non-printed matter, such as audio cassettes or video cassettes, is standard-rated. This includes the storage and dissemination of textual information by electronic, electrical, magnetic, chemical, microfilm, microfiche, or any similar process...'

It is however important to recognise that supplies within category (2), ie those supplied in furtherance of a contract entered into via the Internet may qualify for zero-rating if the subject-matter of the supply comes within a zero-rated group. Table 25 summarises the supplies which are zero-rated, and illustrates the extent to which these types of supply are relevant to Internet transactions, whereby a person enters into contracts for the supply of such goods or services.

---

1 HM Customs and Excise Notice No 701/10/85 (up-dated April 1997).

2 Ibid, Section 1, para 2. See also *Walker (AE) v Customs and Excise Commissioners* [1973] 1 VATTR 8, *Customs and Excise Commissioners v Colour Offset Ltd* [1995] STC 85.

3 Oxford University Press, 1993.

4 HM Customs and Excise Notice No 701/10/85, Section 1, para 5.

5 Ibid, para 6.

6 Ibid, para 16.

Table 25

Group	Classification	Relevance
1	Food	Relevant
2	Sewerage Services & Water	Not Relevant
3	Books	Relevant
4	Audio Books for the Blind	Relevant
5	Construction of a Building	Not Relevant
6	Reconstruction of a Protected Building	Not Relevant
7	International Services	Not Relevant
8	Transport	Not Relevant
9	Caravans & Houseboats	Not Relevant
10	Gold	Not Relevant
11	Bank Notes	Not Relevant
12	Goods Dispensed under Prescription	Not Relevant
13	Imports and Exports	Relevant
14	Tax Free Shops	Not Relevant
15	Charities	Not Relevant
16	Clothing or Footware for Young Children	Relevant

Additionally, goods within the classifications summarised in the above Table which are acquired in the UK from another Member State, or a country outside the Member States, are not chargeable to VAT.[1] VAT is also zero-rated on a supply of goods which are exported outside the EU.[2] No VAT is charged where the place of supply is outside the UK.[3]

1 VATA 1994, s 30 (3) except as otherwise provided in Sch 8.
2 Ibid, s 30 (6).
3 See **14.19.2**.

Chapter 15

E-COMMERCE AND THE SELECTION OF TAX SUPPLIERS IN THE GLOBAL MARKET PLACE – THE CASE FOR LOW DIRECT TAX JURISDICTIONS[1]

15.1 INTRODUCTION

A business person interested in e-commerce, standing back and looking at what is literally a world of choices, will notice that there are many jurisdictions willing to supply an assortment of public sector goods and services in exchange for varying proportions of the revenue or capital of any e-commerce business. Governments may also supply international business with preferential access to selected fiscal regimes established by other governments with whom they have treaties. In general, however, the public sector goods and services which governments supply are rapidly becoming commodities with little to distinguish them aside from price. E-commerce businesses which choose to adopt a global perspective for the global market place will recognise that they need to exercise as much, or more, care in the selection of their tax supplier as they would to any other significant supplier.

This chapter deals with taxation issues from the point of view of business persons and businesses which operate outside of, or have the potential to operate outside of, high tax jurisdictions. As every business person knows, tax in its various forms is one of the largest expense components of any successful business operating within a high tax environment. Start-up and marginal businesses may be caused to fail or may be prevented from growing by tax.

The traditional assumption of the majority of business persons in the industrial age was that tax was an obligatory cost item for which there was only one supplier. This assumption was valid for the vast majority of traditional businesses which were tied to a single geographic location and had only local suppliers of physical goods and a local customer base. The changing nature of commerce has brought this assumption into question for many forward thinking business people. Exposure to tax cost is now becoming subject to the same type of cost-benefit analysis to which all other components of a business plan are subjected.

1 This chapter was written by Dr Christopher Rose.

15.2 CHOICE OF JURISDICTION AND FISCAL CONSIDERATIONS

E-commerce provides global opportunities for the development and expansion for existing businesses, both large and small, and vast scope for starting new businesses. E-commerce also means global competition for many types of business. The legislative and regulatory environment in which a business operates may have a significant influence on the competitiveness and ultimate success of any business. The fiscal environment in which a business operates is a major component of its legislative and regulatory environment.

Tax should rarely be the principal or first consideration in the location of any business. Businesses may choose to locate in high tax jurisdictions for a number of reasons. It would be entirely reasonable for a business to choose to locate in a high tax jurisdiction if that jurisdiction provided government services which provide a benefit to the particular business commensurate with the tax costs. At the other end of the spectrum, there would appear to be little business incentive to establish any business in an environment in which the lack of benefit from government goods and services rendered the fiscal regime entirely punitive. Non-business considerations which may affect the location of many smaller businesses, are very often significant factors in determining business location but such considerations are beyond the scope of this chapter.

Businesses which are highly taxed tend to have less money for reinvestment and also tend to provide a lower rate of return for equity investors and a higher risk for both equity and non-equity investors than comparative businesses which have a lesser tax burden. Businesses which are forced to spend time and money on tax compliance do not have those resources available for productive areas of business. Businesses whose resources are consumed by unproductive activities tend to lose if they are involved in competition with businesses which do not bear such burdens.

Equity and non-equity investors, who are themselves highly taxed, require a pre-tax rate of return which generally exceeds that of investors who are not so highly taxed for the same business risk. In this manner, businesses in high tax jurisdictions are also made less competitive in comparison with comparable businesses in jurisdictions with lower overall tax costs for that type of business. This loss of competitive advantage for businesses may be accentuated where governments waste tax revenues.

An awareness of the comparative costs to business of various fiscal regimes has led many global businesses to recognise that it is prudent to examine fully the location for each and every part of any business. Failure to consider the fiscal implications of business location may be very expensive.

Digitised products and services can be delivered from anywhere on the planet to anywhere on the planet, provided that adequate telecommunications exist. Activities within individual businesses, which can be conducted digitally, can be situated anywhere on the planet with no need for physical proximity to other activities conducted by that same business. Activities within a particular business requiring a large highly trained technical workforce can be conducted wherever such a workforce exists on economical terms. Other digital activities, such as data entry for the same business, can similarly be conducted wherever it is most economical to do so, even if it is conducted on the other side of the planet.

Investors, including those who invest intellectual capital, time and labour as well as those who invest money, will naturally seek out the most favourable business environment. Prudent investors assessing existing and new e-commerce business opportunities must assess all factors relevant to the location from which businesses are conducted from a global perspective. Factors that are relevant to decisions regarding the jurisdictional location of e-commerce business include:

- political stability;
- the regulatory environment;
- the availability and general level of cost of relevant goods and services, including professional and financial services;
- the aggregate effective cost (including compliance costs) of the applicable taxation systems;
- the availability and cost of suitably qualified human resources; and
- the cost and availability of the relevant telecommunications infrastructure.

The relative weight of each of these factors varies from business to business. It is not possible to identify any single jurisdiction which can be said to be optimal for all forms of e-commerce at any particular point in time. An advantage offered by a particular jurisdiction in one regard, may be outweighed by disadvantages in other regards. Fortunately for investors, there are a number of jurisdictions which offer advantages in regard to each particular factor.

In general, investors and entrepreneurs may choose to establish a decision tree. The first decision is often whether or not the political, legal and regulatory environment is sufficiently well run and 'business friendly' to justify further investigation. Obviously, unstable and unfriendly jurisdictions are no place to contemplate establishing new businesses unless there is some overriding reason for doing so. The next level of decision is often to draw up a shortlist of jurisdictions which have available, or will allow to be imported, the necessary human and technological resources on economically reasonable terms. The final level of consideration is often the effective after tax yield offered by similar investments in shortlisted jurisdictions. In the following section, consideration will be given primarily to the tax considerations which may be involved in the choice of a jurisdiction.

15.3 E-COMMERCE AND DIVERSITY IN FISCAL REGIMES

Governments around the world have followed different paths in determining the size and cost of the public sector in their particular jurisdictions. Certain societies impose greater demands for governmental services and have a correspondingly higher overall level of taxation in order to pay for government services. Similarly, governments have developed a variety of mechanisms for raising the revenues required for government services. Taxation has taken different forms in different jurisdictions over time, based upon various considerations including the social, political and cultural values which are predominant in a given jurisdiction at any given time.

The optimal regime of taxation for e-commerce activities, as viewed from the perspective of investors, would naturally be one which efficiently supports the minimal governmental infrastructure which e-commerce requires, and in so doing imposes the lowest effective overall cost of taxation on e-commerce business activities. Considerations of the overall rate of taxation for investors in e-commerce must include not only considerations of income, profit, capital gains and turnover taxes, but additionally the cost of any compulsory taxes, levies or fees related to payroll, employment, health, social security, pension or other matters. The availability of tax treaties and tariff-free zones, may also be a significant consideration for certain e-commerce business applications. In all cases, the costs of compliance in regard to taxation must also be a consideration. The greater the range of taxes and the greater the complexity of each, the higher the cost will be to business.

There has been increasing awareness of the advantages of locating certain businesses engaged in e-commerce in jurisdictions which do not tax income, profit, capital gains or turnover. Such jurisdictions generally raise revenues for the operation of government from import duties, stamp duties, user fees, consumption taxes and infrastructure fees. Not only may the effective rate of overall taxation (expressed as a function of gross revenues) be much less in such jurisdictions, but also the compliance costs required by such taxation systems are generally much lower than in jurisdictions with excessively complex fiscal regimes.

Jurisdictions which do not impose taxes on income, profit, turnover, or capital gains are often referred to as 'low direct tax' jurisdictions. The terms 'tax haven' and 'zero tax' jurisdictions, while popular in the tabloid press and in works of fiction, are obviously not correct, and in certain contexts have even become pejorative. The use of such terms, has to a certain extent entered the vernacular, most likely on the basis that these terms appeal to the desire of many persons in high tax jurisdictions to escape what they view as oppressive and wasteful tax systems which penalise endeavour, ingenuity and productivity. It must be kept in mind however that all governments need revenue, and in this regard the low direct tax jurisdictions are no different. The peoples of the low direct tax jurisdictions in general merely choose to have less 'welfare industry' activities and to have low compliance cost and low administration cost taxation systems based primarily upon taxation of the utilisation of scarce resources within their communities.

In certain situations, jurisdictions tax their own residents in a manner which is distinct from the manner in which they tax non-residents. By way of a simple example, the UK taxes interest income earned within the UK by its residents, but not interest income earned within the UK by non-domiciled non-residents. In this regard the UK may be said to be a 'tax haven' for certain non-resident persons in regard to interest income. The UK is not alone in having such features within its fiscal regime.

Recently, there have been a number of attempts by various cartels and special interest groups in the international forum to define the term 'tax haven' in such a manner as to facilitate the extension of fiscal enforcement into the arena of public international law. These same cartels and groups are at the same time attempting to eliminate competition in fiscal regimes rather than increasing the productivity of their own fiscal regimes. These initiatives are in part aimed at preventing international competition for e-commerce business, other than on terms favourable to these cartels and groups. These initiatives will be discussed in detail later in this chapter.

The term 'offshore', when used to describe a jurisdiction, also needs to be defined for purposes of the present discussion. In general, any location which is beyond the jurisdiction of a particular authority may be said to be 'offshore'. Thus, the UK is 'offshore' with regard to France, not only in terms of geography, but also in terms of the effective fiscal regime which operates. However, using the frame of reference usually employed in the tabloid press, the term 'offshore' has generally been taken as referring to a number of small States and dependencies which have fiscal regimes qualifying them as low direct tax jurisdictions, and which also have the expertise and regulatory environments favouring their financial services sectors. This narrow view of the concept of doing business 'offshore' is, however, far too narrow for business planning considerations.

15.4 TAX CONSIDERATIONS WHEN CHOOSING BUSINESS VENUES FOR E-COMMERCE

The range of business activities which will utilise e-commerce in the future is difficult to predict, but will almost certainly include forms of business that do not even exist at present. In some instances, business products and services will be unique and will not be subject to competitive pressures. In other instances, suppliers of products and services will face global competition and those that enjoy a higher after tax yield on their productive efforts may enjoy an advantage.

In this section, a series of examples will be considered to give an overview of the range of e-commerce activities, which might give rise to considerations of the optimal choice of jurisdiction for e-commerce business at the present time. It must be noted that the considerations set out here are very general in nature and are not to be taken as recommendations for specific business structures for any particular purpose. In all cases, appropriate advice must be obtained prior to the establishment of any business structure.

It is essential that each and every business obtains appropriate advice regarding the regulatory requirements of each jurisdiction in which it will, or may, be deemed to be operating for purposes of taxation, as well as all other regulatory requirements. These regulatory requirements vary from jurisdiction to jurisdiction. As a general rule, the aggregate regulatory requirements and compliance costs present in low direct tax jurisdictions tend to be less than in high tax jurisdictions, if for no other reason than the absent or minimal tax compliance requirements and costs. Each e-commerce business entity or prospective business entity should identify whether there is any advantage to be gained from locating part or all of its operations in a low direct tax jurisdiction.

There are unique non-tax considerations that will apply in each jurisdiction. By way of example, most jurisdictions do not allow foreign persons or enterprises to establish businesses as of right. In many jurisdictions, there are regulations which specify the conditions under which such foreign persons and enterprises may establish themselves within the jurisdiction. In certain circumstances, it may be advantageous to appoint a local company management organisation in order ensure compliance with local regulations.

There are a range of roles which low direct tax jurisdictions may usefully serve in international commerce. This range of roles extends from one end of the spectrum in which all aspects of a business, inclusive of all management and control, are performed within the low tax jurisdiction, to the other end of the spectrum where only a single task within the overall business is performed within the low direct tax jurisdiction.

The following series of examples may serve to illustrate the variety of types of e-commerce activities which may involve the use of a tax efficient jurisdiction. Each of the examples focuses on a small business activity for the sake of simplicity. The persons, products and services referred to in the examples set out below are completely fictitious and any similarity with real persons, products or services is unintended and purely coincidental.

Example 80

Mr A, is and always has been a citizen only of a low direct tax jurisdiction ('LDTJ'), and is and always has been domiciled, resident, and ordinarily resident solely within the LDTJ. The LDTJ imposes no income, corporation, or capital gains tax. One day while walking along a beach in the LDTJ, Mr A has the idea of setting up a company in the LDTJ to sell music which he composes and digitally records, over the Internet. Mr A is the sole shareholder, officer, director and employee of the company. No person, other than Mr A, has any interest, whether legal or equitable in the company. Neither Mr A nor his company have any interest in any company or enterprise operating outside of the LDTJ. The company pays to Mr A an amount equal to 75 per cent of the profits of the company each month. The company has no other agents. The server which is located in the premises of Mr A's company has a direct connection to the Internet. Mr A's company allows persons from anywhere on the planet to download Mr A's music from the company's server upon the purchaser entering into a contract with Mr A's company. The relevant contract specifies that the contract is subject to the laws of the LDTJ, that payment may be made only to Mr A's company, that payment is deemed to have been made only when received by Mr A's company within the LDTJ and that the purchaser shall be deemed to have taken delivery of the music within the LDTJ at the point in time when an electronic copy of the music leaves the company's server. Mr A's company sells a large amount of music and is highly profitable. Neither Mr A nor his company pay any income, or corporation tax on the profits of Mr A's company or on the moneys paid by the company to Mr A.

In the context of the above example, it is unlikely that Mr A's company could be said to have a taxable presence within any jurisdiction other than the LDTJ in which the company is located. Similarly, it is unlikely that Mr A could be said to have a taxable presence within any other jurisdiction other than the LDTJ. Mr A is happy.

Example 81

Mr B is and always has been a citizen only of the UK (and now the EU), and is and always has been domiciled, resident, and ordinarily resident solely within the UK. One day while walking through the freezing rain on a bleak winter's day, Mr B makes the determination that he needs to change his domicile and residence to a more hospitable environment. Mr B consults with his professional advisors, sells all of his possessions, severs all ties to the UK and moves permanently to the LDTJ where Mr A lives. Some time later while walking along the beach, Mr B has an idea. He decides to set up a company in the LDTJ and to sell the graphics which he creates, over the Internet. Mr B consults with appropriate advisors in the LDTJ, obtains the necessary permits and establishes a company for the purpose of selling the graphics in digital form over the Internet. Mr B's company rents space on a server from a company which does not operate outside the LDTJ. The business arrangements between Mr B and his company, and between Mr B's company and its customers are essentially the same as those which exist between Mr A and Mr A's company and between Mr A's company and its customers as set out in Example 81 above. Mr B's company sells a lot of graphics and is highly profitable.

In the context of Example 81, it is unlikely that Mr B's company could be said to have a taxable presence within the UK, or in any jurisdiction other than the LDTJ. Similarly, it is unlikely on the facts given that Mr B could be said to have taxable income in the UK in any tax year commencing following Mr B's departure from the UK. Mr B pays no income or corporation tax in the LDTJ. Mr B is happy.

Example 82

Ms C is and always has been a citizen only of Canada, and is and always has been domiciled, resident, and ordinarily resident solely within Canada. Ms C owns a Canadian company which utilises computer aided manufacturing to make custom tools. The proprietary computer software which Ms C's company had developed for its own use, was less than satisfactory and this was causing Ms C considerable stress. One day while walking through a blizzard on a bleak winter's day, Ms C decided that she was in need of a vacation. She took a holiday in the LDTJ where Mr A lives. One day during her holiday, while walking on the beach she realised that she needed to change not only the company's software, but also the company's manner of doing business. Ms C realised that the computers which ran the software, and which control the manufacturing machinery do not need to be in Canada. The computers running the software could be anywhere on the planet, provided that they were connected through the Internet to the machinery in her Canadian plant. Ms C also realised that the same software, located and running on computers located anywhere on the planet, could also be licensed on a per use basis to other manufacturers anywhere on the planet that have adequate Internet connections. Ms C consulted with appropriate professional advisors in Canada and the LDTJ and with their assistance establishes the following business plan.

Ms C's company caused to be incorporated in a low direct tax jurisdiction which has a double taxation agreement with Canada, a company ('the treaty jurisdiction company' or 'TJC'), to which was sold at fair market value such intellectual property as Ms C's company had regarding the defective software which Ms C's company was at that time using, plus the requirements and specifications for the software which needed to be created. The TJC in turn set up a software development subsidiary ('SDS') in the LDTJ and contracted with SDS in the LDTJ to produce the desired software. The SDS employed persons in the LDTJ to develop the software. The SDS then licensed the software to the TJC which in turn licensed the software to Ms C's company and any other company which required such software. The SDS maintains its central management and control in the LDTJ. The TJC may have its central management and control in either the LDTJ or the TJC. The board of directors of each of the SDS and the TJC exercise effective management and control, and of course the majority of the board members were not to be residents of Canada. There were other conditions which were required to be met in order to satisfy the tax authorities in the treaty jurisdiction concerned and in Canada. At the end of the day, the new software running on a computer in the LDTJ operates machinery all over the planet 24 hours per day. The SDS and the TJC are very profitable. The tax payable by Ms C and her Canadian company are minimised. Ms C is happy.

In the context of Example 82, on the assumption that all of the requirements are met, the income earned by the TJC may be able to flow back to Canada tax-free at appropriate times as exempt surplus. Ms C and Ms C's company will however, otherwise be subject to Canadian taxes for such time as they are resident in Canada.

Example 83

Ms D is and always has been domiciled, resident, and ordinarily resident solely within the UK. Ms D is a software developer who had a wonderful idea for a totally new software application. The only trouble was that she did not have much money and in order to change her idea into an actual software product which could be marketed and sold, she needed investors. She talked to people that she knew, but was unable to find anyone to invest in her idea on anything like reasonable terms. Ms D discovered that potential investors in the UK are also concerned with after tax profit and therefore require a substantial return. One day while sitting in front of her computer and staring at the freezing rain outside, she had another bright idea. She accessed her favourite Internet search engine and searched for information on sources of venture capital. She was surprised to discover that there are such things as companies which run 'incubators' which specialise in providing venture capital and business support for software development. She was even more surprised to discover that some of these incubators require that the software be developed in warm and friendly jurisdictions such as the LDTJ. Ms D decided to contact the 'incubator' company in the LDTJ and, being a wise person, consulted with, and took the advice of her UK professional advisors. She also obtained the advice of a professional advisor with specialist knowledge in the LDTJ. Ms D made the determination that it would be advantageous to her to change her residence by moving to the LDTJ in order to develop the software with the assistance of the LDTJ incubator company. Ms D obtained appropriate market valuations on what was at that point in time only an idea for a software product, as at the date of her leaving the UK to take up residence in the LDTJ. Ms D gave up her residence within the UK, severed all commercial ties with the UK and moved to the LDTJ. On the day after giving up her UK residence and acquiring a new residence in the LDTJ, Ms D wrote out her idea for the first time and caused the written idea to be sold at fair market value to a company which she had caused to be incorporated in the LDTJ on the day after her arrival in the LDTJ. With the assistance of the LDTJ incubator company, Ms D's software company developed the software within the LDTJ. When the development of the software had been completed and tested satisfactorily, Ms D's company sold all of the rights to the software which it had developed to another LDTJ company unconnected with Ms D and earned a very substantial capital gain in the process. Ms D then caused her LDTJ company to be wound up immediately after it had distributed all surplus cash to her. Ms D is pleasantly surprised that the effective cost to her of the assistance provided by the LDTJ incubator was much less than the UK capital gains tax would have been had she stayed in the UK and been able to find investors willing to invest at a reasonable rate.

In the context of Example 83, any capital gain payable by Ms D on the sale of the bare idea immediately after the time of her departure from the UK would likely be comparatively small. The value of the software product would be created after her departure from the UK by a company which was incorporated after her taking up residence outside of the UK. Given that the LDTJ does not have any capital gains, corporation, or income tax, Ms D is happy and contemplating her next software development project.

Example 84

Mr E was domiciled, resident and ordinarily resident in the UK. Mr E is an architect who is comfortable working in an electronic environment. Mr E specialises in designing the renovation and conversion of large outdated commercial buildings and complexes. Mr E recognised that he is able to do most of his work from home and he also realised that he could make his home anywhere on the planet which has adequate telecommunications. Mr E took appropriate advice and decided to give up his residence in the UK, to move to the LDTJ and to set up a company in the LDTJ which would employ him to carry on the business of architectural design consulting. Mr E's LDTJ company caused to be incorporated an Irish non-resident company to act as the EU representative of Mr E's LDTJ company. The Irish company in turn established and maintained a representative office in the UK to facilitate communications with UK based clients who are not comfortable in an electronic environment. Mr E's company has clients from other parts of the world as well, but deals with these clients solely by electronic means from the LDTJ. The representative office in the UK is quite small, employing only one part time secretary. Phone calls and fax messages to the office can be automatically forwarded to the appropriate person wherever that person happens to be at the time. Ordinary mail and parcel deliveries are forwarded to the appropriate person by the secretary. Blueprints and reports produced by Mr E's company can either be transmitted electronically directly to clients, if they have appropriate software and hardware, or they can be transmitted to the representative office in the UK where they can be printed out and shipped to clients by courier or post. Mr E also uses independent sub-contractors in the UK to do surveying and other tasks which would otherwise require his presence within the UK. All of the creative activities of the business occur outside the UK and Mr E does not engage in any gainful occupation in any jurisdiction other than the LDTJ. Each of the contracts which Mr E has, specifies that the contracts are subject to LDTJ law and are fulfilled entirely within the LDTJ.

In the context of Example 84, the Irish company formed by Mr E's company would potentially be subject to both low rate Irish corporate tax and UK corporate tax on a portion of its corporate profit derived from the UK representative office as discussed in preceding chapters. With appropriate planning, this tax burden would be relatively small. Mr E's LDTJ company would not have to pay any corporation tax in the LDTJ. Similarly, Mr E would not be subject to tax on his personal income on the facts given, as there is no income tax in the LDTJ.

Example 85

Ms F is an immigrant to the LDTJ, now resident and domiciled in the LDTJ. Ms F owns a company registered in the LDTJ which purchases the international distribution rights for children's toys and then markets the toys to various unrelated wholesalers in Europe and North America which in turn, sell to large retail stores. Ms F's company contracts electronically with both its suppliers and its customers. Inventory, shipping, receipt confirmation, accounting and payments are all similarly controlled electronically from the LDTJ. The toys are produced under contract by manufacturers in various jurisdictions around the world and are often warehoused in the jurisdictions in which they are produced prior to being shipped. Ms F's company contracts with external quality assurance personnel in regard to the monitoring of toy production and also contracts with outside personnel in regard to quality assurance matters at the point of physical supply to the wholesalers. The toys are normally shipped from the warehouses to either the wholesalers or occasionally directly to the large retail stores. Ms F's company conducts all of its business from the LDTJ and all of its contracts are based in the LDTJ. Ms F's company is organised so that it has no need for representative offices outside of the LDTJ.

In the context of the facts given in Example 85, Ms F's company would have no taxable presence outside of the LDTJ and since there is no corporate tax in the LDTJ, the tax burden for Ms F's company is minimal. The commercial trade off is the cost of contracting with other organisations to provide the services which could otherwise be provided by a potentially taxable representative office if Ms F's company had chosen that business structure.

As can be seen, the spectrum of business activities which may utilise both aspects of e-commerce and the efficiencies of a low direct tax jurisdiction is quite broad. No doubt any person reading this book will be able to think of many other examples.

15.5 INTERNATIONAL TAX RELATED INITIATIVES

Tax is being increasingly recognised by business people around the world as a significant burden to business and a factor which business must consider in choosing the locations from which it operates. At the same time, governments recognise that the comparative advantages and disadvantages of their tax regimes influence the level of inward investment, the competitiveness of businesses which operated within their jurisdictions, and as a result, the employment of their domestic taxpayers.

The larger industrialised nations tend to share a heavy reliance on taxation of business activities to support their large public sectors. In response to present and anticipated pressures on their business tax bases, these governments have moved toward common action to preserve and expand their share of the global market place and to prevent any increased pressure on their existing internal inefficiencies. Many of the governments of the larger industrialised nations view the productive capacity currently or potentially within their fiscal control as their 'property' and are attempting to 'lock in' this productive capacity with its associated tax base through changes in domestic legislation as well as through attempts to force approximation and harmonisation of tax regimes on a global basis. These governments tend to view available alternatives, which would involve rapid increases in efficiencies within their public sectors or improvements in the business environment within their jurisdictions, as politically less expedient if not completely unpalatable. At the same time, many of these governments are supporting measures such as the Multi-lateral Agreement on Investment sponsored by the OECD which will have the effect of enlarging and providing greater security for the portions of their tax bases derived from the income of multinational corporations domiciled within their Member States, but operating in non-member countries.

The principal initiatives which came into existence in the late 1990s are being orchestrated by a number of cartels including:

(1) the Organisation for Economic Co-operation and Development;
(2) the European Union;
(3) the Group of 7 leading industrial nations ('the G7');
(4) the International Monetary Fund/World Tax Organisation ('IMF/WTO').

These initiatives are highly interrelated. Not only are the memberships in these organisations overlapping, but there is formal cooperation in the formation of strategy among the dominant participants in each group. It is beyond the scope of this chapter to go into any of these initiatives in detail. Rather, aspects of the two most detailed initiatives produced by the OECD and the EU will be presented in the context of global e-commerce.

15.5.1 The OECD 'Harmful Tax Competition' initiative

The member states of the OECD comprise most of the rich and powerful nations of the industrialised world including the US, all of the Member States of the EU, Japan, Switzerland, Canada, Turkey, Norway, Finland, Australia, New Zealand, Mexico, the Czech Republic, Hungary, Poland, and Korea. In May 1996, following many months of internal strategy development, the OECD issued a Ministers' Communique which announced the OECD's determination 'to develop measures to counter the distorting effects of harmful tax competition'. In May 1998 the OECD released a report entitled, 'Harmful Tax Competition – An Emerging Global Issue' ('the Report') which is discussed in Chapter 16.

A detailed criticism of the Report and its assumptions would be extremely lengthy and is beyond the scope of this chapter. For the present purposes a brief commentary will be provided on an alternative perspective of the OECD initiative.

It is natural for the political and bureaucratic establishments in the high tax jurisdictions which have responsibility for setting tax collection protocols and spending tax revenues to want to enhance and preserve their powers by whatever means they perceive to be available. Powerful nations have always tried to impose their will on their weaker neighbours. Smaller nations, which developed more efficient public sector systems or more competitive products or services have always been subject to various sanctions and impositions originating from more powerful nations which find their commercial and political interests challenged. The actions of the powerful have frequently been justified as necessary to save the souls of the inhabitants of their less powerful neighbours or to avenge or prevent some often contrived or non-existent wrong.

One interpretation of the principal argument in the OECD initiative is in essence:

> 'Fiscal regimes which offer more efficient alternatives to the regimes presently existing within the member states of the OECD offer a competitive advantage which the OECD chooses not to meet for its own internal political reasons. If this competitive advantage potentially available to non-cartel members is allowed to persist or if subject tax payers are allowed to have any meaningful choice, then there is the potential for the tax bases of the OECD member countries to decline which would do "harm" to our expectations of future tax revenues. The OECD is therefore justified in any attempt to use its power and influence to fabricate international norms which will justify our existing fiscal regimes and label more efficient regimes as "harmful". "Harmful" tax competition as we define it cannot be allowed to do us "harm". We are therefore justified in taking preemptive measures to prevent "harm" to ourselves.'

It is a common feature of the oppression of the less powerful by the more powerful, that the more powerful feel compelled to develop a self-justifying moral position, be it based on 'fairness' or otherwise. Contrived morality is a useful tool when logic and consideration for basic human rights do not produce the desired result.

The principal factor separating the opinions of those representing the high tax jurisdictions which support the Report and the low direct tax jurisdictions which do not, is the absence of shared assumptions and objectives. The supporters of the OECD initiative seem to assert the dogma that competition among private sector suppliers of goods and services is a very good thing, which increases efficiency and provides benefits for the public, whereas competition among public sector suppliers of goods and services is somehow 'harmful'. Indeed, most of the governments which support the OECD initiative have regulatory mechanisms to monitor and prevent anti-competitive activities in the private sector. It is perhaps unfortunate that within the international context, there is no monopolies commission or other anti-trust watchdog.

The OECD is also actively involved in considerations of the implications of e-commerce for the fiscal regimes of its members. A report prepared by the OECD Committee on Fiscal Affairs ('the Committee') for the Ministerial meeting of the OECD in October 1998 entitled 'Electronic Commerce: Taxation Framework Conditions', sets out the then current guidelines which the OECD wishes to see adopted. Of particular importance within the framework is the stated desire to implement taxation of e-commerce within the existing framework of taxation of conventional commerce. If adopted by the member states of the OECD, this should provide for greater certainty for those planning international business with e-commerce components.

The Committee proposes that, in principle, all business decisions should be made on the basis of economic factors excluding tax. This proposal may find difficulty in the real world as tax is a significant factor in the bottom line of most businesses operating within high tax jurisdictions. There are only two situations in which this proposal would seem logical. The first is a situation in which the benefit to business derived from the public sector was equal to the tax cost of operating within that jurisdiction. Many high tax jurisdictions are a long way from achieving that situation. The only other situation would appear to be forced 'harmonisation' of tax levels among jurisdictions.

The Committee recognises that within the international political arena, there will be the necessity of jurisdictions maintaining the right of self-determination in fiscal matters, and that double taxation should be avoided with respect to e-commerce business activities. The Committee also recognises that what it calls 'unintentional non-taxation' should be avoided by governments. From the perspective of business entities, however, the Committee should also recognise that unintentional taxation is more of a problem than unintentional non-taxation. Unintentional taxation arises whenever a business does not consider the available alternatives on a global basis and as a result locates within a jurisdiction in which it pays more in tax than was necessary in order to achieve maximal business efficiency.

15.5.2 The European Union initiatives on tax harmonisation

The Member States of the EU have committed themselves to somewhat poorly defined fiscal policy objectives related to the deployment of the single currency and the prevention of 'harmful' competition between different fiscal regimes within the Union. There is also a stated objective of 'tax harmonisation' within the EU, which received increasing attention throughout the late 1990s to the extent that it was identified as a principal objective of the German Presidency of the EU in the first half of 1999.

Businesses involved in or contemplating involvement in e-commerce within the EU should pay particular attention to developments in this area. It is likely that if the proposed 'tax harmonisation' measures are implemented, business taxes will rise creating a further competitive disadvantage for many e-commerce businesses based within the EU. Businesses located within the EU should constantly monitor the level of public sector benefit which they derive compared with the level of taxation they pay. Businesses which fail to monitor constantly this factor risk becoming the victim of unintentional taxation.

Low direct tax jurisdictions which are dependencies of EU Member States view the EU initiatives with some interest. Most have efficient fiscal regimes and no desire to move to higher rates of taxation with the inherent risks to business survival which higher rates of taxation bring. Fortunately the EU Member States have acknowledged that the constitutional positions of many dependencies should allow the dependencies to avoid the pitfalls being approached by their European relatives. Low direct tax jurisdictions which are independent States view the EU initiatives as a potential source of additional revenue and employment as it is anticipated that businesses will seek to move out of the EU in search of more hospitable business environments.

15.6 LOW DIRECT TAX JURISDICTIONS AND E-COMMERCE

There are a large number of low direct tax jurisdictions which businesses may wish to consider in choosing the location for an e-commerce business. The very brief summaries of selected factors regarding the four English speaking jurisdictions presented below, are provided to illustrate the general type of comparative analysis which might be undertaken by businesses considering establishing themselves within a low direct tax jurisdiction. Any person or corporation anticipating locating an e-commerce business within any jurisdiction, whether low direct tax or otherwise, should consult with appropriate advisors in regard to the evaluation of a selection of appropriate jurisdictions. None of the jurisdictions listed here have DTAs which are thought to be useful for most e-commerce activities. Businesses requiring tax planning involving DTAs should consult appropriate specialist advisors within the jurisdiction of their principal place of business.

15.6.1 Anguilla

Anguilla is a UK Overseas Territory located in the eastern Caribbean. Anguilla has a stable political environment with a Governor appointed by the Government of the UK. The financial sector has modern companies legislation in place and is well regulated. The types of goods and services required for the majority of e-commerce activities are available on the island or may be easily imported from North America or elsewhere. Prices for goods and services are generally comparable to what would be experienced in Europe or North America. Anguilla has recently reduced duties on computer equipment to 5 per cent in recognition of the importance of the information economy in Anguilla's future. There is no income tax, corporate profits tax, or capital gains tax. Human resources for many business activities may be found within the local population. If necessary expertise cannot be found locally, businesses may apply for work permits for overseas personnel which it requires to carry on business. At the time of writing, there is a monopoly telecommunications provider in Anguilla. Telecommunications facilities, including Internet access up to E1 level (1.5 megabits per second) are available, although the costs greatly exceed the costs for comparable telecommunications services in North America and Europe. Relative to other low direct tax jurisdictions, telecommunications costs are in the mid-range in the cost spectrum.

15.6.2 Bermuda

Bermuda is a UK Overseas Territory located in the western Atlantic off the coast of the southern USA. Bermuda has a stable political environment with a Governor appointed by the Government of the UK. The financial sector has modern companies legislation in place and is well regulated. The types of goods and services required for the majority of e-commerce activities are available on the island or may be easily imported from North America or elsewhere. Prices for goods and services range from generally comparable to, to moderately more than the prices for similar goods and services in Europe or North America. There is no income tax, corporate profits tax, or capital gains tax. Human resources for many business activities may be found within the local population. If necessary, expertise can not be found locally, businesses may apply for work permits for overseas personnel which it requires to carry on business. Telecommunications facilities, including Internet access in excess of E1 level are available, although the costs greatly exceed the costs for comparable telecommunications services in North America and Europe. Relative to other low direct tax jurisdictions, telecommunications costs are in the mid-range in the cost spectrum.

15.6.3 Cayman Islands

The Cayman Islands is a UK Overseas Territory located in the western Caribbean. The Cayman Islands has a stable political environment with a Governor appointed by the Government of the UK. The financial sector has modern companies legislation in place and is well regulated. The types of goods and services required for the majority of e-commerce activities are available on the island or may be easily imported from North America or elsewhere. Prices for goods and services range from generally comparable to, to moderately more expensive than what would be experienced in Europe or North America for similar goods and services. The financial services sector in the Cayman Islands is particularly well developed. There is no income tax, corporate profits tax, or capital gains tax. Human resources for many business activities may be found within the local population. If necessary, expertise can not be found locally, businesses may apply for work permits for overseas personnel which it requires to carry on business. At the time of writing, there is a monopoly telecommunications provider in the Cayman Islands. Telecommunications facilities, including Internet access up to E1 level are available, although the costs greatly exceed the costs for comparable telecommunications services in North America and Europe. Relative to other low direct tax jurisdictions, telecommunications costs are in the mid- to high-range in the cost spectrum.

15.6.4 Turks and Caicos Islands

The Turks and Caicos Islands is a UK Overseas Territory located in the eastern Caribbean. The Turks and Caicos Islands have a stable political environment with a Governor appointed by the Government of the UK. The financial sector has modern companies legislation in place and is well regulated. The types of goods and services required for the majority of e-commerce activities are available on the islands or may be easily imported from North America or elsewhere. Prices for goods and services are generally comparable to what would be experienced in Europe or North America although some items attract high import duties. There is no income tax, corporate profits tax, or capital gains tax. Human resources for many business activities may be found within the local population. If necessary, expertise can not be found locally, businesses may apply for work permits for overseas personnel which it requires to carry on business. At the time of writing, there is a monopoly telecommunications provider in the Turks and Caicos Islands. Telecommunications facilities, including Internet access up to E1 level can be made available by the monopoly provider, although the costs greatly exceed the costs for comparable telecommunications services in North America and Europe. Relative to other low direct tax jurisdictions, telecommunications costs are in the mid-range in the cost spectrum.

15.7 SUMMARY

E-commerce offers enormous opportunities for present and future businesses. The realisation of the true potential of e-commerce will only be achieved by those who employ a global perspective. The industrial age paradigms regarding the location of business activities should be left behind. Businesses now have new choices to make in their selection of tax suppliers.

Chapter 16

INTERNATIONAL PROPOSALS FOR TAXING E-COMMERCE

16.1 INTRODUCTION

In November 1997, the OECD hosted a conference in Turku, Finland. This conference was used to identify the challenges to tax administrations and taxpayers of e-commerce. During the year following the Turku conference the Committee on Fiscal Affairs of the OECD concentrated on understanding the issues raised by e-commerce. Revenue authorities have sought to develop their awareness of how the Internet operates and the way in which it can be used for commercial purposes. Special attention is being given by the OECD to the tax impact on small and medium sized enterprises who are likely to find themselves operating for the first time in the more complex international tax arena because of e-commerce.

16.1.1 Problems

E-commerce poses challenges to both tax authorities and taxpayers throughout the world. Traditional concepts of taxation based upon a physical presence within a jurisdiction are quickly being surpassed by technological developments in commerce. The rapid growth of the Internet now means that there is no requirement to establish branches within a jurisdiction. Such technological development directly challenges the application of concepts such as tax residence based upon the existence of a branch or agency. The VAT legislation is not immune from the Internet virus. Concepts such as place of supply in respect of services and its use of a fixed establishment are exposed to the ability of Internet technology to be used to mutate the business operations of Internet traders, and so avoid the requirement to impose VAT. The Turku conference raised the possibility of altering the place of supply of services to where the customer is based. This would not be without problems because as the conference participants recognised avoidance could still be possible.[1]

One of the many problems of Internet technology is that it is essentially anonymous. There is no way in which tax administrations will be able to check the identity of Internet traders operating the computer systems. The world has also become significantly smaller with the advent of modern technology. Increasingly more people are able to gain access to offshore finance centres. These offer the use of numbered

1 OECD conference 'Electronic Commerce: The Challenges To Tax Authorities And Taxpayers' (1997), para 67.

bank accounts. The ability to identify transactions through such accounts will be limited.

Many Internet traders will have little incentive to establish themselves within low tax jurisdictions when they can trade without any tax risk from offshore centres such as the Cayman Islands and pay no tax. The ability to tax non-resident traders, is as described earlier, capable of being achieved by the application of an income tax charge. However, in practice the Inland Revenue is going to face two fundamental problems. How will it be possible to identify when a non-resident is exercising a trade in the UK? How will it be possible to enforce a tax charge on a non-resident with no physical presence in the UK?[1] Precisely how to solve the many problems arising from interaction of tax with Internet trade is far from clear. This tax vacuum for offshore traders is likely to continue for the foreseeable future. The EU has taken the stance that no new taxes should be applied on e-commerce, and of the existing tax concepts no one is precisely sure how these can be adapted to meet the danger that offshore centres pose to national tax revenues.

After a very long wait, the OECD, in October 1998, issued a policy document on 'the rules of the road' for taxing e-commerce. This statement of policy is well overdue, not merely because of the rapid growth of such trade, but also because of the threat posed to e-commerce by various splinter organisations suggesting among other things, 'bit' taxes, and the imposition of obligations to collect consumption taxes via credit card issuers. In October 1998 the UK tax authorities issued a policy statement on UK tax and e-commerce.[2]

The OECD material published after a conference held in Ottawa, Canada proposes what 'the rules of the road' for taxing e-commerce should be throughout the world. Before continuing further, it is of use to note how the Internet Tax Freedom Act passed by the US defines e-commerce. When we talk about 'the rules of the road' for e-commerce it is important to understand what is meant. The term is defined in the Act as meaning:

> 'any transaction conducted over the Internet or through Internet access, comprising the sale, lease, licence, offer, or delivery of property, goods, services, or information, whether or not for consideration, and includes the provision of Internet access.'[3]

OECD-proposed 'rules of the road' formulated in Ottawa relate to such commerce. However, it should be emphasised that e-commerce is a mechanism of facilitating business. In many instances, it will not produce a tax result any different than if other methods of concluding a transaction had been used.[4]

---

1 In *Clark (Inspector of Taxes) v Oceanic Contractors Inc* [1983] 1 All ER 133, at p 139 Lord Scarman said of the direct tax legislation: '... the Income Tax Acts impose their own territorial limits. Parliament recognises the almost universally accepted principle that fiscal legislation is not enforceable outside the limits of the territorial sovereignty of the kingdom. Fiscal legislation is, no doubt, drafted in the knowledge that it is the practice of nations not to enforce the fiscal legislation of other nations.'

2 See Appendix 1.

3 Internet Tax Freedom Act, s 155(4).

4 See Appendix 3.

16.2 KEY RESULTS OF OTTAWA

The Ottawa conference is important for a number of reasons. Broadly, Ottawa resulted in agreement:

(1) between government and business on the appropriate way forward;
(2) on taxation framework conditions;
(3) on application of existing tax principles;
(4) on reform of Tax Rules only in so far as not discriminatory;
(5) that tax administration should be streamlined by the use of information technologies;
(6) on broad principles for application of consumption taxes;
(7) that international taxation should be clarified; and
(8) on a future work programme.

16.2.1 Joint declaration adopted by government and business

The Ottawa conference resulted in the issue of a joint declaration by business and government delegates representing a broad spectrum of views. Represented were the European Commission, the Centre for Inter-American Tax Administrations and the Commonwealth Association of Tax Administrators. A diverse range of business representatives also attended. The common views expressed were:

(1) As a matter of priority the implementation of a tax framework for e-commerce, with appropriate administrative back-up to support that framework.
(2) Use of information technologies to enhance taxpayer service, and simplify tax systems.
(3) The implementation of reporting mechanisms so as to maintain 'neutral and effective' administration of tax systems.
(4) Neutral tax treatment between conventional commerce and e-commerce.
(5) The creation of advisory groups made up of public and private sector representatives to provide an input of business views to government.

16.2.2 Tax Framework Conditions Report

The Ottawa conference endorsed a Taxation Framework Conditions Report. Before examining the detail, the broad position adopted by Ministers is that no country's tax regime should discriminate against e-commerce. By the same token, a tax regime should not favour e-commerce as against conventional commerce, for example, by non-taxation.

The Taxation Framework Conditions Report was prepared by the Committee on Fiscal Affairs of the OECD. In addition the European Commission and the World Customs Organisation provided direct input into the Report.

The main conclusions of the framework document are as follows:

(1) Conventional commerce tax principles to apply to e-commerce.

(2) Tax systems can and should be changed to deal with e-commerce, but only to the extent that new measures are intended to assist in the application of existing tax principles.
(3) However, implementation of new measures must not discriminate against e-commerce.
(4) Any alteration of tax principles must be 'structured to maintain the fiscal sovereignty of countries, to achieve a fair sharing of the tax base from electronic commerce between countries and to avoid double taxation and unintentional non-taxation'.

16.2.3 Administration of tax law and collection of tax revenue

The Taxation Framework Conditions Report recognises the potential benefits that IT can bring in the administration and collection of tax. The overall conclusion in this respect is that information technologies should be used by revenue authorities to improve taxpayer access to information, for example, by establishing web sites where tax legislation and forms can be accessed, minimising business compliance costs by promotion of norms for acceptance of electronic material, and promote electronic assessment. For example, the possibility of sending revenue mail to taxpayers' e-mail addresses is an option. Electronic filing of returns is actively being considered, although such a course would require appropriate safeguards such as taxpayer ID. Electronic collection of tax is another possibility. The option may eventually be available for electronic payments by an employer of payroll taxes. It is no doubt envisaged that tax will effortlessly and without any pain be collected electronically from bank accounts. However, many problems stand in the way of these objectives. For example, identity of taxpayers, and unlocking encrypted details of a transaction where the taxpayer has 'forgotten' the key.

16.2.4 Tax principles

The Report recommends five principles which should govern the taxation of Internet activity.

(1) The Report recommends that in taxing e-commerce the rules should be neutral and equitable between different forms of e-commerce, for example, the supply of digital products and supply of tangible products ordered via web trading sites. It is emphasised that Internet traders should be motivated by economic considerations alone. A tax regime should not impact upon the choice of business practice.
(2) A further principle emphasised is that the taxing mechanism should promote efficiency. This means minimisation of compliance costs.
(3) All tax regimes applicable to e-commerce should be certain and simple to understand. Each and every taxpayer whether an individual or multinational, should be able to anticipate the tax consequences in advance of a transaction. The Report states that this in effect means that the taxpayer should be able to know when, where and how tax is to be accounted.
(4) Tax avoidance and evasion should be minimised by implementation of counter-active measures. These measures are recommended to be proportionate to the risks posed by e-commerce.

(5) The Report recommends that any mechanism introduced should be sufficiently flexible to match developments in IT and commercial practice in respect of e-commerce.

16.2.5 Consumption taxes

The Report tackles the application of consumption taxes to e-commerce. The Report highlights that any decision concerning liability to tariffs is a matter for the World Trade Organisation which has responsibility for agreements on the application of tariffs to trade. The primary conclusions are that:

(1) In the context of cross-border trade, consumption taxes should only apply in the jurisdiction where consumption takes place. The post-Ottawa agenda includes seeking a consensus on when a supply is deemed to be consumed in a jurisdiction.
(2) For the purposes of consumption taxes the supply of digital products is to be treated as a supply of services. This is now UK practice. Clearly such digital products are not subject to customs controls, nor handled by intermediaries. The Committee of Fiscal Affairs ('CFA') comment that such practice, ie treating digital products as a supply of services, is to prevent tax base erosion that could occur under some systems if these products were to be considered goods. The policy also clearly simplifies compliance issues for a taxpayer.
(3) Where services and intangible products are acquired from outside another jurisdiction concepts such as the reverse charge should be implemented to protect domestic tax bases, and the competitiveness of domestic suppliers. In other words, a domestic business recipient would be required to account for VAT on international service supplies. This happens within Europe under the Sixth VAT Directive.
(4) Appropriate systems should be developed in consultation with the World Customs Organisation, and carriers to identify how tax can and should be collected on the importation of physical goods ordered via electronic trade. However, the Report recommends that such systems should not hinder the efficient delivery of products. The World Customs Organisation recommends a simplified customs clearance process. One idea is to require suppliers to calculate and account for taxes to the revenue authority in the place of consumption, and for electronic filing of customs documentation.

16.2.6 Tax base erosion

The Report recognises that the nature of e-commerce may result in significant erosion of tax bases for the reasons set out in the Turku conference papers. For example, the information superhighway offers greater access to offshore numbered bank accounts. Traders may locate businesses in offshore jurisdictions without ever establishing a physical presence within jurisdictions. Taxpayers with no physical or agency representation cannot have tax assessments enforced against them. Tax authorities face the real difficulty of matching an Internet business identity (ie a domain name) with a physical business identity (ie a registered company).

Against this background, the Report states that revenue authorities will intensify the use of existing cooperative arrangements, explore options for multilateral assistance, and examine the recommendations relating to geographically mobile activities contained in the OECD report on Harmful Tax Competition with a view to their application to e-commerce.

16.2.7 OECD Report on Harmful Tax Competition

The Report on Harmful Tax Competition, issued in April 1998, received the endorsement of the G7 at the Summit held in the UK during 1998. The Report recommends a number of ways to combat harmful tax competition in relation to geographically mobile activities. The focus of the Report is on tax havens and harmful preferential tax regimes.

The Report comments that:

> 'If nothing is done, governments may increasingly be forced to engage in competitive tax bidding to attract or retain mobile activities. That "race to the bottom", where location and financing decisions become primarily tax driven, will mean that capital and financial flows will be distorted and it will become more difficult to achieve fair competition for real economic activities.'

The threat of harmful tax practices in the context of e-commerce is significant. Jurisdictions with no tax scheme are already acting as a significant magnet for Internet business. Participation in low tax jurisdictions is growing 'exponentially'.

Harmful tax practices are identified as those where:

(1) country A is a tax haven and, as such, generally imposes no tax on income; and
(2) country A, collects revenues from tax levied on income at the individual or corporate level, but its tax system has preferential status for certain relevant income which is subject to low or no taxation.

The Report identifies four factors which are common to harmful preferential tax regimes, which are:

(1) the regime imposes a low effective tax rate;
(2) the regime is 'ring-fenced';
(3) the operation of the regime is non-transparent; and
(4) the jurisdiction operating the regime does not effectively exchange information with other countries.

The Report recommends a number of measures which are designed to tackle harmful tax practices. If applied in the context of e-commerce, this may prevent the transfer of such activities which would otherwise operate to reduce tax revenues. The broad purpose of the recommendations is to prevent 'aggressive competitive bidding by countries for geographically mobile activities'.

The recommendations can be summarised as follows:

(1) Adoption of Controlled Foreign Company rules.
(2) Restrictions on participation exemption, and other methods of exempting foreign income in the context of harmful tax competition. In other words, foreign income that has benefited from tax practices deemed as constituting harmful tax competition should not qualify for relief under the exemption method as used as a means of eliminating double taxation.

(3) Adoption of rules for reporting international transactions, and foreign operations of resident taxpayers.
(4) Adoption of the OECD's 1995 Transfer Pricing Guidelines, and that countries refrain from applying their transfer pricing rules in a way which constitutes harmful tax competition.
(5) Removal of legal barriers to tax authorities gaining access to banking information. This effectively means altering confidentiality laws as a method of counteracting harmful tax competition.
(6) Intensification between tax authorities in exchange of information relating to transactions in tax havens and preferential tax regimes.
(7) Removal of DTA benefits for entities and income covered by measures constituting harmful tax practices.
(8) Countries consider termination of DTAs with tax havens.
(9) Implementation of coordinated enforcement programmes, such as specific exchange of information projects.
(10) Countries review their rules relating to enforcement of tax claims of other countries. The Committee of Fiscal Affairs proposes drafting provisions that could be included in DTAs.

(11) Countries which have links with tax havens to ensure those links whether political, or economic do not contribute to harmful tax competition.

However, Luxembourg and Switzerland have not approved the Report. Both countries believe that the Report is unbalanced, and do not share the implicit belief that bank secrecy is a source of harmful tax competition.

16.2.8 International tax arrangements

Working Party No 1 of the Committee on Fiscal Affairs of the OECD has recently adopted changes to the Commentary on Art 12 (Royalties) of the OECD Model Tax Convention. The proposals relate to the characterisation of computer software.

Proposed amendments:

(1) Recognition that software can be transferred electronically, and via the media of a CD-ROM (Art 12(1)).
(2) That the character of payments received for the transfer of computer software depends on the nature of the rights that the transferee acquires regarding use and exploitation of the program (Art 12(2)).
(3) Payments made for the acquisition of partial rights in copyright, for example, the granting of a licence to reproduce computer software, or to modify and publicly display the program, will represent a royalty (Art 13(1)).
(4) Method of transfer of computer programs is irrelevant in characterisation of payments. For example, there is to be no distinction between transfer via a computer disk, or an electronic network (Art 14(1)).
(5) Utilisation rights, such as the right to copy a program onto a computer's hard drive, or random access memory, or making an archival copy are steps necessary to utilising the program. Such rights connected with effective operation of the program by the user are to be disregarded in characterisation of transactions. Payments in this context are governed under Arts 7 or 14 of the Model Tax Convention (Art 14).

(6) Rights granted for the making of multiple copies for use within a business are regarded as 'site licences' or 'network licences'. Such rights are regarded as solely enabling the user to make multiple copies of a program for use within a business. Payments for such rights are regarded as commercial income subject to Arts 7 or 14 (Art 14(2)).
(7) Only payment for the use of partial rights ie to reproduce software and issue to third parties will be governed by Art 12.

16.2.9 Post-Ottawa agenda

The post-Ottawa agenda can be summarised as follows.

(1) Development of international consensus on ways to simplify tax regimes so as to minimise cost of tax compliance.
(2) Develop uniform identification practices sufficient to permit digital signatures to be accepted as evidence in tax matters.
(3) Achieve international consensus on specific terms, such as place of consumption, definitions of services and intangible property.
(4) Clarify how concepts in the OECD Model Tax Convention apply to e-commerce, such as 'permanent establishment', classification of income etc.
(5) Monitoring of challenges to tax administrations presented by e-commerce, and alteration in light of that knowledge.
(6) Improvement in use of agreements for administrative assistance.
(7) Consideration of how harmful tax competition for e-commerce is to be avoided in the context of the OECD recommendations on geographically mobile activities contained in the Report on Harmful Tax Competition.

16.3 RECENT ACTIVITY IN THE USA

16.3.1 US position statement

The overall tax policy of the US in relation to e-commerce was stated by the US Treasury Deputy Assistant Secretary to the Senate Finance Committee in July 1998 as being:

> 'To encourage the growth of this technology and the resulting social and economic benefits, it is crucial that governments act responsibly and fairly regarding the Internet and electronic commerce. The Administration's key objectives are no new Internet taxes and neutrality in taxing electronic commerce. Overall, it is the view of the Administration that there should be no tax rules at the national, international, federal or sub-federal levels that inappropriately impede the full development of these exciting new technologies.
>
> Neutrality is a fundamental principle that should guide the development of tax rules in this area. Neutrality requires that the tax system treat economically similar transactions equally, whether such transactions occur through electronic means or through conventional channels of commerce. In addition, tax rules should be consistent across jurisdictions, so as to minimize the possibility of multiple or no taxation, and the rules should be transparent and easy to administer, so as to protect the revenue base.'

16.3.2 Internet Tax Freedom Act

The Internet Tax Freedom Act (HR 4105) is part of US law. The broad effect of the Act is to impose a three year moratorium on sub-national taxation of the Internet including taxes on Internet access and bit taxes. Additionally, the Act will prohibit multiple and discriminatory taxes on e-commerce.

The Act is also noteworthy because it establishes an Advisory Commission on Electronic Commerce. The Commission will comprise Secretaries of the US Treasury, the Attorney-General, and representatives of business. Their function will be to examine domestic and international taxation of the Internet and e-commerce. However, the Commission will not consider Federal Level Taxation.

The US is also actively engaged in promoting the removal of international tariffs and discriminatory taxation relating to e-commerce.

Part VI

APPENDICES

Appendices

Appendix 1

ELECTRONIC COMMERCE: UK POLICY ON TAXATION ISSUES OECD CONFERENCE IN OTTAWA, CANADA, 8–9 OCTOBER 1998

The Inland Revenue and HM Customs and Excise today issued a joint paper on UK tax policy regarding electronic commerce.

The taxation principles that the UK will follow include neutrality, certainty, effectiveness and efficiency. Tax must not be allowed to stifle the growth of electronic commerce. The aim should be for tax rules and tax compliance to be neutral between electronic commerce and more traditional forms of commerce.

Both tax departments make a commitment to positive use of the opportunities for improving services to taxpayers.

The paper enlarges on the tax issues in 'Net Benefit: The Electronic Commerce Agenda for the UK' which the Department of Trade and Industry are publishing today. The DTI paper highlights the great benefits that electronic commerce can bring.

The Organisation for Economic Co-operation and Development (OECD) is holding a Ministerial conference on electronic commerce in Ottawa, Canada on 8 and 9 October where taxation will be one of the issues to be discussed at the conference and at a government and business dialogue on taxation and electronic commerce on 7 October.

DETAILS

1. Electronic commerce has the potential to be one of the great economic developments of the 21st Century, spurring growth and employment throughout the world.

2. Tax policy and administration must keep pace with these developments, and it is important that business benefits and opportunities are not stifled by taxation. It is also important that tax revenues remain secure so that public services can be adequately funded.

3. A major policy principle for the UK is that taxation should aim to be neutral between electronic commerce and more conventional forms of commerce so that no form of commerce is advantaged or disadvantaged.

4. Current taxes are sufficiently robust to mean that the UK does not believe it is necessary, at this stage, to make any major changes to existing tax rules. But some work is necessary to ensure the effective and consistent operation of VAT systems, when dealing with international transactions, and to clarify how certain aspects of the

OECD Model Tax Treaty apply to electronic commerce. In the future it is possible that some changes in domestic tax rules and international tax treaties may become necessary to ensure that they continue to work effectively.

5. Internatinal co-operation between revenue authorities is essential. The Inland Revenue and HM Customs and Exise have been actively working on the issues through the OECD, and Customs has also contributed to work on VAT issues in the European Community.

6. The two departments are also convinced of the importance of consulting with business, and will continue to do so both directly and through OECD.

7. The Inland Revenue and HM Customs and Excise will be attending and participating in the tax dialogue and the conference in Ottawa. There will also be a joint seminar by live video link between the tax dialogue in Ottawa and the Annual Congress of the International Fiscal Association in London.

ELECTRONIC COMMERCE: UK TAXATION POLICY

Preface

1. At their meeting in Birmingham, UK in May 1998, the G8 Finance and Foreign Ministers concluded that 'Information and communication technologies offer all countries – industrialised, emerging and developing – the opportunity to revolutionise their quality of life and economic well-being. The potential impact of electronic commerce on global growth and employment is profound. They undertook to 'work with the international institutions and the private sector to offer the best opportunities for the future: a predictable and stable environment and a seamless, decentralised global market place where competition and consumer choice drive economic activity.'

2. The Department of Trade and Industry has published a paper 'Net benefit: The Electronic Commerce Agenda for the UK'. This highlights the great benefits that electronic commerce can bring and the role of government. It includes a brief summary of UK taxation policy on which this paper enlarges.

Introduction

3. Tax policy and administration must keep pace with the scope of electronic commerce and with the growth of the global market place generally. It is important that commercial and business benefits and opportunities, both domestically and internationally, are not stifled by taxation. And it is important that tax revenues remain secure, so that public services can be adequately funded. With these aims, the Inland Revenue and HM Customs and Excise have been consulting widely with business; both directly, and through the OECD, the international forum which has been examining the tax implications of electronic commerce in a global context. And for VAT, Customs and Excise have been actively involved with European Community consultation with business. There is broad consensus between Government and business on the nature of the challenges and opportunities, and on the priorities for meeting and exploiting them.

4. UK businesses have indicated that, amongst their tax priorities, they need:

- certainty about the tax rules;
- neutrality between electronic and conventional commerce;
- no double or unintentional non-taxation;
- compliance costs should be as low as possible;
- no new taxes on electronic commerce; and
- the use of modern technology by our tax administrations to improve the service they offer their customers.

5. The Government recognises these priorities. So far as possible, it will have regard to them in the development of UK tax policy on electronic commerce. And it is committed to extending the use of new technologies to improve the quality of service to taxpayers and make it easier for them to comply with their tax obligations.

6. Other countries have similar objectives. And it is in the interests of business and governments alike to co-operate in agreeing a framework for the taxation of electronic commerce that will secure countries' appropriate tax bases. Effective international co-operation will avoid the risk of individual countries taking unilateral action which could create double taxation and/or excessive compliance burdens which would damage international business in general, and UK business in particular.

7. The Inland Revenue and Customs and Excise have been working very closely together in the development of UK tax policy on electronic commerce. They have also been working with their international counterparts and with other Departments. And they have been consulting with business representatives; and will continue to do so.

8. The OECD is the most appropriate international forum for bringing together examination of all tax issues with also, for VAT, the European Community. OECD has been working on the tax issues raised by electronic commerce for more than two years, has been consulting with business representatives and intends to step up the involvement of business in this area of its work. And it is fully committed to an outreach programme to bring non-OECD member countries into the debate. The UK has been playing a major role in the work being done by the OECD, and will continue to do so. In particular, the UK has actively contributed to and supports the taxation framework conditions for electronic commerce developed by OECD and to be presented to its Ministerial conference in Ottawa in October 1998. The UK has also contributed to and supports the principles for VAT recently agreed by European Finance Ministers.

Broad Policy Principles

9. The Government has concluded that the following broad principles should apply to the taxation of electronic commerce:

Neutrality – the taxation of electronic commerce should seek to be technology neutral so that no particular form of commerce is advantaged or disadvantaged.

Certainty and Transparency – the rules for the taxation of electronic commerce should be clear and simple so that businesses can anticipate, so far as possible, the tax consequences of the transactions they enter into.

Effectiveness – the tax rules should not result in either double or unintentional non-taxation, and risks from increased evasion and avoidance should be kept to a minimum. The overriding aim should be that the right amount of tax is paid at the right time and in the right country. And the rules will need to be sufficiently flexible to continue to achieve this as technology develops.

Efficiency – the tax rules should be efficient, keeping the compliance costs of business and the administration costs of government to the minimum compatible with effective tax administration. Measures to counter evasion or avoidance should be proportionate to the risks which they seek to address.

10. The Government does not believe it is necessary, at this stage, to make any major changes to existing tax legislation and regulations, or to introduce new taxes. As the technology develops, it is possible that some changes may become necessary to existing domestic rules to ensure that they continue to work effectively. (For instance, the scope of the Controlled Foreign Companies legislation may need to be reviewed.) In the international context, the UK is actively participating in the examination by OECD of the adequacy of the current international standards.

Customer Service Opportunities

11. The Departments are increasingly taking advantage of modern methods of communication, processing of information and payments. They will consider extending the use of Internet technology in particular, so as to continue to improve the quality of service to their taxpayers, simplify and streamline procedures where possible, reduce costs to business and Government and encourage voluntary compliance. In particular, the Departments:

- will continue to develop their web sites. They will aim to provide clear, easily accessible guidance on tax obligations and how to meet them.
- will consider, as cryptography systems and digital signature technology develop, wider use of e-mail as a means of secure communication with their customers. This could speed up communications and reduce costs to taxpayers and Government alike.
- have developed systems for the electronic filing of returns and will seek to encourage their greater use. And they are currently developing electronic 'intelligent' forms in close co-operation with the private sector.
- are already using facilities for direct bank to bank payment and repayment of tax. Developments in other electronic payments systems will be monitored and their use considered once security problems have been overcome.

12. As technology develops, the Departments will explore, together with the private sector, how it might be used by businesses to collect and process information relevant to their tax liabilities. By facilitating more accurate return information, less time will be spent by both business and the tax administrations in correcting errors and tracking down missing information, and compliance costs will be driven down.

Tax Administration and Compliance Issues

13. Electronic commerce has the potential to amplify significantly some existing areas of risk to tax compliance. UK tax policy must ensure that our tax base is adequately

secured. And it is important that businesses which play by the rules are not disadvantaged because others use some of the opportunities offered by electronic commerce to flout them. The Department are therefore looking very carefully at the emerging risks from:

- taxpayers using the Internet to conceal their identity, their location and/or particular transactions;
- encryption of documents and financial records or the holding of them in other jurisdictions to try to prevent the tax administrations gaining access to them;
- any electronic record keeping systems which allow transactions to take place without leaving an audit trail or where the trail may be easy to alter or destroy.

14. Information is the key to addressing these risks and to maintaining the effective administration of both direct and indirect taxes. The Inland Revenue and Customs and Excise must continue to have access, to the same extent as with physical commerce, to reliable information which will identify and verify taxpayers and transactions. They will monitor whether their current powers for information gathering are adequate in an electronic environment. At the same time, any measures considered necessary to deter, uncover or rectify non-compliance should have proper regard to the costs they may impose on business.

15. And the Departments will need to monitor all developments in electronic commerce which could result in significantly increased risk to tax compliance, such as the widespread use of unaccounted electronic payment systems. They will work through OECD and with their treaty partners to improve exchange of information with the tax authorities of other countries. OECD is also considering how mechanisms for international assistance in the collection of tax should be developed, and the UK is participating fully in that debate.

Direct Tax Issues

16. The Inland Revenue is working with business and through the OECD to find solutions to a number of direct tax issues.

Royalties

17. The UK, like many other countries, requires tax to be withheld from royalty payments in some circumstances, ie payments for the use of, or the right to use, a copyright. The current rules which distinguish between such payments and payments for goods or services, from which tax does not usually need to be withheld, were developed in relation to physical products.

18. It is increasingly possible for images of certain products to be transmitted electronically rather than in physical form, eg various forms of written text (such as newspapers, or magazines or reference material), and photographs. Customers may have to pay a fee before being allowed to view the images; and will in any event usually have to pay a fee before being allowed to download a copy of the product. And the operation of computer software can be viewed in a similar way before customers download a copy after payment of a fee. In future, it may also be possible to download music easily. Customers may be allowed to modify downloaded products or to incorporate them in products which they develop themselves, either for their own use

or to seel to others. It is not always clear whether payments to view and download such products for those various purposes are, in whole or in part, payments for the use of, or for the right to use, a copyright on the one hand or, are payments for the purchase of goods or services. If they are the former, practical issues arise concerning whether, under UK law, the customer should deduct and account for tax when making the payment.

19. OECD is reviewing the guidance which it has already given on the nature of payments for computer software in the OECD Model Tax Convention on Income and on Capital. OECD is also looking at the issues mentioned above and the Inland Revenue is participating fully in those discussions. It is clear that further work needs to be done to analyse and clarify the situation. The Inland Revenue will continue to work on this through the OECD so as to ensure that there is international consensus on the way forward. And the Inland Revenue will be guided by the principle of neutrality.

Permanent Establishment

20. The UK taxes non-residents trading here on their UK source income. But where we have a tax treaty with the person's country of residence, we only exercise our taxing rights if the person has a permanent establishment here as defined in the tax treaty (the UK generally adopts the definition of permanent establishment in the OECD Model Tax Convention). Questions have been raised about the continuing relevance of the permanent establishment concept.

21. The use of permanent establishment as a threshold for taxation is a long-standing and widely supported one, and the Government sees no need at the present time to depart from it. To do so could have far reaching implications for all types of businesses, and for UK businesses trading abroad as well as for non-residents trading in the UK. The Inland Revenue will instead continue to work closely with the OECD to keep under review the continuing appropriateness of the concept.

22. The Government does however believe that the detailed application of the permanent establishment concept to electronic commerce needs clarifying. In particular, the UK is aware that business is concerned to know whether a web-site on a server could be a permanent establishment and, if so, in what circumstances. The UK is therefore working with OECD to up-date the explanatory commentary to the OECD Model Tax Convention.

Transfer Pricing and Attribution of Income to Permanent Establishment

23. Electronic commerce is likely to have the effect of increasing the complexity of arrangements required to be examined under the arms length principle used to determine the appropriate prices for transactions between associated persons in different jurisdictions. The number of such complex arrangements is also likely to increase. And it could become more difficult to identify where relevant functions have been performed, to quantify the value added in relation to business conducted over the Internet, and to establish where any such value has been added.

24. At present there is no reason to suppose that the arm's length principle, and in particular the methods to apply that principle recognised by the OECD's 1995

Guidelines on this subject, should not continue to work. However, the Inland Revenue will continue, with OECD, to monitor the position.

25. The Inland Revenue is also contributing to the work currently being done by OECD on the subject of the attribution of profits to permanent establishments, and taking into account situaitons likely to arise in the electronic commerce field.

Indirect Tax Issues

Value Added Tax (VAT)

26. For VAT, the implications of the development of electronic commerce can be examined in relation to three broad categories of transaction, namely:

- supplies of physical goods to both business and private consumers;
- business to business supplies of services; and
- business to private consumer supplies of services and of 'digitised' products.

27. At present the vast majority of electronic commerce based supplies fall into the first category of supplies of physical goods, and most are business to business transactions within a single country. Typically in these cases the Internet is used as a means of communication to place an order. Existing VAT rules (including those applicable to intra-EC and international trade) are, in general, readily applicable to such physical deliveries of goods purchased using electronic means.

28. The second category of transactions – business to business supplies of services – should similarly be capable of accommodation within existing rules. In particular, where UK businesses buy certain services from suppliers based outside the UK, they already make use of an existing VAT accounting mechanism ('reverse charge') whereby the UK business customer accounts for VAT. This mechanism ensures that UK suppliers are not unfairly disadvantaged (as compared with non-UK suppliers), that VAT is properly accounted for, and that the non-UK supplier is not required to register in the UK. Such arrangements could usefully be extended to take account of the likely growth in provision of services over the Internet.

29. The third category of transactions – supplies of services to private consumers – presents potentially the greatest tests to effective tax administration. But it is also the least well developed and so remains very small. Trading models in this sector are still evolving in tandem with technological developments. Satisfactory VAT arrangements for this category of transactions will have to be developed. The UK is working with all interested parties in this field (such as infrastructure providers and software developers) to this end.

30. In addition to the principles outlined earlier in this paper, the EC has recently agreed a set of general principles which provide a useful foundation for further, more detailed work. In outline, these are:

- the focus of activity should be in adapting existing VAT provisions to accommodate electronic commerce based on internationally established guidelines. In this context, no new taxes are envisaged at this stage;
- 'digitised' products supplied by electronic means should be treated, for VAT purposes, as supplies of services;

- the place of taxation of services supplies by electronic means should, in principle, be the place of consumption;
- the tax system as it applies to such services should be readily enforceable by tax administrations;
- paperless electronic invoicing should be facilitated for VAT purposes, taking account of the need for adequate controls. International co-operation to facilitate such invoicing is essential;
- compliance with tax rules should be easy and as simple as possible. Businesses should be able to fulfil fiscal obligations by means of electronic declarations and accounting.

Customs Duties

31. When establishing the treatment of imported supplies for customs duties purposes, a distinction needs to be drawn between goods ordered electronically but delivered by traditional means and direct on-line delivery of digitised products.

32. In line with the WTO Declaration on Global Electronic Commerce, goods ordered and supplied electronically will continue to be treated as 'services' and as such be free of import duties, but remain liable to VAT. Goods ordered electronically but delivered physically from outside the EU will continue to attract the rate of duty appropriate to that commodity. However, no additional import duties will be introduced relating to electronic transmissions.

33. With the increased use of electronic media as a method of ordering goods, there is likely to be a parallel increase in the number of small packages imported from outside the EU. Customs and Excise are committed to reviewing the tax treatment of small packages at importation with a view to introducing simplified customs clearance procedures and duty/tax concessions for those consignments below prescribed de-minimis value limits.

34. Part II of the Information Technology Agreement (ITA II) seeks to extend the product coverage of ITA I, under which tariffs on a range of IT goods are due to be eliminated by the year 2000. Discussions on ITA II are currently stalled due to a lack of agreement between producing countries of consumer electronics (eg TVs and VCRs) and certain importing countries, who are opposed to the extension of tariff elimination to such goods. The TWO is due to present compromise proposals shortly with a view to commencing implementation of further phased tariff reductions from 1 January 1999.

Betting and gaming duties

35. Electronic commerce has the potential to facilitate the growth of Internet-based betting and gaming, so threatening the tax base of certain of the UK's duties in this sector. For example, 'virtual casinos' on the Internet, when not established in the UK, currently escape UK duties. International co-operation to examine the implications of this and identify suitable safeguards, is vital. The UK intends to play an active role in these discussions.

Future Work

36. The above is a fairly brief analysis of the main, current issues for taxation raised by electronic commerce, and an outline of UK policy in respect of them. There is still much work to be done both domestically and at an international level. The Inland Revenue and Customs and Excise will continue this work, particularly within OECD, and for VAT, within the EC. And they will continue to consult closely with business and with other Government Departments.

Appendix 2

DTAs WHICH LIMIT THE UK'S POWER OF TAXATION ON A NON-RESIDENT TO PROFITS OF A BUSINESS DERIVED FROM A PERMANENT ESTABLISHMENT

Double Tax Agreement	*Reference*
Argentina	Convention of 3 January 1996, art 7(1)
Armenia	SI 1986/224, art 6(1), SP 3/92
Australia	SI 1968/305, art 5(2)
Austria	SI 1970/1947, art 7(1)
Azerbaijan	SI 1995/762, art 7(1)
Bangladesh	SI 1980/708, art 7(1)
Barbados	SI 1970/952, art 6(1)
Belarus	SI 1986/224, art 6(1), SP 3/92
Belgium	SI 1987/2053, art 7(1)
Belize	SR & O 1947/2866, art 3(2)
Bolivia	SI 1995/2707, art 7(1)
Botswana	SI 1978/183, art 7(1)
Brunei	SI 1950/1977, art 3(2)
Bulgaria	SI 1987/2054, art 7(1)
Canada	SI 1980/709, art 7(1)
China	SI 1984/1826, art 7(1)
Croatia	SI 1981/1815, art 7(1), SP 6/93
Cyprus	
Czech Republic	SI 1991/2876, art 7(1), SP 5/93
Denmark	SI 1980/1960, art 7(1)
Egypt	SI 1980/1091, art 7(1)
Estonia	SI 1994/3207, art 7(1)

Double Tax Agreement	*Reference*
Falkland Islands	SI 1984/363 art 7(1)
Faroe Islands	SI 1950/1195, art 3(2)
Fiji	SI 1976/1342, art 8(1)
Finland	SI 1970/153, art 8(1)
France	SI 1968/1869, art 6(1)
Gambia	SI 1980/1963, art 7(1)
Georgia	SI 1986/224, art 6(1), SP 3/92
Germany	SI 1967/25, art 3(2)
Ghana	SI 1993/1800, art 7(1)
Greece	SI 1954/142, art 3(2)
Grenada	SI 1949/361, art 3(2)
Guernsey	SI 1952/1215, art 3(2)
Guyana	SI 1992/3207, art 8(1)
Hungary	SI 1978/1056, art 7(1)
Iceland	SI 1991/2879, art 7(1)
India	SI 1993/1801, art 7(1)
Indonesia	SI 1994/769, art 7(1)
Ireland	SI 1976/2151, art 8(1)
Isle of Man	SI 1955/1205, art 3(2)
Israel	SI 1963/616, art 3(2)
Italy	SI 1990/2590, art 7(1)
Ivory Coast	SI 1987/169, art 7(1)
Jamaica	SI 1973/1329, art 5(2)
Japan	SI 1970/1948, art 8(1)
Jersey	SI 1952/1216, art 3(2)
Kazakhstan	SI 1986/224, art 6(1), SP 3/92
Kenya	SI 1977/1299, art 8(1)
Kiribati and Tuvalu	SI 1950/750, art 3(2)
Korea	SI 1996/3168, art 7(1)
Kyrgystan	SI 1986/224, art 6(1), SP 3/92
Latvia	SI 1996/3167, art 7(1)

Double Tax Agreement	Reference
Luxembourg	SI 1968/1100, art 7(1)
Macedonia	SI 1981/1815, SP 6/93
Malawi	SI 1956/619, art 3(2)
Malaysia	SI 1973/1330, art 6(1)
Malta	SI 1995/763, art 7(1)
Mauritius	SI 1981/1121, art 7(1)
Mexico	SI 1994/3212, art 7(1)
Moldova	SI 1986/224, art 6(1), SP 3/92
Mongolia	SI 1996/2598, art 7(1)
Montserrat	SR & O 1947/2869, art 3(2)
Morocco	SI 1991/2881, art 7(1)
Myanmar	
Namibia	SI 1962/2352, art 3(2)
Netherlands	SI 1980/1961, art 7(1)
New Zealand	SI 1984/365, art 8(1)
Nigeria	SI 1987/2057, art 7(1)
Norway	SI 1985/1998, art 7(1)
Pakistan	SI 1987/2058, art 7(1)
Papua New Guinea	SI 1991/2882, art 7(1)
Philippines	SI 1978/184, art 7(1)
Poland	SI 1978/282, art 7(1)
Portugal	SI 1969/599, art 7(1)
Romania	SI 1977/57, art 7(1)
Russian Federation	Convention of 15 February 1994, art 7(1)
Sierra Leone	SR & O 1947/2873, art 3(2)
Singapore	SI 1967/483, art 4(1)
Slovak Republic	SI 1991/2876, art 7(1), SP 5/93
Slovenia	SI 1981/1815, art 7(1), SP 6/93
Solomon Islands	SI 1950/748, art 3(2)
South Africa	SI 1969/864, art 6(2)
Spain	SI 1976/1919, art 7(1)

Double Tax Agreement	***Reference***
Sri Lanka	SI 1980/713, art 7(1)
St Kitts (St Christopher) and Nevis	SR & O 1947/2872, art 3(2)
Sudan	SI 1977/1719, art 7(1)
Swaziland	SI 1969/380, art 8(1)
Sweden	SI 1984/366, art 7(1)
Switzerland	SI 1978/1408, art 7(1)
Tajikistan	SI 1986/224, art 6(1), SP 3/92
Thailand	SI 1981/1546, art 8(1)
Trinidad and Tobago	SI 1983/1903, art 7(1)
Tunisia	SI 1984/133, art 7(1)
Turkey	SI 1988/932, art 7(1)
Turkmenistan	SI 1986/224, art 6(1), SP 3/92
Uganda	SI 1993/1802, art 7(1)
Ukraine	SI 1993/1803, art 7(1)
USA	SI 1980/568, art 7(1)
Uzbekistan	SI 1994/770, art 7(1)
Venezuela	SI 1996/2599, art 7(1)
Vietnam	SI 1994/3216, art 7(1)
Yugoslavia	SI 1981/1815, art 7(1)
Zambia	SI 1972/1721, art 8(1)
Zimbabwe	SI 1982/1842, art 7(1)

TABLE OF COUNTRIES WITH WHOM THE UK HAS NO DTA

In the case of countries with which the UK has no DTA, corporation tax will be charged where a trade is carried on through a branch or agency, or in the absence of that charge income tax will be applied solely where a non-resident is trading within the UK. Where a DTA exists with a country based on the OECD Model Tax Convention (as listed in Appendix 2) there must also be a permanent establishment in the UK for tax to be applied. Where this is the case, profits of an Internet trade will not normally be captured. It is important to check whether the UK has entered into DTAs with any of the countries listed below since publication.

Country	*Country*
Afghanistan	Chad
Albania	Chile
Andorra	Columbia
Angola	Congo
Anguilla	Costa Rica
Bahamas	Cote D'Ivoire
Bahrain	Cuba
Benin	Dominica
Bermuda	Dominican Republic
Bhutan	El Salvador
Brazil	Equatorial Guinea
Burundi	Ethiopia
Cambodia	Federated States of Micronesia
Cameroon	Gabon
Cape Verde	Gibraltar
Cayman Islands	Guatemala
Central African Republic	Guinea

Country	***Country***
Guinea-Bissau	Pitcairn Islands
Haiti	Puerto Rico
Honduras	Qatar
Hong Kong	Republic of Yemen
Hungary	Rwanda
Iceland	San Marino
Iran	Sark
Iraq	Saudi Arabia
Jordan	Senegal
Kuwait	Seychelles
Laos	St Lucia
Lebanon	St Vincent and Grenadines
Lesotho	Syria
Liberia	Taiwan
Libya	Tajikistan
Liechtenstein	Tanzania
Madagascar	The Comoros
Maldives	Togo
Marshall Islands	Tonga
Mauritania	Turks and Caicos Islands
Monaco	United Arab Emirates
Mozambique	Uruguay
Nauru	Vanuato
Nicaragua	Virgin Islands
Niger	Virgin Islands of the USA
Palau	Western Samoa
Paraguay	Zaire
Peru	

TERRITORY OF THE EC FOR THE PURPOSES OF VAT

Country	*Excluded territories*	*Included territories*
Austria		
Belgium		
Denmark	Faroe Islands	
Federal Republic of Germany	the Island of Heligoland the territory of Busingen	
Finland	Greenland Aland	
French Republic	the overseas departments	Principality of Monaco
Greece	Mount Athos	
Ireland		
Italy	Livigno Campione d'Italia the Italian waters of Lake Lugano	
Luxembourg		
Netherlands		
Portugal		
Spain	Ceuta Melilla the Canary Islands	
Sweden		
United Kingdom of Great Britain and Northern Ireland	Gibraltar	Isle of Man

Other exclusions:

(1) The Channel Islands;
(2) Andorra;
(3) San Marino;
(4) All other countries not specifically referred to in this appendix.

References: Art 3 of the Sixth VAT Directive, Directive 77/338; Art 229 of the Treaty Establishing the European Economic Community; and the Value Added Tax (General) Regulations 1985, SI 1985/886.

Appendix 3

HOUSE OF COMMONS SELECT COMMITTEE ON TRADE AND INDUSTRY 7th REPORT 'BUILDING CONFIDENCE IN ELECTRONIC COMMERCE'

Correspondence between Mr Derek Wyatt MP and Dawn Primarolo MP, Financial Secretary, HM Treasury

E-Commerce and Taxation

I buy a new car for £20,000 from a virtual garage web site. The site is maintained in London but the garage warehouse is in (say) Portugal and the company running that site is registered in (say) the Cayman Islands.

I buy a new Mac computer for $1000 from a virtual computer store on the net; it is registered in Malaysia.

I buy monthly CDs and CD-ROMs to the value of £100 from www.amazon.com as opposed to www.amazon.co.uk. I wonder out aloud about when I order from the USA site whether it doesn't pass the order along to its UK site (but how would I know and how would the government know?)

These are three examples I have plucked from mid-air. I'm expecting a virtual garage to be launched this year, I've bought software and CD-ROMs off the net.

I would like to know how and where we would pay UK tax on these three transactions.

On the buying of a car from Portugal – where cars are currently the cheapest in Europe – would I pay TVA/VAT there or in the UK? When it arrived at my house (driven by a member of the supply chain) would he have had to pay customs duty (if so how much?) A couple of points to ponder, it is in the UK's interest for me to buy a car in Portugal from a virtual web site as we lose corporation tax and much else besides. Is the inevitable outcome of this purchase in (say) three years time the ending of TVA/VAT across Europe? And then greater harmonisation of corporation tax despite subsidiarity in the Masstricht Treaty and then income tax?

On the purchase of software (some of which can now be downloaded for free or for rent or for a fee), I cannot see a solution. Inevitably, as America has about 90 per cent of all internet trade it wants a no tax haven. Again though the Treasury is the loser.

As for CDs and CD-ROMs, UK prices are much more expensive and internet trade gives us greater choice but again there are implications for the Treasury.

To enable the move to internet trading could the Treasury offer a one year tax break or a incentive to move our economy to the net so that we compete with America and challenge Europe?

I shall look forward to your responses.

Derek Wyatt, MP

Derek Wyatt MP

Thank you for your letter of 12 January to Barbara Roche about electronic commerce and taxation. I am replying as the Treasury Minister responsible for Customs matters.

You set out three examples of purchases that can be made using the Internet. In all the examples you cite the Internet is used as a communictions medium and an order (and maybe payment) would be transmitted, followed by the delivery of physical goods by traditional means. It may be helpful to explain that for VAT purposes physical goods are generally taxed according to where they are. Thus goods coming to the UK will be subject to UK VAT on their arrival.

Your first example is of a new car purchased from a company registered in the Cayman Islands, and which supplies the car from a garage in Portugal. In this example you would be purchasing a car that is located in another member state of the EC and that will be moved either by yourself, or by an agent acting on your behalf, to the UK.

VAT on the purchase of a new car is always due in the member state of destination, where the vehicle will be kept and used. Each member state has made special arrangements that allow a VAT free supply where the new car is to move to another country within the EC, charging VAT on those which arrive within it borders. An individual who purchases a new means of transport (including a car) can employ someone to act on their behalf to transport the car to the UK. The purchaser in the UK is still the person who is responsible for notifying Customs that the vehicle has been brought to the UK and for paying the VAT that is due in the UK. Similar rules would apply if you were instead to bring the car in from a country that is not part of the EC. The car would be liable to customs duty and VAT at importation. You will need to acquire VAT papers from Customs before you can register the car with the DVLA.

In your second example a new computer is purchased. Using the Internet the order is placed with a Malaysian company. The VAT treatment would depend on the country from which the goods were delivered. The Malaysian supplier may have stocks in a warehouse in the UK, in another member state of the EC, or outside the Community. Where the computer is delivered from stocks held in UK the supplier would be liable to UK VAT in the same way as any other UK based supplier. Where the computer is delivered to a customer in the UK from another member state, the customer will be charged either the VAT of the country from which the computer was delivered, or UK VAT. The treatment depends on whether the supplier has breached certain turnover thresholds for business transacted in the UK (known as the 'distance selling scheme'). Where the computer is imported into the UK from a country outside the EC, the customer would be liable to pay VAT and duty (where applicable) to Customs before taking delivery of the shipment. In each case VAT is payable.

Your third example consists of CDs and CD-ROMs to the value of £100 purchased from Amazon com (based in the USA). In this case, Amazon would post the CDs to your address in the UK, with a Customs value declaration stuck to the parcel. The Post Office would deliver these CDs, but would collect from you VAT and duty (if applicable) before releasing the goods. If you refused to pay the charges then the Post Office would return the package to Amazon. For small value shipments up to approximately £18 value (including delivery costs) a low value exemption exists, and no taxes would be collected.

As you see, for each of your examples the means of communication of the order has no effect on the VAT treatment. It is the destination of the physical goods that determines where VAT is due. You are also concerned about the treatment of software that is downloaded electronically rather than beling delivered to you on, say, a CD-ROM. VAT would not be due where no charge is made for software regardless of its provenance – VAT is normally levied on the consideration (what is paid) for a product. Other taxes such as corporation tax are levied on profits, and again a free supply would not give rise to a corporation tax charge. At present, business customers who pay for and download a piece of software from a supplier that is based outside the UK would be liable to declare a self-assessed charge on their normal VAT return. This is not practical for private persons, and at present when such a purchase is made from supplier outside the EC, no VAT will be due.

As you have illustrated, the Internet is opening up many opportunities for cross-border trading and more customer choice. The extent to which UK corporation tax would be due in the situations you describe would depend on the precise facts. But it is certainly true that the Internet makes it easier for residents of the UK to buy goods and services from overseas companies which do not have a presence in the UK sufficient to require them to pay corporation tax here. At the same time, the Internet offers UK companies the opportunity to export goods and services more easily to residents of other countries, and those companies will pay corporation tax here. If this trade by UK companies is strong and increases, there could be an overall increase in our tax revenues.

To help achieve this it is important that tax is not an obstacle to the growth of electronic commerce in the UK, and our policy is set out in a paper published jointly by the Inland Revenue and HM Customs and Excise on 6 October last year. As noted in the paper and the accompanying Press Release, we believe that current taxes, including corporation tax and VAT, are sufficiently robust to mean that major changes to existing tax rules are not necessary at this stage. But some work is needed to clarify how certain aspects of the OECD (Organisation for Economic Co-operation and Development) model tax treaty apply to electronic commerce and to consider the adequacy of the current international standards. International co-operation between revenue authorities is essential, and the UK is taking a leading role in this work through the OECD, and for VAT the European Community.

Underpinning the work of the OECD is a framework document which all member countries agreed last year. The document sets out a future work plan for the OECD, as well as a number of principles which all member countries have agreed to, including the aim that there should be neutrality between the taxation of electronic commerce and the taxation of more traditional forms of business.

I am sorry to reply at such length, but trust you find this useful.

Dawn Primarolo, MP.

Appendix 4

TAX RATES 1999/2000

Corporation tax

Full rate:	30%
Small companies rate:	20%
Small companies limit:	£300,000
Upper marginal limit:	£1.5 million
Effective marginal rate:	32.5%

Income tax

£0–£1,500	10%
£1,501–£28,000	23%
£28,001 and above	40%

Capital gains tax

Individuals	20/40%
Companies	20/30%

Value added tax

17.5%
Registration limit: £51,000
Deregistration limit: £49,000

FURTHER READING

1. Books

Information Technology

Campbell *International Information Technology Law* (John Wiley & Sons, 1997).

Lloyd *Information Technology and the Law* (Butterworths, 1997).

Macdonald and Rowland *Information Technology Law* (Cavendish Publishing, 1997).

Internet

Dickie *Internet and Electronic Commerce Law in the EU* (Hart Publishing, 1999).

Edwards and Waelde (ed) *Law and the Internet* (Hart Publishing, 1997).

Gringras *Laws of the Internet* (Butterworths, 1997).

Smith *Internet Law and Regulation* (FT Law and Tax, 1997).

Taxation

Baker *Double Taxation Agreements and International Tax Law* (Sweet & Maxwell, 1994).

Bramwell *Taxation of Companies and Company Reconstructions* (Sweet & Maxwell, 1999).

British Master Tax Guide (CCG, 1999).

De Voil's Indirect Tax Service (Butterworths, loose-leaf).

Doernerg and Hinnekens *Electronic Commerce and International Taxation* (Kluwer Law International, 1998).

Model Tax Convention on Income and on Capital (OECD, 1997).

Morse Davies, Williams and Salter *Principles of Tax Law* (Sweet & Maxwell, 1996).

Shipwright and Keeling *Revenue Law* (Blackstone Press, 1998).

Simon's Direct Tax Service (Butterworths, loose-leaf).

Taylor *Double Taxation Relief* (Tolley's, 1996).

Terra and Wattel *European Tax Law* (Kluwer Law International, 1997).

Tiley and Collison *UK Tax Guide* (Butterworths, 1999).

Customs Duty

Snyder *International Trade and Customs Law of the European Union* (Butterworths, 1998).

Swartze *European Adinistrative Law* (Sweet & Maxwell, 1992).

Walsh *The Customs Code of the European Union* (Butterworths, 1995).

2. Articles

Becher 'Taxation of Electronic Business in a Globalizing World – Ten Demands for an Adaptation' (1998) *Intertax*, Vol. 26, p 410.

Dittmar and Selling 'How to Control Internet Transactions? – A Contribution from the Point of View of German Tax Inspectors' (1998) *Intertax*, Vol 26, p 88.

Fairpo 'Already Behind The Times' (1998) *The Tax Journal*, Issue No 449, p 12.

Fairpo 'What Direction? Tax and the Internet' (1998) *The Tax Journal*, Issue No 453.

Fairpo 'Taxation of Electronic Commerce: Residence' (1999) *The Tax Journal*, Issue No 483.

Geurts 'How to Tax Electronic Commerce Transactions? (1998) *Intertax*, Vol 26, p 301.

Hickey 'Electronic Commerce' (1998) *Taxation*, Vol 141, No 3656, p 169.

Hickey 'Electronic Commerce' (1998) *Taxation*, Vol 141, No 3657, p 200.

Hickey 'Offshore Electronic Commerce, Taxing Difficulties and Planning Opportunities' (1998) *European Taxation*, Vol 38, No 8, p 255.

Hinnekens 'The Challenges of Applying VAT and Income Tax Territoriality Concepts Rules to International Electronic Commerce' (1998) *Intertax*, Vol 26, p 52.

Hinnekens 'Looking for an Appropriate Jurisdictional Framework for Source-State Taxation of International Electronic Commerce in the Twenty-first Century' (1998) *Intertax*, Vol 26, p 192.

Horner and Owens 'Tax and the Web: New Technology, Old Problems' (1996) *The Bulletin for International Fiscal Documentation*, p 516.

'International Tax Issues in Cyberspace' (1997) *Intertax*, Vol 25, with contributions from the UK, Japan, US, Canada, Germany and France.

Jenkins 'E-Commerce: Future State: The likely indirect tax treatment in the European Union' (1999) *The Tax Journal*, Issue No 486, p 13.

Jenkins 'Indirect Taxes and E-Commerce' (1999) *The Tax Journal*, Issue No 508, p 12.

Jenkins 'VAT and Telecommunications within the European Union' (1995) *VAT Monitor*, Vol 6, No 5, p 286.

Kortenaar and Spanjersberg 'Taxation and E-Commerce: Dutch Tax Policy Implications' (1999) *Intertax*, Vol 27, p 180.

Lejeune, Vanham, Verlinden, Verbeken 'Does Cyber-Commerce Necessitate Revision of International Tax Concepts' (1998) *European Taxation*, Vol 38, No 1, p 2.

Lejeune, Vanham, Verlinden, Verbeken 'Does Cyber-Commerce Necessiate a Revision of International Tax Concepts?' (1998) *European Taxation*, Vol 38, No 2, p 50.

Loten 'Doing Business on the Internet' (1996) *The Tax Journal*, Issue No 361.

Oberson and Piaget 'Electronic Commerce and Taxation: a Swiss Perspective' (1998) *The Bulletin for International Fiscal Documentation*, Vol 52, No 12, p 535.

O'Donnell and DiSangro 'United States Tax Policy on Electronic Commerce' (1997) *Intertax*, Vol 25, p 429.

Ollerenshaw 'Electronic Lodgement and Employers' (1999) *The Tax Journal*, Issue No 497, p 17.

Postma 'Netherlands Issues Internet Discussion Paper' (1998) *Intertax*, Vol 26, p 303.

Schon 'The Likely Impact of the Internet on International Tax Policy' (1997) *The Tax Journal*, Issue No 387, p 9.

Schwarz 'Transfer Pricing and Electronic Commerce' (1999) *The Bulletin for International Fiscal Documentation*, p 286.

Sprague and Hersey 'Letter to OECD re Electronic Commerce' (1999) *Intertax*, Vol 27, p 40.

'Taxation of Internet Trading' (1998) *Tax Planning International Review*, contributions from UK, Ireland, Italy, Germany, Spain, The Netherlands, and Switzerland.

Tillinghast 'The Impact of the Internet on the Taxation of International Transactions' (1996) *The Bulletin for International Fiscal Documentation*, p 524.

Toshiaki Katsushima 'Internet and Electronic Commerce – The Next Frontier' (1998) *Intertax*, Vol 26, p 86.

3. Monthly News

'E-Commerce' *Tax Planning International* (BNA International Inc).

INTERNET SITES

Australia
Australian Tax Office
http://www.ato.gov.au/
Australian Treasury
http://www.treasury.gov.au/
Taxation Institute of Australia
http://www.taxia.com.au/index.html

Belgium
Minsitry of Finance
http://minfin.fgov.be/

Canada
Canadian Revenue
http://www.rc.gc.ca/
Department of Finance
http://www.fin.gc.ca/
Canadian Tax Foundation
www.ctf.ca/index.htm

Denmark
Minsitry of Finance
http://www.fm.dk/english.htm

Ireland
Revenue Service
http://www.revenue.ie/

The Netherlands
Loyens and Volkmaars
www.lovotax.nl

New Zealand
Revenue service
http://www.ird.govt.nz/

South Africa
Revenue service
http://www.sars.gov.za/

United Kingdom
HM Customs and Excise

http://www.hmce.gov.uk/c&ehome.htm
HM Treasury
http://www.hm-treasury.gov.uk/
Inland Revenue
http://www.inlandrevenue.gov.uk/home.htm
Institute for Fiscal Studies
http://www1.ifs.org.uk/

United States of America
Internal Revenue Service
http://www.irs.gov/
Department of the Treasury
http://www.ustreas.gov/

International organisations

OECD
General
http://www.oecd.org
E-commerce (Tax)
http://www.oecd.org/daf/fa/e_com/e_com.htm
Opportunities and Challenges for Government (The 'Sacher Report')
http://www.oecd.org/dsti/sti/it/ec/act/sacher.htm
Electronic Commerce: The Challenges to Tax Authorities and Taxpayers (Turku)
http://www.oecd.org/daf/fa/e_com/turku.htm

CATA (Commonwealth Association of Tax Administrators)
http://www.open.gov.uk/cata/
{**HYPERLINK "http://www.ciat.org/"**}
http://www.ciat.org/

European Commission: Indirect Tax
http://europa.eu.int/en/comm/dg21/dg21.html

Global Information Infrastructure Commission
http://www.giic.org/focus/ecommerce/ectax.html

International Monetary Fund
http://www.imf.org/

The European Commission
http://europa.eu.int/comm/

International Fiscal Association
http://www.ifa.nl/

International Fiscal Association (US Branch)
http://www.usa.ifa.org/

INDEX

References are to paragraph numbers. References to a Table are followed by the page number where the Table is set out, for example Table 13 at p 104; italic page references are to Appendices.